# WRITING and THINKING in the SOCIAL SCIENCES

*Sharon Friedman*

Associate Professor
Gallatin Division
New York University

*Stephen Steinberg*

Professor
Department of Urban Studies, Queens College, and
Department of Sociology, Graduate Center,
City University of New York

PRENTICE HALL, Englewood Cliffs, New Jersey 07632

Library of Congress Cataloging-in-Publication Data

Friedman, Sharon.
    Writing and thinking in the social sciences / Sharon Friedman,
Stephen Steinberg.
        p.    cm.
    Bibliography: p.
    Includes index.
    ISBN  0-13-970062-5
    1. Social sciences—Research.  2. Social sciences—Authorship.
I. Steinberg, Stephen.  II. Title.
H62.F727  1989
300'.72—dc19                                            88-27589
                                                            CIP

Editorial/production supervision and
  interior design: Fred Bernardi
Cover design: Ben Santora
Manufacturing buyer: Arthur Michalez / Laura Crossland

 © 1989 by Prentice-Hall, Inc.
A Division of Simon & Schuster
Englewood Cliffs, New Jersey 07632

Printed in the United States of America

10   9   8   7   6   5   4   3   2   1

ISBN 0-13-970062-5

Prentice-Hall International (UK) Limited, *London*
Prentice-Hall of Australia Pty. Limited, *Sydney*
Prentice-Hall Canada Inc., *Toronto*
Prentice-Hall Hispanoamericana, S.A., *Mexico*
Prentice-Hall of India Private Limited, *New Delhi*
Prentice-Hall of Japan, Inc., *Tokyo*
Simon & Schuster Asia Pte. Ltd., *Singapore*
Editora Prentice-Hall do Brasil, Ltda., *Rio de Janeiro*

To Danny and Joanna

# CONTENTS

v

# PART III   THE FORMS OF ACADEMIC WRITING

*Chapter 10*
## THE SUMMARY   *139*

*Chapter 11*
## THE CRITICAL PAPER   *146*

*Chapter 12*
## THE RESEARCH PAPER   *158*

*Chapter 13*
## THE ESSAY EXAM   *174*

*Appendix A*
## SELECTIVE REFERENCE WORKS IN THE SOCIAL SCIENCES   *179*

# INTRODUCTION: THE INTERPLAY BETWEEN WRITING AND THINKING

The purpose of any composition course is to teach students "how to write." Yet writing specialists have come to realize that one does not learn to write simply by acquiring a set of abstract skills. Rather, one begins to write effectively when there is a desire to develop and communicate ideas. We write *about* something, and in doing so, we deepen our understanding of our subject. We write to learn, and in the process we learn to write.

This is what is meant by the term "composition with content." The premise is that students will improve their writing through a process of reading and thinking in conjunction with writing on a regular basis with feedback from instructors and peers. This premise has changed how writing is taught. In addition to general composition courses designed to upgrade writing skills, specialized courses are offered where students read, write, and think within their chosen field of inquiry—the humanities, the natural sciences, or the social sciences. In these courses students are discouraged from inventing topics "off the cuff," or from speculating about issues by parroting conventional opinions. Instead, students are asked to write on topics that they have studied to some extent, so that their writing will be informed by prior reading and thought.

*Writing and Thinking in the Social Sciences* draws upon six disciplines: anthropology, economics, history, political science, psychology, and sociology. Although each discipline has its own characteristic research tradition, it is also the case that there is much common ground in terms of subject and method, and in terms of writing as well.

Our goal is to teach you, as social science students, how to make use of your background knowledge and interests to become effective writers in your chosen field of study. We hope to demonstrate how the act of writing clarifies the subject matter, and conversely, how mastery of a subject helps to produce coherent writing. This is our overall purpose. We approach it through three related steps, corresponding to the three major divisions of this book:

In Part I (Chapters 1 to 5) we provide general instruction on the writing process and the distinctive character of social science writing. An underlying rationale of these chapters is that before students can write social science they have to grasp how social scientists think.

In Part II (Chapters 6 to 9) we examine the tools that are commonly employed in social science research—the experiment, observation, the interview, and the document—and explore the implications that research method has for the writing process. In each instance we present a sample essay drawn from the social science literature.

These sample essays are taken from the disciplines of educational psychology, history, and sociology. Note, however, that the chapters are organized not by discipline, but by method—the experiment, observation, the interview, and the document. It is true that each method tends to be associated with a particular discipline—the experiment with psychology, observation with anthropology, the interview with sociology and political science, the document with history. But it is also the case that all these methods are used, to a greater or lesser extent, in each discipline. For example, although interviews are most identified with sociology and political science where they are used to gauge popular attitudes and opinion, psychologists use "depth interviewing" to probe the inner states of mind of subjects, and anthropologists engaged in field studies routinely use informants who are "interviewed" in order to elicit information about the people or community under study. Even historians have recently developed a field of "oral history," which is based on detailed interviews with individuals who have firsthand knowledge of some historical event or phenomenon. Thus, it would hardly be possible to represent the broad spectrum of research and writing in any one discipline with a few sample essays. By focusing on method rather than on discipline, however, we are able to illustrate the general *forms* that govern research and writing in the social sciences.

Each of the four chapters in Part II begins with a general introduction to the method, presents the sample essay, and ends with a critical analysis of this essay in terms of both "composition" and "content." Through a close reading and analysis of these four sample essays, you will begin to acquire a basic literacy in "the language of social research," a literacy that is indispensable for your writing as students in social science courses.

Perhaps we should add that these sample essays, which were written by leading scholars, do not represent the kind of original research and writing that is expected of undergraduates. Our purpose in including these essays is to demonstrate the ways in which professional social scientists frame research questions and gather, organize, and interpret evidence in an attempt to answer these questions. These are mental operations that you will need as students even if you do not conduct original research. Papers assigned in courses typically require you to synthesize information gathered by others who *have* conducted original research. To do this effectively, you need to know what kinds of strategies are appropriate for addressing certain kinds of questions, and how these strategies are useful in collecting and analyzing research material. As we emphasize throughout this book, reading, writing, and thinking are interrelated skills. To write well, one needs to know how to read and interpret what *others* have written.

Moreover, even if you are not expected to undertake full-fledged research projects, it is likely that you will be asked to carry out simplified exercises that employ social science methods. For example, you may be asked to work with original documents, to conduct a survey of students on campus, or to observe, record, and interpret a situation or event. David Hamilton, a composition theorist, calls these research exercises "serious parodies of science." Although they are done with fairly simple means, they require exacting thought. In the following passage Hamilton suggests the range of possibilities:

> One can move toward the social sciences by framing and assessing the behavior of people much as you might describe the movement of wind or of stars. Traffic patterns, study habits, the way people behave on elevators or in other stylized situations all present problems. If you introduce a variable [a new factor], say a stuck elevator, there is more to describe. You can treat a common local event such as a homecoming parade as an exotic native rite in order to study the terms "exotic," "native," "rite," and so on. It helps to force distance on these latter problems.[1]

Unlike scholars who do research in order to advance the frontiers of knowledge, students typically carry out these more limited research projects in order to advance their understanding and appreciation of a particular subject, or to learn more about a method by putting it into practice. With this in mind, research exercises are provided at the end of Chapters 6 to 9. However, whether you are actually doing research, or writing about research conducted by others, it is essential that you have an understanding of how social scientists go about addressing problems.

In Part III (Chapters 10 to 13) we examine the forms of academic writing that students are likely to encounter in social science courses—the summary, the critical paper, the research paper, and the essay exam.

All of these papers require that you be an analytical reader as well as a skillful writer. That is, you must be able to understand and interpret the writing of professional social scientists. Again, this was our rationale for presenting and analyzing the four sample essays in Part II. As students enrolled in social science courses, you will be expected to develop your own point of view on a topic or issue, based upon your reading, and to effectively communicate it in writing. You must be able to distill an argu-

---

[1]David Hamilton, "Interdisciplinary Writing," *College English*, 41 (March 1980), 786.

ment, comprehend its parts, and make judgments about its validity and significance.

Thus, skillful writing is based on skillful reading. However, this process also works in reverse. Writing a paper, or even an exam, will sharpen your understanding of a work, and force you to develop ideas about it. You may balk at the prospect of writing papers and essay exams, but this is the surest way to master the material in your courses.

Finally, we would like to make one observation about student attitudes toward writing. For most students writing is a difficult and even painful process. Students are all too willing to admit that they "hate to write." In our view, this is a symptom, not a cause, of poor or defective writing. As you improve your writing skills, you will begin to take pleasure in writing—not necessarily because writing is intrinsically satisfying, but because you will find yourself thinking more clearly and communicating your ideas with greater conviction.

*Sharon Friedman*
*Stephen Steinberg*

# ACKNOWLEDGMENTS

One's development as a writer is necessarily interwoven with one's life. Each of us would like to acknowledge our appreciation to individuals who inspired and tutored us in the craft of writing.

*Stephen Steinberg:*
As a fledgling graduate student, I collaborated on a research project, resulting in a book, with Gertrude Jaeger. It fell upon me to crank out a rough first draft, which Gertrude would then overhaul. My education as a writer came as I observed my purple prose transformed into writing that was lucid and polished, and like its author, free of affectation. Gertrude always respected the immortality of the written word, and this is how I remember her.

My next lesson came from Ileene Smith who, as a young editor at Atheneum, was assigned to copyedit my book, *The Ethnic Myth.* She had the cheek, at our very first meeting, to tell me that I was wordy. I was taken aback since I had always thought of myself as terse. By the time we completed the editing several months later, I conceded the point. Her scrupulous and unrelenting editing made me a better writer. As I have come to understand, to write is to write again.

*Sharon Friedman:*
My interest in the teaching of writing began in graduate school. The Department of English Education at New York University has been a pioneer in the theory and pedagogy of composition. Its faculty encouraged graduate students to pursue research in a field that traditionally was considered tangential to literature and language study. This experience prepared me for a unique opportunity to work as a graduate fellow in an innovative composition program at Queens College.

The chief architects of this program were Robert Lyons and Donald

McQuade. They assembled a dynamic group of doctoral students from universities in the New York metropolitan area. To their credit, they did not simply march us into classrooms to teach composition. With other faculty members, they organized workshops around a broad range of topics dealing with both theory and practice. As a group we produced exciting syllabi, new approaches to the pedagogy of writing, and a rich file of ideas that "worked" in the classroom. We had a genuine sense of mission that we could help students see the value of learning to write well. More than a few of these graduate fellows went on to make the teaching of writing central to their careers, and several of them—Lennard Davis, Janice Forman, Bella Mirabella, Anne Schotter, and Joanna Semeiks—are still my friends as well as intellectual compatriots.

We want to thank Phil Miller, executive editor at Prentice Hall, for his faith in this project and his infinite patience. The raw manuscript fell into the competent hands of Fred Bernardi, our production editor, whose editorial skills and judgment are especially appreciated. A number of people served as readers at different stages in the writing of this book: Pat Belanoff (State University of New York at Stony Brook); Joseph Bensman (City College and Graduate Center, CUNY); John T. Harwood (Pennsylvania State University); William B. Julian (Central College); Kate Kiefer (Colorado State University); William G. Roy (University of California, Los Angeles); and Dean Savage (Queens College and Graduate Center, CUNY). We received much thoughtful criticism that we heeded as we revised the manuscript.

We also want to thank our friends "across the disciplines" who provided us with useful source material: Lisa Fleisher (educational psychology); Floyd Hammack (education); Michael Krasner (political science); William Muraskin (history); Jon Peterson (history); Alice Sardell (political science); and Andrew Schotter (economics).

As is customary, we would like to end by thanking our respective spouses. In this case it can truly be said that without them this book would not have been possible.

*Chapter 1*
# SOCIAL SCIENCE AS A DISTINCT FORM OF INQUIRY

## SOCIAL SCIENCE AND COMMON SENSE[1]

Knowledge about "man and society" did not wait upon the establishment of social science in institutions of higher learning, which is mostly a twentieth-century phenomenon. Throughout history sages, mystics, and poets in their various guises have pondered the human condition, often with extraordinary insight. Who can deny that Shakespeare comprehended the complex machinations of the unconscious long before psychology emerged as a discipline? Or that Machiavelli's astute analysis of how a prince might enhance his power is as relevant to the modern nation-state as it was to sixteenth-century Florence? Certainly Herodotus, the ancient Greek scholar who is regarded as the father of history, is an inspiration to present-day historians, despite the fact that he wrote his history of the Persian Wars in the fifth century B.C.

What, then, is unique about social science? How is knowledge obtained through social science different from knowledge obtained by individuals relying on intuition or common sense? Clearly, the truth or falsity of a proposition cannot be gauged by who is advancing it—whether a social scientist or a social seer. Notwithstanding their claim to scientific objectivity, social scientists have been known to make grievous errors. One noto-

---

[1]The first two sections of this chapter were influenced by Ernest Nagel, *The Structure of Science* (New York: Harcourt, Brace & World, Inc., 1961) chapters 1 and 2.

rious example is the considerable body of research and writing early in this century that "proved" the inferiority of certain races. As this example shows, the scientific method is less than a perfect safeguard against error. On the other hand, social seers at times have advanced ideas that may be profoundly true, even if they lack scientific rigor.

But how are we to determine whether or not a proposition is true? It is this concern with *verification* that defines social science and distinguishes it from other kinds of knowledge. The characteristic refrain of the social scientist is, "Yes, but how do we *know* that?" It is well and good to speculate that the Republicans will go down to defeat in the next election, or that the poor will one day rise in revolt, or that the economy is heading for another depression, or that Hitler was a madman, or that human beings are innately good or innately evil, and so on. There has never been a dearth of pundits to issue opinions on such matters, often with a passion that can be quite compelling. But social scientists, by profession, are skeptics. They need to be convinced. For the passion and conviction of the seer, they substitute dispassionate inquiry and a willingness to suspend belief. Evidence becomes something of an obsession, for it is through evidence, systematically garnered in accordance with fixed procedures, that social scientists arrive at "truth." This insistence on evidence is the hallmark of social science—the single most important factor that distinguishes it from knowledge derived from other sources.

This does not mean that social seers are indifferent to evidence. Even the fortune teller who dazzles her clients with her "uncanny powers" has mastered the art of detecting and interpreting such social indicators as dress, speech, and body language. For social scientists, however, observation is less an art than a craft—one that is practiced in accordance with strict rules designed to minimize the chances of error. And unlike the fortune teller who jealously guards her trade secrets, the social scientist is obliged to present all the evidence, thereby dispelling any aura of mystery.

In short, contrary to knowledge based on intuition, abstract thought, or revelation, knowledge in the social sciences is based on the scientific method. The essence of the scientific method is *controlled inquiry*, or the systematic collection and analysis of evidence. Thus, before a proposition is accepted as true, it must be demonstrated to be consistent with the available evidence, and must withstand the critical scrutiny of other researchers and critics.

In this respect social science is also different from the "conventional wisdom," a term that is applied to the common sense explanations of social phenomena that enjoy wide popular currency. The trouble with these everyday beliefs is that they are typically accepted uncritically, and held irrespective of the evidence. Often the conventional wisdom consists of empty platitudes or vague generalizations that do not even lend themselves to an empirical test, and thus cannot be either confirmed or disconfirmed.

For example, according to one familiar tenet of conventional wisdom, "Prejudice is fear." Undeniably, this statement has a kernel of truth. However, the blanket statement that "prejudice is fear" is so ambiguous as to be virtually useless as an explanation of prejudice. It does not specify what people are afraid of, why they should be afraid, or why these assumed fears afflict some people and not others. Nor can the conventional wisdom explain why some groups are singled out for hostility, or why prejudice that is dormant one year can erupt into mass violence in the next. On closer examination, the assertion that "prejudice is fear" raises more questions than it answers.

As this example suggests, the commitment to controlled inquiry often pits social science against the conventional wisdom. There is a "debunking motif" running through sociological writing, as Peter Berger noted in his *Invitation to Sociology*.[2] Rooted in an insistence on hard evidence, this debunking motif manifests itself in a tendency to question and, if necessary, to challenge prevailing opinion, which all too often is selective, biased, self-serving, simplistic, or merely trendy—certainly not based on deep thought or careful investigation.

Thus one assumption underlying social science is that the world is not always as it appears or as we are told it is. Aside from the pitfalls of commonsense explanation alluded to above, every society propagates myths that gloss over its contradictions and failures. Promulgated as they are at the highest levels of society, these myths are not easily resisted, least of all by people who are not inclined to question basic values and assumptions. But part of the mission of social science is to get behind the facade of official society, and to adopt a critical stance toward established institutions and prevailing beliefs. Thus, if social science has a credo, it is that nothing is to be accepted on faith alone, that even the most cherished assumptions must be subjected to critical scrutiny. This is what Max Weber, one of the pioneers of modern sociology, meant when he wrote that the social scientist should be a "disturber of the intellectual peace."[3]

It should come as no surprise, therefore, that social science is a field where there is much intellectual ferment, where different writers and schools engage in spirited debate, sometimes in classrooms and symposia, more often in print. Compared to the natural sciences, knowledge in the social sciences is not given to absolute and fixed answers, and notwithstanding all attempts to marshal evidence and establish proofs, social science is fraught with ambiguity. It is not a field for people who tend to view the world in black and white terms, or who are wedded to simple dichotomies—between right and wrong, truth and error. On the other hand, those with a high tolerance for ambiguity, who are willing to question

[2]Peter Berger, *Invitation to Sociology* (New York: Doubleday, 1963), p. 38.

[3]Max Weber, "Science as a Vocation," in Hans Gerth and C. Wright Mills, *From Max Weber* (New York: Oxford University Press, 1946), pp. 129–56.

the conventional wisdom, and who can break with the equation that "whatever is, is good," will find social science to be provocative and illuminating.

As noted earlier, much social science deals with subjects that are more or less familiar, though imperfectly understood. The excitement of learning comes not from discovering previously unknown terrain, but rather from reassessing old assumptions and gaining new insight into aspects of social life previously taken for granted. Thus, even for students in a first encounter with social science, the moment of discovery is not likely to evoke a shout of, "Eureka!" (which, in Greek, means "I have found"). Rather it is apt to take a more sobering and reflective expression as one realizes, "I never thought of it that way before."

Again, the unique character of social science is perhaps best understood against the background of the natural sciences. By comparison, there are few, if any, obvious frontiers in social science; few, if any, breakthroughs that call into question whole systems of thought or open up entirely new vistas. There is nothing in social science to compare with the discovery of the atom, or the cure for polio, or the development of genetic engineering. However, it is in the best tradition of social science to shed new light on old problems, to establish relationships among apparently disconnected events, and to find deeper meaning in aspects of social life that are only superficially understood.

Given these objectives, it is all the more important that social scientists communicate their findings effectively. Muddled thinking can hardly be remedied with turgid or unintelligible prose. If social science is to fulfill its mission of bringing greater clarity to our understanding of the world around us, then it must uphold standards of excellence in writing as well as research.

## THE MANY MEANINGS OF "WHY"

All science, indeed all knowledge, attempts to answer the question, "Why?" However, this question assumes different meanings, which in turn yield different answers. Therefore, it should not be surprising that the various social sciences typically approach the same general question from vastly different perspectives, employ different research strategies, and reach different conclusions.

As an illustration, let us turn again to the question, "Why prejudice?" This question can be approached on two different levels of analysis. The one most commonly employed in social research asks, "Why are some individuals prejudiced and others not?" Even this question has multiple meanings. It can be construed to mean, "How do *individuals* acquire their prejudiced beliefs?" Attention is thus directed to the socialization process, and the role of various institutions—the schools, the mass media, the state—in either propagating prejudice or upholding norms of tolerance. On the other hand, concern with the sources of prejudice in the individual may lead to an exploration of the psychological needs that are served by prejudice, for example, in blaming innocent minorities for one's own frustrations or failures. Or the search for individual motives may be directed toward the material interests that are served by prejudice, for example, in reducing competition for jobs. Indeed, there is an enormous body of research in each of the social sciences that has explored the gamut of historical, social, economic, and psychological factors that help to determine whether or not individuals are prejudiced in their beliefs and actions.

The question, "Why prejudice?" can be approached on a second, more abstract level of analysis. In this instance what is being explained is not individual variations in prejudice, but the entire *system* of prejudice. Implicitly, it is assumed that prejudice will have special appeal to certain individuals, depending on such factors as their upbringing, their values, and their personalities. But where do prejudiced beliefs come from in the first place? What are their historical sources? What is the constellation of societal forces that explains their persistence down to the present? Why has racial and ethnic prejudice been so pronounced in the United States, as compared to other nations?

What is involved here is a difference between *microscopic* and *macroscopic* levels of analysis, a distinction that can be applied to virtually any area of social inquiry. A microscopic approach focuses on *individual* manifestations of a particular phenomenon. In the case cited above, prejudice is treated as an attribute of discrete individuals, and thus the "causes" of prejudice are presumed to reside within individuals—their personalities, their cultural values, or their social milieu.

In contrast, a macroscopic approach treats prejudice as an attribute of a social system, and thus looks for systemic rather than individual factors that account for the level and intensity of prejudice. On this view, individual prejudice is but a last link in a long chain of causation, reaching back to factors that have little or nothing to do with individuals. To be sure, there could be no prejudice if there were no bigots. Nevertheless, from a macroscopic perspective individual beliefs and actions are influenced and constrained by factors over which they, as individuals, have little or no control. Individuals may be held morally responsible for their prejudice, but from a macroscopic perspective the "root causes" or "ultimate sources" lie far outside the individual.

For example, according to one macroscopic theory of slavery, Africans were not enslaved because of some preexisting or spontaneous racial hatred on the part of whites toward blacks. Rather, slavery was a system that was instituted in order to provide cheap labor—the cheapest of all labor, slave labor—to southern agriculture, which produced the raw cotton that was essential to the textile industry both in the north and in Britain. Racial prejudice, as we know it, evolved in order to give moral justification and political legitimacy to what at bottom was a system of labor exploitation. Thus, blacks were not enslaved because they were hated; it would be more accurate to say that they were hated so that they might be enslaved. How does the individual fit into this model? Not only slaveholders, not only southerners, but the entire nation had a stake in slavery. Even after slavery was abolished, a caste system was instituted that nourished and reinforced belief in black inferiority. The end result was a pervasive racism that was reflected in white beliefs, feelings, and actions, and that was passed down from one generation to the next. From a macroscopic perspective, the individual is but the last link in a long chain of causation.

Clearly, microscopic and macroscopic approaches are both useful, although they address different questions and yield different insights. Furthermore, the various social sciences, and different schools within a particular discipline, have tended to focus on one or another of the meanings of "why" alluded to above. The following breakdown does not attempt to summarize the large and diverse body of research in each discipline, but only to suggest a main thrust or emphasis in terms of the specific questions that have governed research on prejudice.

*Psychology.*  The emphasis in psychology is on the role that psychological factors play in the formation of prejudice, and in determining how individuals respond to established systems of prejudice. The psychological classic on this subject is *The Authoritarian Personality*, which was undertaken in the aftermath of the Second World War in order to better understand the genocide of European Jews.[4] The authors concluded that prejudice is an integral part of a much larger syndrome of psychological traits, comprising an "authoritarian personality." In their view, individuals acquired a predisposition for an authoritarian personality in early childhood, partly as a result of repressive childrearing practices. As this example suggests, psychologists tend to treat prejudice as a problem of the individual, resulting from deep inner conflicts that are "acted out" on defenseless minorities. Consistent with this view, some psychologists have actually proposed mass therapy as the only means of eliminating prejudice.

*Sociology.*  Unlike psychologists, sociologists tend to treat prejudice not as a personal aberration, but as "normal" behavior, in the sense that it is often granted political and social legitimacy, and is acquired through routine processes of social learning. The sociological classic in this area is Gunnar Myrdal's *An American Dilemma*.[5] Myrdal viewed racism as representing a glaring contradiction between American ideals and practices. Blacks, he argued, were trapped in a vicious circle, in that they were forced to live under degrading conditions, which reinforced racist attitudes among whites, thus forming the basis for further discrimination. According to Myrdal, this vicious cycle can be broken either by convincing whites, presum-

[4]Theodor Adorno and others, *The Authoritarian Personality* (New York: Harper, 1950).
[5]Gunnar Myrdal, *An American Dilemma* (New York: Harper, 1944).

ably through educational programs, to abandon their prejudice, or by upgrading the condition of the black minority. Though this model has its critics, it has dominated sociological thinking on prejudice for over three decades.

*History.*   As a discipline history has been preoccupied with questions concerning the origins and evolution of different systems of prejudice, and their impact on the groups involved. For example, in *White Over Black* Winthrop Jordan traced the development of racism from the earliest encounter between Englishmen and Africans in the sixteenth century to the establishment of slavery in the United States.[6] There is also a large canon of studies that document the history of particular groups in meticulous detail, often focusing on specific places and periods. For example, in *Harlem: The Making of a Ghetto*, Gilbert Osofsky traced the history of blacks in New York City between 1890 and 1930, and in *The Promised City*, Moses Rischin conducted a similar study of Jews in New York between 1890 and 1914.[7]

*Political Science.*   The distinctive focus of political science is not on individual prejudice, but on the state and its role in fomenting or legitimating prejudice. For example, in his 1950 study of *Southern Politics in State and Nation*, V. O. Key documented the various contrivances that southern states employed to circumvent the Fifteenth Amendment which granted blacks the vote.[8] These included the poll tax, literacy tests, and the white primary, not to mention intimidation and outright violence, which resulted in the disfranchisement of virtually the entire black population. As race history has changed, so has the research focus. More recently, political scientists have conducted studies on the civil rights movement, the ghetto "uprisings" of the 1960s, and the various public policies designed to combat racism and to reduce racial inequality.

*Economics.*   The chief contribution that economists have made to the study of prejudice has been to establish the key role that economic factors play in producing and maintaining inequalities among racial and ethnic groups. Some economists—for example, Gary Becker in *The Economics of Discrimination*—have focused on the factors that either provide an economic rationale for discrimination in the marketplace or make it unprofitable.[9] Others, like William Tabb in his book *The Political Economy of the Black Ghetto*, have analyzed the broad economic forces that relegate blacks to impoverished ghettos, and deny them access to the more desirable jobs that would allow them to break out of the "cycle of poverty."[10]

[6]Winthrop D. Jordan, *White Over Black* (Baltimore: Penguin Books, 1969).

[7]Gilbert Osofsky, *Harlem: The Making of a Ghetto* (New York: Harper, 1966). Moses Rischin, *The Promised City: New York's Jews, 1870–1914* (Cambridge: Harvard University Press, 1962).

[8]V. O. Key, *Southern Politics in State and Nation* (Knoxville: University of Tennessee Press, 1977).

[9]Gary Becker, *The Economics of Discrimination* (Chicago: University of Chicago Press, 1957).

[10]William Tabb, *The Political Economy of the Black Ghetto* (New York: Norton, 1970).

Economists have also played a leading role in formulating and evaluating public policies designed to provide assistance and opportunity to disadvantaged groups.

*Anthropology.* Through countless cross-cultural studies, anthropologists have documented the great variability that race relations assumes in different parts of the world. In some countries—South Africa is the most notorious example—racial difference is the basis of the utter subjugation of one race by another. But in other countries—Brazil and Mexico, for example—intermarriage between settlers and natives was commonplace, resulting in a racially mixed population where racial distinctions are relatively unimportant. In still other countries—Cuba is a recent example—racial differences persist but are no longer a basis for domination and hierarchy. From an anthropological perspective, there is little support for the popular notion that prejudice and conflict are inevitable in racially mixed societies.

As can be gleaned from this discussion, there is no single or simple answer to the question, "Why prejudice?" Prejudice is a complex, multi-dimensional phenomenon. It can be, and has been, studied from many different vantage points, and instead of a single all-encompassing theory, there are numerous partial explanations that pertain to different facets of the problem.

Recognition of this principle has one major implication for both research and writing. It is extremely important to be clear about exactly what questions are being addressed. Confusion on this point is the source of much muddled thinking and writing. Professional social scientists, not to speak of less skilled practitioners, too often engage in fruitless debate over which of two competing theories is correct when, on closer examination, they are not inconsistent or contradictory, but are merely addressing different facets of a problem.

## SUGGESTIONS FOR WRITING AND THINKING

1.  It was once generally accepted that women were by nature passive and emotional, and suited only for domestic labor and childrearing. Discuss how the prevailing wisdom on this issue has changed. In what ways do you think social science has contributed to this change?

2.  In the section of this chapter titled "The Many Meanings of 'Why'" we showed how different disciplines approach the question of why prejudice exists. Think of another social phenomenon or event, and show how it would be approached differently by an economist, a historian, a psychologist, a political scientist, and a sociologist. You might consider an issue such as teenage pregnancy or the war on drugs, or an event such as a presidential election or the closing of a factory.

## Chapter 2
# THE WRITING PROCESS

An underlying assumption of this book is that reading, thinking, and writing are integrally related activities in the learning process. This process, however, is not a simple linear one: step one, reading; step two, thinking; step three, writing. Rather, reading, thinking, and writing are a series of cyclical, back and forth, overlapping acts that build on one another.

This is sometimes misunderstood even by graduate students who, when writing their master's or doctoral thesis, think that they must read everything on a given subject before putting pen to paper. As a consequence, the reading goes on and on, often without focus, and students become lost in a mire of facts and ideas, overwhelmed and unable to write.

To be sure, it is imperative to read before you begin to write, since reading will help you locate ideas and identify questions around which topics might be developed. If the reading is to be of maximum benefit, however, you must find a direction, a line of thought which is personally meaningful and that makes sense of this material so that the writing and subsequent reading will have a purpose. Writing can help you to find that direction as you begin to connect and organize facts, observations, and insights into a coherent whole. Furthermore, in the act of writing and grappling with the substance of a paper, writers invariably confront gaps in their knowledge, or arrive at new insights that warrant further reading and thought.

For these reasons writing can and should take place at various points in the learning process. "Writing to learn" begins with putting thoughts on paper, taking notes, keeping journals in which you comment on readings and class discussions, and exploring topics for formal compositions. As Janet Emig put it, writing is "a record of the journey from jottings and notes to full discursive formulations."[1] This record is then available for you to review and revise.

C. Wright Mills, the eminent sociologist, had this in mind when he advised students to keep a file, which he described as "a growing store of facts and ideas, from the most vague to the most finished." Organized around topics, the file could include "ideas, personal notes, excerpts from books, bibliographical items and outlines of projects." Rewriting and rearranging these entries often stirs the mind to grasp relationships among ideas not previously understood. Keeping a file, according to Mills, is "a sociologist's way of saying: keep a journal. Many creative writers keep journals; the sociologist's need for systematic reflection demands it."[2]

In short, writing stimulates and deepens thought. It is a way of thinking out loud and yet recording our thoughts so that we can catch hold of significant ideas, key phrases, and useful terms. It is a way of organizing our knowledge in relation to a topic or question. Finally, writing is the way we communicate our understanding of the relationship among questions, findings, interpretations, and conclusions.

## STAGES IN THE WRITING PROCESS

As we have suggested, writing a formal paper is a process that occurs in overlapping stages. Let us distinguish four such stages:

1. the discovery of ideas
2. the arrangement of ideas
3. the composition of drafts
4. the revision of drafts

We want to emphasize that the writer does not necessarily go through these stages in serial order. A writer may shift back and forth between stages, and different writers will give more attention to one stage than another. After describing these stages below, we include a student paper that illustrates how one writer worked through these stages, and in the process developed insights that she did not have at the outset.

### Discovery

In this first stage you, in effect, "write before writing"[3] by plunging in without much preparation and spilling out whatever ideas or fragments of thought occur to you. This is sometimes called "brainstorming." Its purpose is to allow your thoughts to surface and to get something on paper with

---

[1]Janet Emig, "Writing as a Mode of Learning," *College Composition and Communication,* 28, no. 1 (May 1977), 127.

[2]C. Wright Mills, *The Sociological Imagination* (New York: Oxford University Press, 1959), pp. 196, 198, 212.

[3]Donald M. Murray, "Write Before Writing," *College Composition and Communication,* 29, no. 4 (December 1978), 375–81.

which to work. For example, you could brainstorm a series of words, phrases, or ideas that you associate with your subject and that you might later use to develop a paper. In writing down these kernels of thought you may discover connections among them, or whole new lines of inquiry that can then be used in the further development of the paper.

Another way to "write before writing" is to let your mind wander from an initial idea to wherever it leads you. This is called "freewriting." It is like brainstorming except that it is less fragmentary. Begin with whatever idea engages you, perhaps one suggested by your brainstorming list. Then freewrite for a paragraph or more without censoring your thoughts. Sooner or later, however, you must move toward what Peter Elbow calls a "center of gravity," a summing up that indicates a focus or theme.[4]

How do you get to this "center of gravity"? When you freewrite, you can either write for a limited time (say, a series of ten-minute intervals), or you can keep a journal in which you write each day. Review what you have written, and try to identify major ideas that might serve as a basis for further exploration. Write these ideas as assertions in declarative sentences, and then write again, this time using these declarative sentences as your point of departure.

Eventually your freewriting should help you develop a *preliminary thesis statement*. This is a unifying idea, expressed in one or two clear sentences, that asserts or argues a major point about the subject. The preliminary thesis statement will begin to focus your research and writing.

Let us illustrate this strategy with a paper from a sociology course on racial and ethnic minorities. The original assignment was as follows:

> Write a paper developed around an oral history—that is, an interview with a person who has experienced a sociologically relevant aspect of ethnic history. It is not enough to write an interesting life story. You should do background reading that will allow you to see this person as reflecting the larger history of his or her group, and conversely, to use ethnic history to illuminate this person's life.

During class the instructor gave students twenty minutes to freewrite on their topic. Afterwards, he instructed them to read over what they had written, find a major idea, and write again. The next step was to generate a preliminary thesis statement that could serve as a focus for the paper. This material would allow him to provide feedback and guidance while the paper was being written. One student, Diane Chessen, decided to write about her immigrant grandmother, Mary Mendelow. Here is a copy of her freewrite:

> My grandmother, who is of Russian descent, came to the United States in the 1920s. She worked as a saleswoman in clothing stores until she married. From speaking with my grandmother about her early experiences in Russia, I get the feeling that she found being in this country had

---

[4]Peter Elbow, *Writing Without Teachers* (New York: Oxford University Press, 1973), p. 20.

improved her life in many ways. She talks about how superstitious and scared she was growing up in Russia. When she came here I think she was pretty eager to assimilate and to become part of American society. When she first went to work, she changed her name from Miriam to Mary because Mary sounded American, and tried to conceal her Jewish identity. She often prides herself on the period of her life in which she worked as a saleswoman.

Preliminary Thesis Statement: Coming to America and taking on a new role and lifestyle which were not available to her in Russia was a positive experience for my grandmother.

*Teacher's Response*: Your preliminary thesis statement begins to focus the paper, but should be more specific. Clearly, you wish to explore the positive aspects of your grandmother's experience as an immigrant. Exactly what were her "new role and lifestyle"? How do you account for her eagerness to assimilate?

Since she prides herself on her work as a saleswoman, perhaps you should explore this further. What specifically did she do, and how did her work affect other aspects of her life—for example, her status in her family, her identity as a woman, and her sense of herself as an American rather than an immigrant?

In advancing her preliminary thesis, Diane sought to focus her thoughts, and to make connections between large ideas (immigration to America, new role and lifestyle, positive feelings) that emerged in her freewrite. Because Diane was somewhat vague about what contributed to her grandmother's positive feelings, her instructor suggested that she pursue her observation that her grandmother took pride in her work, and relate this work experience to her "new role and lifestyle."

Obviously, a freewrite is only a first step in the writing process. However, through writing and rewriting Diane selected, expanded, and connected the idea-fragments in her freewrite, and developed them into a coherent paper.

We want to emphasize that the purpose of freewriting is not just to spew out ideas, but to move toward a focus or theme. As this focus begins to emerge, you should freewrite around it in order to develop a set of ideas and a direction for the paper.

Still another way to discover ideas about a subject is to interrogate it—that is, to ask questions that will guide further reading, writing, and thought. It is often helpful to begin with the journalist's questions: *who? what? when? where? how?* and *why?* The *why* and *how* questions involve analysis rather than simple description. (The significance of these questions for writing and organizing a paper will be discussed in Chapter 4, "Rhetorical Strategies.")

Of course, the analytical questions *how* and *why* assume different meanings within the context of different disciplines. All social science is concerned with these questions, but as we showed in Chapter 1, each discipline applies them to different facets of social life. Thus, when you pose the question "Why?," you should incorporate key terms and concepts associated with your discipline.

Below are the questions that Diane posited as she thought about the events, circumstances, and attitudes that comprised her grandmother's experience. Note that these questions incorporate sociological terms and concepts, such as status, identity, assimilation, and discrimination. Also note that, prompted by her instructor's feedback, Diane framed a number of questions around her grandmother's work:

1. What kinds of work opportunities were available to immigrant women in the 1920s?
2. What were the prevailing attitudes among Americans toward working women? Toward immigrant working women? Was there much discrimination?
3. What were the prevailing attitudes among Russian-Jewish immigrants toward working women?
4. Were immigrant women treated differently on the job and in the hiring process than native women?
5. How did the language barrier affect one's opportunities in the job market?
6. What were job conditions like? Hours, work environment, wages, benefits?
7. What did my grandmother do with the money she earned? Was it for her personal use or did it go into the family budget? How did her earnings affect her role and status in the family? Her feelings about herself?
8. As she became more assimilated, did more opportunities open up for her?
9. As a recent immigrant, did she feel torn between old and new cultures? Did she feel confused about her identity? From her perspective, what did she gain and what did she lose?
10. To what extent did her attitudes reflect currents of thought in the Jewish immigrant community at that time?

Although Diane did not explore all of these questions in the actual paper, they guided her thinking and writing, and identified promising areas of inquiry as she explored the central question: Why was her grandmother's experience as an immigrant a positive one, notwithstanding obvious hardships and adversities?

### Arrangement

The discovery stage may well leave you with a hodgepodge of ideas and facts that lack unity and coherence. Of utmost importance is that you make the transition from *subject* to *topic*. This involves carving out of a general subject area, a specific topic that has clear boundaries and is narrower in scope. Once you whittle down the subject to more manageable proportions, you will be able to explore it in greater depth and detail, and to make a significant statement about it. Let us illustrate this process by referring again to our student paper:

Subject: The Immigrant Experience in America

Gradual Focus: My grandmother's experience as a Russian-Jewish immigrant in the 1920s

Tentative Topic: My grandmother's attitudes toward her assimilation into American society

Preliminary Thesis Statement: Coming to America and taking a new role and lifestyle which were not available to her in Russia was a positive experience for my grandmother.

The next step is to arrange the ideas and facts that you generated during the discovery stage in some logical order. You do this by selecting, classifying, and ordering dominant and subordinate ideas in relation to each other, and to the major controlling idea of the paper (the preliminary thesis statement).

In many composition courses, students are asked to plot out their ideas in outline form. The trouble with this approach is that it is difficult to produce a detailed outline of a paper that has yet to be written. An alternative approach is to write a first draft of the paper and then to extrapolate a formal outline. This will help you to see the implicit structure of your paper, and to detect gaps or disjunctions.

In lieu of a formal outline, composition theorists have devised new ways of plotting ideas that help students structure their ideas. One such strategy is called "nutshelling." Linda Flower and John Hayes provide this apt description of nutshelling:

> Find a listener/fellow-student/long-suffering friend to whom you can condense and explain the essentials of your thinking. In two or three sentences—in a nutshell—lay out the whole substance of your paper. Nutshelling practically forces you to make the relationship between your major ideas explicit. . . . Nutshells put noisy supporting information in its place and help you focus on the essentials of what you have to say.[5]

Below is a nutshell of Diane's paper on her immigrant grandmother:

> When my grandmother first came to this country at eighteen years of age in 1920, her family encouraged her to adapt to American culture. The circumstances in which they lived necessitated certain adjustments in her life. Because she is basically positive in her account, I would like to understand in personal and historical terms how she made this adjustment. The history of her immigration (attitudes toward Jews in Russia, what made them leave, details of her family's experience in the old country, the quality of their lives as newly arrived immigrants in America); her work experiences; her interpersonal relationships within and outside her community—all these factors might help to explain her journey toward becoming an American, as well as her attitudes toward this experience. Furthermore, my grandmother's experience might help to illuminate the experience of other immigrants at the time.

In this nutshell one can see the broad outlines of the paper, the emerging focus, and the kind of detail that will fill it out. Clearly, this student's goal is to chronicle her grandmother's experience as an immigrant, and to explain

---

[5]Linda S. Flower and John R. Hayes, "Problem-Solving Strategies and the Writing Process," *College English,* 49, no. 4 (December 1977), 456.

how her circumstances affected her attitudes. In addition, she will try to locate these circumstances and attitudes within the broader contours of immigrant history.

### Composition

Once you have generated some preliminary ideas or goals for your paper and "arranged" them, however tentatively, you are ready to compose a first draft. You can begin by writing an introduction, or you may want to defer this until a later draft and begin with the heart of your paper. Whichever you choose, you should experiment to find the most effective way of presenting material so that your intentions are clear to the reader. Above all, remember that you are communicating your goals to an audience, and ask yourself three questions:

1. In terms of the subject, what goal do you share with your readers that you can use to engage their attention?
2. What information do you want your readers to remember upon finishing your paper?
3. What do you want your readers to think about this information? That is, what conclusions would you hope that your readers would reach once they have absorbed the information that you have presented?[6]

If you have not already done so, translate your ideas and information into a problem or question that you intend to solve or answer. If your paper is not framed in terms of a problem or question, then you must develop some other rationale. Perhaps you are reviewing the literature on a particular subject. Perhaps you are examining or trying to reconcile opposing points of view. Perhaps you are simply doing a report on a book. Whatever the case, you should integrate your thesis statement or your statement of purpose into your introduction. It is important to sustain this focus as you delve into the body of your paper.

Keep in mind that readers have expectations, biases (what they believe to be true or right), and gaps in knowledge that might lead to different conclusions. You must be ready to confront, circumvent, or consciously ignore what might be in your reader's mind. When deciding which course to take, you should consider what knowledge and assumptions your reader is bringing to your paper.

Returning to our student paper, we can see the overriding goal that is built into the assignment: to communicate a facet of immigrant history through an interpretive rendering of one person's experience. The following excerpts demonstrate how the topic and thesis statement are introduced, and interwoven with information gleaned from Diane's interview with her

---

[6]For a more extensive discussion of these and other questions, see Flower and Hayes, Ibid., pp. 458–59.

grandmother and from library research about Jewish immigration. The preliminary thesis statement, slightly expanded, is underscored.

### EARLY IMMIGRANT EXPERIENCES OF MARY MENDELOW: ATTITUDES TOWARD ASSIMILATION

My grandmother Mary threw up her arms in exasperation. She certainly had reservations about my probing the intimate details of her past, yet she was also eager to relate her story to me. Although my grandmother now feels very much at home living in a neighborhood in the Bronx where there are many ethnic groups, she originally came from a close-knit Jewish enclave in the Ukraine and had very little contact with people from any culture other than her own. When she first came to this country at eighteen years of age in 1920, my grandmother had few reservations about shrugging off many Jewish customs, and saw adapting to American culture as a positive thing. While she still identifies with Jewish culture, she has no desire to live the way she did in the old country or even to live in an exclusively Jewish community.

Diane engages her readers' attention by bringing them into the interview. She does this by describing the emotionally charged atmosphere as her grandmother reveals intimate details of her early life. As readers, we are reminded that we, too, are missing large parts of our own family history. This need or desire to know our past is a concern that we all share, and the paper arouses our interest in this grandmother's saga because we are curious about our own family roots.

Notice that the thesis statement is still somewhat vague. We are told that her grandmother "saw adapting to American culture as a positive thing," but we do not know why this is so, or what facilitated her adjustment from "a close-knit Jewish enclave in the Ukraine," to feeling comfortable "living in a neighborhood in the Bronx where there are many ethnic groups." The paper goes on to recount the saga of Mary Mendelow, and to place her story in historical context:

When my grandmother recalls people and experiences, she becomes very emotional. Sometimes she would insist that I put my pencil down because she didn't want me to record certain memories that were very painful for her, and at other times she emphasized how much love and reverence she felt for certain people.

Her father, Lewis Levy, was one of those people for whom she felt tremendous love and respect. He was the first of her family to come to this country. He came in 1912 with the intention of earning enough money to bring the rest of his family to America. When I asked her about his motives for coming, my grandmother, in disbelief of my ignorance, explained that he came partly because he was trying to avoid being drafted into the Russian army, and also because the situation for Jews in Russia was very precarious. Jews were being massacred and repeatedly chased out of villages. My grandmother recalls running from one town to the next, and crawling into barns to sneak food for her family. In Russia Lewis had worked as a bookkeeper and also candled eggs. When he came to the United States, he found a similar job candling eggs. . . . In 1920 Lewis sent for his wife and four children (including my grandmother). They lived together with a boarder in an apartment in the Williamsburg section of Brooklyn.

My grandmother's account of why and how her family came to this country coincides with historical records of the situation of Russian Jews in the early 1900s. The Harvard Encyclopedia of American Ethnic Groups cites a number of factors, beginning with the assassination of Tsar Alexander II in 1881, which led to a steady increase in Jewish emigration from Russia between 1881 and 1924: "After the assassination of Tsar Alexander II, the new regime introduced policies that encouraged mob violence. Pogroms in 1881 and 1882 struck over 200 Jewish communities and ushered in three decades of anti-Jewish outbursts" (p. 581). Then in 1882, the "May Laws," which expelled Jews from rural centers and put severe restrictions on Jewish trade in cities, were instituted. In 1891 Jews were banished from major cities such as Moscow and St. Petersburg, and by 1900 "more than one in four Jews received some form of charitable aid from the Jewish community" (p. 581). All these conditions, combined with the Russo-Japanese war and the 1905 Revolution, triggered a mass exodus of Russian Jews.

Just as in my grandmother's situation, the article states, "The Russian Jewish father in his twenties or thirties preceding his family was typical" (p. 581). After Russian Jews arrived in the United States, most of them lived in Jewish communities which preserved a lot of the ethnic flavor through newspapers and various organizations. However, other immigrants were becoming established in America and were eager to become part of the American culture around them. According to the Harvard Encyclopedia, the Yiddish Press even publicized citizenship and Americanization programs.

As fewer Jewish immigrants entered the country, the tendency to want to assimilate quickly increased. The year after my grandmother arrived in this country—1921—was the peak year for Jewish immigration. To quote the Harvard Encyclopedia again: "Nearly 120,000 Jewish immigrants entered the United States, most joining families that had arrived earlier. After the passage of the Immigration Restriction Act of 1924, Jewish immigration fell to 10,000; thereafter new immigrants assumed a marginal place in American Jewish life and rapid acculturation shaped the society" (p. 588).

When my grandmother came to this country, she was already eighteen years old, and there was no question in her mind that she was part of the Jewish community and always would be. She made no conscious effort to preserve her culture because doing things according to Jewish culture was the only way she knew. However, my grandmother's circumstances did encourage her to learn English and to adapt to American culture. When she first came here, she was sent to what she called a "prep school" for immigrants. There she was taught English, arithmetic, and American customs. Her three younger brothers attended public school, except for the oldest of them who also went to the prep school. Although the eldest of the brothers, George, went on to college and became an engineer, my grandmother was not permitted to further her education. Since she was a woman, nobody had any expectation that she would need a career.

The remainder of the paper recounts her various work experiences, her social relations, and her troubled marriage. It is not until the conclusion that the student brings together these disparate elements, and assumes a more analytical stance toward what her grandmother has told her:

> In looking back at my grandmother's early experiences in this country as an immigrant, I can see that her economic and family circumstances allowed her very little choice except to assimilate the American culture around her. It was necessary for her to work, and through work she became exposed to a variety of cultures and to the American way of doing things. I sense, though, that my grandmother felt this exposure to American life was liberating. When I asked her about her Jewish heritage, she said, "I'm still Jewish, I haven't thrown my Jewishness away. I think the Jewish culture will go on although it won't be the same way as we did it." Thus, even though my grandmother is proud of and appreciates many aspects of her Jewish heritage—such as its music, humor, history, and literature—she has not limited herself exclusively to the Jewish community for her economic or social needs.

Here, then, is a good example of thoughts emerging through writing. The idea that economic need compelled her grandmother to work, that work functioned as a bridge to American culture, and that this was experienced as a kind of personal liberation had not been fully anticipated by the student at the outset of her paper. Now, with this new insight, our student-writer must consider revising the paper in order to integrate these new ideas into her thesis and the body of the paper.

### Revision

One of the most grievous errors that students make is in treating their first draft as the final draft. There is yet another critical step in the writing process: revision.

Revision is a pervasive activity. Even as you write, you review and reflect on what you have written, and make appropriate changes. Nevertheless, there is always a need to look at your writing with a fresh eye. After some time has passed you can, in effect, approach your own manuscript as a reader as well as a writer. With a fresh eye you may see inconsistencies in logic. You may realize that you need more information to substantiate a point. You may see a connection that eluded you as you were enmeshed in an earlier draft.

At the very least, revision involves refining and polishing a penultimate draft (the next to the last one). Spelling errors are corrected, sentences are rewritten for grammatical reasons, and an occasional word is changed for accuracy or clarity. However, revision can involve a more extensive overhaul of an earlier draft, especially if you have had the benefit of feedback from an instructor or some other critical reader. Your revision might involve rewriting—adding, cutting, and/or reordering. When engaged in this kind of revision, you need to resist becoming so enamored with your prose that you are unwilling to let go of language or ideas that do not "work," and thus detract from the paper.

If, as suggested earlier, writing and thinking are related, and we advance our thinking in the very act of writing, then it is inevitable and altogether desirable that first drafts will require considerable revision. In other words, once we arrive at new insights or a clearer formulation of what we want to say, then it becomes possible to go back and streamline our thought process, eliminating digressions or sloppiness that crept in as we thought through a problem.

In the case of our student paper, Diane began with an enigma. Her grandmother's experience, as a Russian-Jewish immigrant whose marriage ended in divorce, was undeniably harsh. Yet her grandmother still regards this period of her life as a fulfilling one. How can we make sense of this apparent contradiction? Diane's answer is somewhat complex. Through the process of writing the paper, she came to a new and subtle understanding that could be stated as a paradox: The burdens and tribulations that marked her grandmother's life were real, but nonetheless liberating. Indeed, it was the hardships associated with immigrant life that forced her grandmother into the world of work, and that gave her a sense of independence and pride in having overcome so many obstacles. This is a stunning insight, unanticipated by the writer at the outset of her study—the product of writing and thinking working in concert.

In the final revision, note that Diane has refined her original thesis statement to include the ideas that she arrived at through writing and revising a series of drafts. For our purposes, we have reproduced only the introduction. The revised material is underscored.

### THE ASSIMILATION OF MARY MENDELOW

My grandmother Mary threw up her arms in exasperation. She certainly had reservations about my probing the intimate details of her past, yet she was also eager to relate her story to me. Although my grandmother now feels very much at home living in a neighborhood in the Bronx where there are many ethnic groups, she originally came from a close-knit Jewish enclave in the Ukraine and had very little contact with people from any culture other than her own. What gave my grandmother a bridge to American culture was the experience and education she gained through working outside her family. Although it was out of economic necessity that she worked, this nevertheless gave her an understanding of American mores and customs, and exposed her to people from diverse cultures.

In the old country, she related almost exclusively with family members, and had a role only within her family unit. In the United States she became part of larger social institutions. Having the ability to function in both her own ethnic group and in the larger American society put my grandmother at a great advantage. With an understanding of both the Jewish people and of America, my grandmother was in a freer position to choose which ethnic traditions to incorporate into her life. Today, while she still identifies with Jewish culture, she has no desire to live the way she did in Russia or even to live in an exclusively Jewish community in this country.

Revised thesis statement

In this chapter, we delineated various steps or phases of the writing process, beginning with the discovery and arrangement of ideas, and leading to the composition and finally to the revision of drafts. To repeat, we do not mean to imply a linear series of steps. In the final analysis, writing is a uniquely personal act, and there is no single way to go about composing a paper. One writer might spend time developing elaborate outlines, and then write and revise simultaneously. A second writer might spend a great deal of time jotting down notes, playing with ideas, and then organizing these ideas while writing a series of drafts. A third writer might plunge in with very little preparation, allowing for a free flow of ideas, but expecting that substantial revision will be necessary to give coherence to those ideas. In other words, different writers will work with these stages of writing in different combinations. Through trial and error, you will have to find the combination that suits your temperament and style, and that results in the most effective writing.

## SUGGESTIONS FOR WRITING AND THINKING

1. At the next class meeting of one of your social science courses, begin a journal in which you jot down your responses to key ideas or information presented by the instructor. Reflect on questions or issues that came up in class discussion. Are there any questions or ambiguities that are unresolved in your mind? Do you have any personal experiences that relate to the issues discussed in class? The purpose of this journal entry is meant to help you "discover your ideas," and the writing need not be formal and polished.

2. Take a subject that you might like to explore in a formal paper for a social science course. Brainstorm or freewrite around the subject in order to discover your ideas and formulate a specific topic. Generate a series of questions about this topic in order to further develop your thinking. Is there a single overarching question that will govern the paper? Try to develop a preliminary thesis statement that poses a tentative answer to this question.

*Chapter 3*
# WRITING AND RESEARCH IN THE SOCIAL SCIENCES

Academic writing or discourse generally involves the communication of research findings that address stated problems, and hence is intended to advance the frontier of knowledge. Students, too, are often called upon to conduct original research, or to address some problem in terms of their life experience, personal observation, or library research. Not all writing in social science, however, involves original research. Students and scholars alike often write about research conducted by others. Sometimes this involves reporting on and evaluating a specific study or a body of research. A more common format is the book review, and every discipline has a number of journals that routinely publish reviews of recent books in the field.

More will be said about these different forms of writing in later chapters. The main point here is that whether one is reporting one's own research or attempting to interpret and evaluate the research of others, it is imperative that the writer be familiar with the research process. This is the underlying rationale for Chapters 6 to 9 of this book, which deal with the various methods that are commonly employed in social science research and the implications that each has for composition. As a preliminary step, however, let us consider the role that writing plays in the research process generally.

## THE ROLE OF WRITING IN THE RESEARCH PROCESS

Writing is an integral part of the research process because it is through words on paper that we explore questions, define problems, interpret evidence, and communicate insights.

Just how integral the relationship is between research and writing is not always appreciated. To be sure, they are separate operations in the sense that social scientists first carry out the research and then "write up the results." Rarely, however, does writing consist merely of a rote presentation of research findings. In the first place, it is necessary, through writing, to develop a *context* in which evidence will be presented and interpreted. Its meaning becomes clear only in terms of a frame of reference, the question it purports to answer, the problem it attempts to solve, the body of knowledge to which it contributes. Facts rarely speak for themselves. They need to be interpreted, explained, communicated. It is through establishing connections and relationships with other facts and observations that the full significance of otherwise isolated facts is brought out.

As an example, suppose that a researcher found that there has been a sharp rise in ethnic intermarriage. Taken at face value, this fact speaks for itself. Placed in context with other observations and concerns, however, this "isolated fact" assumes great significance as an indicator of much larger trends, and is subject to very different meanings and interpretations. The upswing in intermarriage may be viewed as a sign that groups once stigmatized as undesirable are enjoying greater social acceptance. From another standpoint, however, it may be viewed as a sign that ethnic bonds have so eroded that the future of these groups may be imperiled. Though not necessarily incompatible, these are two very different interpretations of the raw data. Which interpretation is advanced or emphasized depends on the purposes of the research, the questions posed, and the background information introduced as the context for the investigation.

Thus, the act of writing frames the investigation as researchers wrestle with the statement of the problem, their purpose in pursuing this topic, and the strategies they will use to gather evidence, interpret findings, and communicate a point of view. As Chapter 2 suggested, we use writing to discover our ideas; to learn the full meaning of these ideas by seeing them in relation to each other; and finally, to communicate our understanding in clear, precise language, within a context that is meaningful to our readers. In short, writing clarifies and organizes thought.

## WHAT IS A RESEARCH PROBLEM?

At this juncture it will be useful to give more formal definition to what is meant by a *research problem*, as well as a number of related terms that will be encountered in later chapters: *hypothesis, data, research procedures, sample, instrument,* and *argument.*

When social scientists speak of a *research problem*, they do not necessarily refer to facets of social life that are deemed problematic or troublesome, such as racism, poverty, or crime. Social scientists are equally interested in "the problem of order," that is, how societies regulate social relations, curb aggression, and maintain civic peace. Broadly speaking, a research problem involves any question or issue around which there is uncertainty or doubt, and that will be addressed or resolved by the research. In framing the research problem, the investigator must specify exactly where the uncertainty or doubt lies, since this gives justification to the research—why it is being undertaken. Once the rationale for the research is established, the writer has both a point of departure and an overriding objective or thrust for the research report.

In pursuing a research problem, researchers often, though by no means always, put forward a *hypothesis*, or a statement of the expected findings. The next step is to collect evidence, or *data*, that will test the hypothesis, or provide answers to the research questions. Data are collected through the use of one or another *research procedure*, such as library or archival research, direct observation, or the collection of statistical data. Social scientists draw a distinction between *quantitative data*, which involve numerical or statistical information, and *qualitative data*, which refer to the nonnumerical observations typical of most historical research and field studies. In quantitative studies it is rarely possible to survey the entire population, and therefore a *sample*, or subgroup, is selected, usually through a scientific sampling procedure that assures that the sample is *representative* of the larger population. Finally, the term *instrument* refers to the data-collection procedure—whether an interview or a self-administered questionnaire.

Like *research problem*, the term *argument* has popular connotations that easily lead to misunderstanding. "Argument" does not necessarily mean that the writer is disagreeing with someone else. In developing an argument the writer is setting forth a point of view, a result, or an interpretation—one that is supported by the data that have been collected. The argument may or may not explicitly challenge an opposing set of facts or assumptions. However, not unlike a defense attorney who presents a case to the jury, writers are well advised to anticipate opposing facts or interpretations that are likely to be advanced by critical readers. In this sense a research paper is more than a simple statement of findings: It is an "argument" in defense of a particular conclusion. This is yet another reason why social science demands writing that is clear, precise, and convincing.

## THE RHETORICAL STANCE: SUBJECT, AUDIENCE, AND VOICE

Like all writing, academic discourse is motivated by a desire on the part of the writer to communicate with the reader. Effective communication involves the use of *rhetoric.* This term refers to the means of persuasion, sometimes construed as the "art of writing." The three major elements of rhetoric are *subject, audience,* and *voice.* Writers must always consider the information and/or point of view that they wish to present (subject); the needs and expectations of their readers (audience); and the tone that most clearly reflects their disposition toward both audience and subject (voice).

Wayne C. Booth, a leading writing theorist, refers to the balance among these elements—subject, audience, and voice—as the *rhetorical stance*.[1] In calling for a balance, Booth admonishes the writer not to ignore the reader while expounding on the subject. On the other hand, he warns against concentrating on "pure effect" at the cost of "undervaluing" the subject.[2]

Although subject, audience, and voice are interrelated, it will be helpful if we discuss them separately in the pages that follow.

## Subject

The subject is more than an accumulation of facts or ideas on a given area of study. As we suggested in the previous chapter, through an interactive process of reading, thinking, and writing, the subject is refined to a focused statement that contains the purpose of the writer in communicating specific information. This purpose can be simply a statement of intent—for example, to summarize, report on, or expound on a topic. Or the purpose might contain a full-fledged thesis statement, which develops a dominant idea and a point of view. To fulfill this purpose, the writer needs to organize the material with the audience in mind.

As scholars, social scientists are more intent on presenting their subject clearly and logically than they are on affecting readers' senses and emotions. This does not mean that there is no interaction between writer and reader. Both writer and reader are engaged in a collaborative pursuit of knowledge. The emphasis is on the subject and how we understand it, and thus by presenting a subject clearly and logically, the writer is engaging the reader on the basis of a shared concern for truth.

This kind of writing is called "referential writing," according to a schema classifying the aims of discourse proposed by James Kinneavy.[2] According to Kinneavy, referential writing has three related aims: (1) to explore a question, (2) to argue for an answer, and (3) to provide information. In contrast to his other categories—to express oneself, to entertain, to persuade to an action—referential writing is more oriented to the research question than to the audience. Let us briefly consider each of the three aims of referential writing.

*Exploratory discourse* asks a question, diagnoses a problem, proposes a solution to a problem, or provides a "tentative definition" of some term or concept. This is typically the aim of seminars, symposia, and preliminary studies.

[1]Wayne C. Booth, "The Rhetorical Stance," in *The Writing Teacher's Sourcebook*, eds. Gary Tate and Edward P. J. Corbett (New York: Oxford University Press, 1981), p. 111.

[2]James Kinneavy, "The Basic Aims of Discourse," in *The Writing Teacher's Sourcebook*, eds. Tate and Corbett, pp. 95–96.

*Scientific discourse* attempts to answer a research question either by arguing from accepted premises or by generalizing from particular examples. This is the inherent aim of research, whether it is based on original data or on studies conducted by other investigators.

*Informative discourse* answers a question by reporting on events, facts, and ideas. This is generally the aim of abstracts, reports, and news articles.

Of course, these aims commonly overlap. We cannot prove or argue a point without first exploring an issue, diagnosing a problem, and reporting on what others have said about that problem. Even if our aim is simply to report, without advancing our own point of view, we select and organize information according to some plan or perspective that we hope will make the material clear to the reader.

## Audience

The audience, your intended readers, also influences your selection and arrangement of material, as well as your style of writing. As students, however, you should not write solely for an instructor, even if that person will be the only reader of your paper. The danger is that you will neglect to include enough background information, or to elaborate on key points, because you assume that the instructor already has this knowledge. Even if this is the case, most instructors expect students to demonstrate their understanding of the subject by providing appropriate background information and developing arguments fully. It would be better, therefore, to assume that you are writing not only for your instructor but also for your classmates and others who have an interest in your subject.

There are certain conventions dictated by audience that apply to virtually all writing. For example, readers expect an introduction that conveys the writer's purpose and that provides enough background material to allow the reader to make sense of that purpose. In content and style, the introduction will depend on the audience. If the audience consists of other scholars in the field, the writer will want to place his or her study within the context of the existing literature on the subject. Typically, academic writers begin their articles by pointing to an assumption or understanding that has been put forward by previous writers, and is presumably shared by many readers. The writer's aim is to reaffirm, extend, qualify, or oppose this assumption. If the audience consists of general readers, the writer may also begin by citing a common assumption, but it is likely to be one rooted in public opinion rather than in previous research.

To illustrate how an introduction depends on the intended audience, let us take an article that was initially published in a scholarly journal, and later revised for publication in a popular journal. The research on which these articles were based was designed to test whether the expectations that teachers have of their students influences how well these children actually perform in school. The results were first published in *Psychological*

*Reports* under the bland title, "Teacher's Expectancies: Determinants of Pupils' IQ Gains." It began as follows:

> Experiments have shown that in behavioral research employing human or animal S's [subjects], E's [the experimenters] expectancy can be a significant determinant of S's response (Rosenthal, 1964, in press). In studies employing animals, for example, E's led to believe that their rat S's had been bred for superior learning ability obtained performance superior to that obtained by E's led to believe their rats had been bred for inferior learning ability (Rosenthal & Fode, 1963; Rosenthal & Lawson, 1964). The present study was designed to extend the generality of this finding from E's to teachers and from animal S's to school children.[3]

About a year later the authors published their findings in a popular journal, *Scientific American,* under the less pedantic title, "Teacher Expectations for the Disadvantaged." This version began as follows:

> One of the central problems of American society lies in the fact that certain children suffer a handicap in their education which then persists throughout life. The "disadvantaged" child is a Negro American, a Mexican American, a Puerto Rican or any other child who lives in conditions of poverty. He is a lower-class child who performs poorly in an educational system that is staffed almost entirely by middle-class teachers.
>
> The reason usually given for the poor performance of the disadvantaged child is simply that the child is a member of a disadvantaged group. There may well be another reason. It is that the child does poorly in school because that is what is expected of him. In other words, his shortcomings may originate not in his different ethnic, cultural and economic background but in his teachers' response to that background.[4]

This example illustrates how the audience influences not only the style but form and content as well. In the case of the scholarly article, the study is presented entirely within the context of earlier research conducted on animals. If expectations that experimenters have of rats influence their performance, the authors argue, then perhaps the expectations of teachers have similar bearing on the performance of children. Thus, their research is justified in terms of earlier research, and conceived in terms of the theoretical relationship between expectations and performance.

In the case of the *Scientific American* article, the research is introduced and justified on a far more pragmatic level—the academic problems of disadvantaged children—which was a subject that was widely debated at the time the article was published. Thus, the introduction is designed to engage general readers, and to raise their interest in the results. The previous research, which is given such prominence in the scholarly article, is mentioned only in passing (in subsequent paragraphs not quoted here).

[3]Robert Rosenthal and Lenore F. Jacobson, "Teachers' Expectancies: Determinants of Pupils' IQ Gains," *Psychological Reports,* 19 (1966), 115–18.

[4]Robert Rosenthal and Lenore F. Jacobson, "Teacher Expectations for the Disadvantaged," *Scientific American,* 218 (April 1968), 19.

Another difference between the two versions has to do with language. The writing in the scholarly article is admittedly arid, but precise. By comparison, the writing in the *Scientific American* article is undeniably more engaging, though less detailed. As this example suggests, scholars must sometimes forsake lively writing for technical precision and thoroughness.[5]

As students, your writing usually falls between these two poles, since you are implicitly addressing a mixed audience of professionals and peers. Although you are not likely to have the background to reel off a series of studies that lay the groundwork for your own paper, you can still refer to important works on a topic that have influenced your own thinking. Many instructors expect students to emulate the conventions of a scholarly journal. Whether or not this is the case, you should attempt to adapt your language not just to the general reader but to those who are being schooled, as you are, in the language of social science.

## Voice

Your success in engaging the audience largely depends on your ability to project a voice that is trustworthy. Aristotle referred to this as "ethos," the ethical appeal of someone who has demonstrated that he or she is a person of good sense, good moral character, and good will. In academic discourse, this means the voice of reason, objectivity, and fairness.[6]

Reason, here, is paramount. The "honest face" is not enough, as Mina Shaughnessy and others have contended.[7] The academic voice conveys good sense and worthy intentions through an ability to elucidate, validate, order information, and above all, to extend an argument.

The "ethos" of the social scientist is based on values of reason, objectivity, fairness, and caution in asserting large claims. Some forty years ago, when social science was in its infancy, the sociologist William Ogburn wrote an essay on "scientific writing" in which he argued that emotive language was inappropriate to scientific discourse. For Ogburn clarity and verification were the distinguishing characteristics of scientific writing. As he wrote:

> The object of scientific exposition is to transmit knowledge, not feelings. Words that arouse emotion are generally more suitable to persuasion and entertainment than they are to science. . . . [The scientist's] report should be in such language that his findings are verifiable. . . . Opinion is often a characteristic of unverifiable statements.[8]

---

[5]The *Scientific American* article is reprinted in its entirety in Chapter 6.

[6]Patricia Bizzell, "The Ethos of Academic Writing," *College Composition and Communication*, XXIX (December 1978), 351–55.

[7]Mina Shaughnessy, *Errors and Expectations* (New York: Oxford University Press, 1977), p. 206.

[8]William F. Ogburn, "On Scientific Writing," *American Journal of Sociology*, 52 (March 1947), 385–86.

Ogburn's point is that "the scientist should not try to implant attitudes in readers which the facts do not convey."[9] Indeed, one of the hallmarks of social science is to insist upon sufficient evidence to substantiate a claim. It is this reliance on evidence that imparts the voice with authority. As writers, we rely on evidence to make our arguments convincing. As readers, we listen because the evidence compels us to.

In most scholarly writing, there are a number of organizational features that contribute to the authority and clarity of the writer's voice:

- An *initial overview* of the problem to be discussed, usually at the very beginning of a book or article.
- A *pattern* or *plan* evident through the use of divisions, with appropriate headings and subheadings. A common format for research papers includes the following divisions: Introduction, Previous Research, The Present Study, Findings, Conclusions.
- *Emphasis on important points* either by stressing their importance or by repeating them (perhaps in different language) at appropriate junctures, especially when summarizing key findings, interpretations, and conclusions.

Social scientists also employ certain stylistic features to convey a sense of objectivity:

- Words and phrases that indicate relationships between researcher and subject or among facts, events, and ideas. For example: "On the basis of these observations, we can infer . . ." or: "If we compare X to Y, then we see that . . ." or: "It would therefore appear that X is one cause of Y. . . ."
- Restricted use of the personal pronoun *I*. Instead, the passive voice is common. For example: "It was found that . . ." or: "In order to address this question, survey data were employed. . . ."

Note the objective tone in the following passage, which is taken from an article that analyzed the ideological character of Little Orphan Annie. In the very first paragraph, the author provides an overview of the problem, verifies a claim, and states the study's purpose, all in a tone that conveys seriousness and impartiality:

### A CONTENT ANALYSIS OF "LITTLE ORPHAN ANNIE"

Verification of claim   The most significant characteristic associated with comic strips is their huge audience which includes four-fifths of all adult newspaper readers. If, in the

Overview   face of this popularity, modern comic strips show a tendency to deal with events and issues of the real world, then cognizance must be taken of the emergence of the comic strip as an important mass communication medium.   Passive voice

Purpose of study   In view of these conditions an analysis was made to determine the nature and extent to which a measurable social, political, and economic ideology was contained in "Little Orphan Annie," a nationally syndicated strip.[10]

[9]Ibid.

[10]Donald Auster, "A Content Analysis of 'Little Orphan Annie'," in *Sociology: Progress of a Decade*, eds. Seymour Martin Lipset and Neil J. Smelser (Englewood Cliffs, N.J.: Prentice-Hall, 1961), p. 241.

Note the use of the passive voice. The author has conducted a study of ideological bias in a comic strip, and seems to be going out of his way to establish his own impartiality, which is accented by the use of the passive voice. We hasten to add that the passive voice is often frowned upon, especially by writing teachers. Let us therefore examine this thorny issue further.

Without doubt, the passive voice is unappealing and cumbersome. Nevertheless, there is some rationale for using it in scientific discourse. The tacit assumption in scholarly writing is that although an author is at work, it is the evidence that provides ultimate authority. The writer is behind the scene, as it were, and irrelevant to the truth or falsity of a proposition. Thus, the passive voice helps to create a tone that is formal, authoritative, and impersonal, and is meant to inspire trust in the reader.

However, we do not wish to give the impression that the use of the personal pronouns *I* or *we* is proscribed under all circumstances. On the contrary, the use of the personal pronoun is sometimes appropriate and even necessary. This is especially true of field studies, where the investigator is engaged in personal observation of some social setting. Perhaps because these studies are inherently subjective, at least compared to studies based on "hard data," researchers are often willing to discuss the value premises that they brought to their study. For example, in her observational study of an old-age community, Arlie Hochschild wrote the following:

> Most of my goals concerning Merrill Court coincided with most of theirs. However, as a person of a different age and social class, and as a sociologist, my perspective differed from theirs. I thought that, as welfare recipients, they were poor; they thought they were "average." I initially felt that there was something sad about old people living together and that this was a social problem. They did not feel a bit sad about living together as old people, and although they felt that they *had* problems, they did not think that they *were* one.[11]

This is more than a statement of refreshing candor. Through use of the first person Hochschild creates analytical distance between her subjects and herself. Paradoxically, by openly discussing how her preconceptions changed in the process of doing the research, Hochschild establishes her objectivity.

## THE LANGUAGE OF SOCIAL SCIENCE

As with all fields of specialized knowledge, social science has evolved its own "language." The use of this vocabulary lends authority to the writer's voice in that it demonstrates a working knowledge of one's field. However, when the writer uses this vocabulary imprecisely or as a way of impersonat-

---

[11]Arlie Russell Hochschild, *The Unexpected Community* (Berkeley: University of California Press, 1973), p. 5.

ing the scholar, the results can be disastrous. Instead of technical precision, we get a tangle of phrases that bore and confuse the reader.

Social scientists have gained a certain notoriety for their use of "jargon." Some of the most trenchant criticism has come from humanists who are appalled by what they regard as a perversion of the English language. Fowler's *Dictionary of English Usage* even has an entry on "sociologese," which includes the following uncharitable comment on why sociologists are given to overblown language:

> Sociology is a new science concerning itself not with esoteric matters outside the comprehension of the layman, as the older sciences do, but with the ordinary affairs of ordinary people. This seems to engender in those who write about it a feeling that the lack of any abstruseness in their subject demands a compensatory abstruseness in their language.[12]

Nor has criticism come only from guardians of the English language. A good many social scientists complain about the obscure and often tortuous prose found in most professional journals and books. In a caustic essay entitled "The Smoke Screen of Jargon," Stanislav Andreski lampooned his fellow sociologists for using "impressive-sounding opaque jargon" that tells us nothing we did not know before.[13] Andreski compares the sociologist to a character in one of Molière's plays who answers the question about why opium makes people sleep by saying that it is because of its soporific power.[14] (The dictionary definition of "soporific" is "causing or tending to cause sleep.")

Because the issue of "jargon" has excited so much criticism of social science writing, let us confront the issue squarely. Is jargon merely a smoke screen for banality, as Andreski and others have claimed? Or is it a legitimate and valuable "tool of the trade," as its practitioners would like to think?

To begin with, let us be clear about what jargon is. The *Random House Dictionary* provides two meanings that are often confused.[15] One meaning is "the language, especially the vocabulary, peculiar to a particular trade, profession, or group." Social scientists can hardly be assailed for using this specialized language in their research and writing. When people complain of "jargon," however, they usually have the second meaning in mind: "unintelligible talk or writing, gibberish." Obviously, gibberish is indefensible,

---

[12]H. W. Fowler, *A Dictionary of Modern English Usage* (New York: Oxford University Press, 1965), p. 570. For a recent analysis of the "ills that afflict sociologists' writing," see Hanan C. Selvin and Everett F. Wilson, "On Sharpening Sociologists' Prose," *Sociological Quarterly*, 25 (Spring 1984), 205–22.

[13]Stanislav Andreski, *Social Sciences as Sorcery* (London: Andre Dent, 1972), p. 55.

[14]Ibid., p. 68.

[15]*The Random House Dictionary of the English Language* (New York: Random House, 1973).

even in the name of science. Thus, what needs to be addressed is the difference between legitimate jargon and academic gibberish. The issue is not whether jargon is aesthetically pleasing—it is not—but whether it enhances or detracts from understanding.

### When Jargon IS Jargon

As an example of jargon that clearly detracts from understanding, let us take a passage from a book by Talcott Parsons, who has earned a reputation as the profession's worst jargonmongerer:

> Skills constitute the manipulative techniques of human goal attainment and control in relation to the physical world, so far as artifacts or machines especially designed as tools do not yet supplement them. Truly human skills are guided by organized and codified *knowledge* of both the things to be manipulated and the human capacities that are used to manipulate them. Such knowledge is an aspect of cultural-level symbolic processes, and, like other aspects to be discussed presently, requires the capacities of the human central nervous system, particularly the brain.[16]

What does all this verbiage mean? Andreski offers a simple interpretation:

> As every schoolboy knows, a developed brain and acquired skills and knowledge are necessary for attaining specifically human goals. . . .[17]

In fairness to Parsons, his intended audience was not the general reader, but professional social scientists. Furthermore, as Dennis Wrong has pointed out, Parsons sought to identify what was unique and universal about the human experience, and this forced him to write on a high level of abstraction.[18] Still, the writing in this passage is atrocious. It is not just that the prose is confusing and almost unreadable. To make matters worse, the reader who takes up the challenge and translates the passage into simple English will discover what is already obvious.

It would be easy for us to cite other glaring examples of the misuse of jargon and to join the chorus of critics who decry the debasement of the English language. To do so, however, would beg a larger and more difficult issue: When is jargon legitimate? When does it enhance understanding?

### When Jargon Is NOT Jargon

As we suggested earlier, the first principle of writing is clear, direct, unembellished prose. Generally speaking, it is preferable to use common language over jargon. In other words, jargon should be avoided whenever

---

[16]Quoted in Andreski, pp. 60–61. The original source is Talcott Parsons, *Societies: Evolutionary and Comparative Perspectives* (Englewood Cliffs, N.J.: Prentice-Hall, 1966).

[17]Ibid., p. 60.

[18]Dennis H. Wrong, "Professional Jargon: Is Sociology the Culprit?" *Vniversity* (Publication of New York University), 2 (March 1983), 7–8.

the same idea can be expressed with common language. However, there are at least five occasions when the common language is problematic and the use of jargon is justified:

1. *The common language is often too ambiguous to be useful in social science discourse.*

Precisely because social scientists do not concern themselves with esoteric matters outside the comprehension of the layperson, it is often necessary to find language that is more precise and discriminating than the common language. Everybody knows what it means to "fall in love," but this term is so imprecise, and given to so many different meanings, that it would be useless in any serious study of this phenomenon. As a result, psychological studies are peppered with words such as "affectual systems," "libido," "erogenous needs," and "oedipal substitution." The layperson may scoff at the use of such abstruse language to describe familiar emotions, but the social scientist would not get very far employing the nebulous words, clichés, and euphemisms that are used in common parlance.

Even when social scientists use common words, they often do so in uncommon ways. Thus, when economists speak of "capital," or political scientists of "democracy," or psychologists of "personality," or anthropologists of "culture," or sociologists of "community," they mean more than what is meant or understood when laypeople use these terms. To a layperson, "democracy" probably conjures up a single salient observation, such as popular elections. But to a political scientist the term is associated with a whole constellation of interrelated factors, and embedded in a large body of scholarship concerning the history, theory, and dynamics of democratic systems. Thus, even when social scientists use common words, they often give them technical definition.

2. *Occasionally no words exist in the common language that adequately express a new idea or describe a new phenomenon.*

At times a writer may not be able to find words to express a new idea or insight, and is forced to coin a new term (these are called "neologisms"). This is a perilous step, to be taken only as a last resort.

On the other hand, some neologisms are justifiable, so much so that they eventually make their way into common parlance. Freud, for example, coined the term "narcissism," building on the Greek myth of Narcissus, the youth who fell in love with his own image reflected in a pool. David Riessman coined the term "inner-directed personality," which involved a juxtaposition of familiar words to form a new concept. While Emile Durkheim did not coin the word "anomie," he was the first to introduce it into the sociological lexicon. All three of these words have made their way into the general language.

For example, a recent edition of the *Random House Dictionary of the English Language* defines "inner-directed" as follows:

Guided by internalized values rather than external pressures. Cf. other-directed.[19]

To the extent that social science jargon is incorporated into the common language, then jargon can be seen not as a debasement of language, but as part of the ongoing evolution of language.

Also to be considered is the fact that a body of social science writing is concerned with *change*, and new developments often require new names. For example, in her book *The Origins of Totalitarianism*, Hannah Arendt was among the first to use the term "totalitarianism" to refer to regimes, like that of Nazi Germany, that seek monolithic control over all major social institutions. "Mass society" is another term invented by social scientists to refer to the tendency of modern society to weld its population into a single undifferentiated mass.

3. *The common language is sometimes too concrete to be useful in theoretical analysis.*

All of the social sciences have theoretical branches whose goal is to develop large concepts on the basis of complex patterns of observation. Often the common language is on too low a level of abstraction to denote these large concepts, and social theorists occasionally feel compelled to coin new terms. This is when critics are most likely to inveigh against the mutilation of language.

For example, Talcott Parsons sought to develop a simple schema for classifying all human societies. He began by identifying two traits defined by dichotomies: universalism-particularism and achievement-ascription. Parsons held that all societies could be classified in terms of these two traits, which were found in different combinations, thus producing four distinct types of societies. According to this schema, all modern industrial societies conform to the "universalistic-achievement pattern," whereas traditional societies organized around kinship belong to the "particularistic-ascriptive pattern." Granted, these are jarring terms, and their usefulness can be debated. Their purpose, however, is to raise the analytical focus above the empirical level, and to transcend the limits of the common language.

4. *The common language is sometimes so riddled with value judgments that it thwarts objectivity.*

Consider the following example. After the assassination of Martin Luther King in 1968, there were outbreaks of violence in dozens of American cities. These were termed "riots" by government officials, the media, and the public at large. On closer examination, however, "riot" is anything but value-free. It conjures up images of wanton violence, and of "rioters" bent on looting and mindless destruction. Indeed, the term virtually implies a the-

---

[19]*The Random House Dictionary of the English Language* (New York: Random House, 1987).

ory by suggesting that these are the acts of aberrant and antisocial individuals. Insofar as these value judgments are consonant with prevailing views, the bias inherent in the term "riot" easily escapes notice. The social scientist who uncritically accepts the prevailing wisdom will not hesitate to use the term, as Edward Banfield did in an essay titled "Rioting Mainly for Fun and Profit."[20]

Other social critics, however, interpreted the "riots" as a form of protest against ghetto conditions.[21] While not condoning violence, they argued that "riots" were the inevitable byproduct of smoldering resentments within the ghetto population. These writers insisted that it would be more accurate to refer to these events as "revolts" or "uprisings," as Robert Blauner did in his essay "Internal Colonialism and Ghetto Revolt."[22] Clearly, more is involved here than a quibble over word choice.

The Kerner Commission that was commissioned by Congress to study the "riots" sought a middle ground, and adopted the term "civic disorders."[23] At first blush, one is inclined to wince at such stilted language. Its virtue, of course, is that it is neutral and avoids making prejudgments one way or another. After all, whether violence was wanton or selective, whether its participants were driven by antisocial impulses or expressing rage over their condition—these and other such issues must be resolved through empirical research, not assumed in the very terms of discourse. As this example shows, when the common language is so value-laden that it compromises objectivity, the use of jargon is not only permissible, but probably advisable.

5. *Compared to the common language, jargon is often more concise.*
When adolescents refer to a person as "cool," the term embodies a whole welter of ideas and assumptions shared by those who partake of adolescent subculture. By the same token, social science jargon often functions as a shorthand or a code for much larger ideas. Take the term "sex-role socialization," for example. Admittedly, it is cumbersome. Its virtue is that it compresses into a few words shared assumptions about gender and the social character of gender that would otherwise require elaborate explanation. By obviating further discussion, this shorthand term allows the writer to get on with the argument, thus allowing for greater economy of speech and more cogent writing.

In this chapter we presented the best defense of jargon that we could muster. On the whole, however, we agree with critics who contend that social science writing is marred by an excessive use of jargon. As students in

[20]Edward Banfield, *The Unheavenly City Revisited* (Boston: Little, Brown, 1974), chap. 9.

[21]For example, Robert M. Fogelson, *Violence as Protest* (New York: Doubleday, 1971).

[22]Robert Blauner, *Racial Oppression in America* (New York: Harper & Row, 1972), chap. 5.

[23]*Report of the National Advisory Commission on Civil Disorders* (New York: Bantam Books, 1968).

social science courses, you will be introduced to key concepts that make up the language of social science, and you should incorporate these concepts into your thinking and writing. Remember, however, that the overriding function of writing is to communicate. If communication is enhanced by scientific terminology, you should not hesitate to use it. On the other hand, if the same idea can be expressed in plain language, then jargon should be avoided.

## SUGGESTIONS FOR WRITING AND THINKING

1.  The following abstract is from an article by Claude Fischer on "The Effect of Urban Life on Traditional Values," published in *Social Forces* (March 1975). Rewrite it in plain language as though you were writing for a nonacademic journal intended for an educated audience, such as *Scientific American* or *Psychology Today*.

    Three models predict an association between urbanism and nontraditional behavior: (1) that it is a function of the characteristics of individuals found in cities; (2) that it is due to the anomie* of cities; (3) that it is due to the generation of and consequent influence of innovative urban subcultures. Secondary analysis† of American survey data on religiosity, church attendance, attitudes toward alcohol and birth control confirm the general urbanism-deviance association. . . .Some suggestive data point to Model 3 as the more accurate one.

2.  How would you characterize the language in the above abstract in terms of subject, audience, and voice? Is the use of jargon legitimate? Are there instances where you think jargon is unnecessary or inappropriate?

---

*This term was coined by Emile Durkheim, the "father" of sociology. Literally it means "normlessness"—a condition where individuals are not well integrated into groups that provide moral authority and regulation over their lives.

†This term refers to research based on data collected for another purpose.

# Chapter 4
# RHETORICAL STRATEGIES

In Chapter 3 we discussed the importance of purpose in shaping the content of a paper. One might say that purpose refers to a writer's destination. In this chapter we discuss the rhetorical strategies for reaching that destination. By "rhetorical strategies" we mean the different organizational patterns that recur in all expository writing. Eight rhetorical strategies are discussed in this chapter:

1. Definition
2. Classification
3. Description
4. Narration
5. Illustration
6. Comparison-contrast
7. Cause-effect
8. Argument

Before going any further, we want to stress that these rhetorical strategies are not immutable forms. They are not "muffin tins" into which we pour our academic batter, to use the words of one critic.[1] Writers do not make a conscious decision to adopt one or another strategy, and to adhere to its rules. Rather, in exploring a topic or developing an argument, writers intuitively employ whatever rhetorical strategy helps to clarify and communicate their ideas. Furthermore, different rhetorical strategies may be used within the same paper, depending on purpose and need.

For example, when Durkheim wrote his classic study of suicide, he found it necessary at the outset to define suicide. Next, he developed a classification of different types of suicide, in order to distinguish, for exam-

---

[1]C. H. Knoblauch and Lil Brannon, "Writing as Learning Through the Curriculum," *College English*, 45, no. 5 (September 1983), 468.

ple, between people who sacrifice their life for a cause and those who destroy themselves out of sheer despair. Then he explored differences in the rate of suicide over time and between different countries. In other words, Durkheim used the rhetorical strategies of "definition," "classification," and "comparison-contrast" even though he did not do so as a matter of preconceived design.[2]

Thus, the discussion that follows only makes explicit what is often tacitly understood by writers as they formulate their ideas and commit them to writing. As a self-conscious writer, you will be able to make better use of rhetorical strategies for generating questions, clarifying thought, and organizing material into a coherent exposition.

## DEFINITION

Communication is not possible unless we agree on the meaning of the words that we use. A dictionary will usually suffice to clarify the meaning of particular words. However, the meaning of concepts is not so easily resolved. A common form of writing in all academic disciplines is the extended essay that seeks to define key concepts in all of their ramifications. Indeed, whole volumes have been written explicating concepts such as "capital," "narcissism," "community," and "democracy."

As always, the writer's purpose determines the scope and complexity of the definition. However, there are certain stock methods for defining terms:

- Identify the class to which the subject belongs.
- Cite its essential characteristics.
- Isolate the single, most important characteristic.
- Trace the word's roots.
- Find synonyms or terms that are close in meaning.
- Provide a specific illustration of how it is used.

Needless to say, writers do not use all these methods in defining each term, but only the ones suited to their specific purposes.

In the selection below, Brian Wilson, a sociologist of religion, grapples with the problem of defining "sect." His ultimate purpose is to explain how certain sects resist the tendency to become established denominations, thus preserving their original evangelical ideals. Before addressing this larger question, Wilson had to define what sects are and how they differ from denominations:

> Typically a *sect* may be identified by the following characteristics: it is a voluntary association; membership is by proof to sect authorities of some claim to personal merit—such as knowledge of doctrine, affirmation of a conversion

[2]Emile Durkheim, *Suicide* (Glencoe, Illinois: The Free Press, 1951).

experience, or recommendation of members in good standing; exclusiveness is emphasized, and expulsion exercised against those who contravene doctrinal, moral, or organizational precepts; its self-conception is of an elect, a gathered remnant, possessing special enlightenment; personal perfection is the expected standard of aspiration, in whatever terms this is judged; it accepts, at least as an ideal, the priesthood of all believers; there is a high level of lay participation; there is opportunity for the member spontaneously to express his commitment; the sect is hostile or indifferent to the secular society and to the state.[3]

Wilson then identifies *one* defining attribute of sects: "The commitment of the sectarian is always more total and more defined than that of the member of other religious organizations."[4] Having thus established a clear definition of what a sect is, Wilson then differentiates between different kinds of sects. This brings us to the next rhetorical strategy: classification.

## CLASSIFICATION

If definition answers the question, What is it?, then classification answers the questions, What are its parts? What forms does it take? How do they work together to make a whole? When we are treating a large and complex subject, classification is a way of bringing greater order and clarity to the subject. We do this by formulating categories that divide the subject into discrete but related parts.

Let us return to Wilson's article on sect development. Wilson wants to distinguish the subtypes of sects, and he does so in terms of different "types of mission." Specifically:

> The *Conversionist* sects seek to alter men, and thereby to alter the world. . . . The *Adventist* sects predict drastic alteration of the world, and seek to prepare for the new dispensation. . . . The *Introversionists* reject the world's values and replace them with higher inner values. . . . The *Gnostic* sects accept in large measure the world's goals but seek new and esoteric means to achieve these ends. . . .[5]

With this classification in place, Wilson is in a better position to approach the larger questions that govern his study, which have to do with the conditions under which sects emerge and whether they are able to preserve their original evangelism. Wilson found that different types of sects display different patterns of development, which validates the usefulness of his classification.

---

[3]Brian R. Wilson, "An Analysis of Sect Development," *American Sociological Review,* 24 (1959), 4.

[4]Ibid.

[5]Ibid., p. 5.

## DESCRIPTION

Much social science is concerned with describing some facet of human experience. As a discipline, anthropology has provided graphic descriptions of the multitude of cultures and subcultures that exist in the world today. Sociologists, too, often "go out" into the field to observe social settings, ranging from "typical" towns or suburbs to unusual groups like hippie communes or motorcycle gangs. Political scientists write extensively about political events, economists about economic trends, and so on. The overall purpose of this research is to accurately *describe* some aspect of social life. When done effectively, readers are left with a clear mental picture of the event or phenomenon being studied, even if they have never observed it firsthand.

Presumably, the social scientist's description will be different from that of the legendary "casual observer." Of course, social scientists may also disagree among themselves. Indeed, this is the point of departure for many writers who, in one way or another, are challenging popular or prevailing views. For example, a study titled "Fear and Loathing at a College Mixer" began as follows:

> The predominant view expressed in the sociological literature on dating is that the social events and interactions are "fun" for the participants. An adult observer of adolescents at a social gathering would see them dressed up for the occasion, flirting with one another, dancing to loud music, engaging in light conversation, and generally seeming to be enjoying themselves.[6]

The researchers, however, provide a very different assessment of the college mixer. According to them, it is "a serious socialization process with potentially negative consequences for the individual."[7] Contrary to appearances, it is fraught with tension and anxiety, and often destructive of a person's sense of self-worth.

As this example suggests, description is never random or capricious. In the first place, the selection of detail is governed by social science concepts. In this case the concept of socialization led the observer to record the dress, the gestures, and the conversation of adolescents learning to court one another in a social setting. Secondly, in order to create a clear mental picture, researchers must have some principle for organizing and presenting their observations. As McQuade and Atwan have written:

> . . . whether we are picturing something concrete (the furniture or appliances in the kitchen) or something abstract (the spirit in a room during a holiday)— the process of writing an effective description remains essentially the same.

[6]Pepper Schwartz and Janet Lever, "Fear and Loathing at a College Mixer," *Urban Life*, 4 (January 1976), 413.

[7]Ibid., p. 414.

> We should start with an overview of whatever we want to describe. We should then proceed to select the most striking and significant details and develop them in an intelligible sequence that produces the effect we intended to create.[8]

To move from the general to the particular in this manner allows the writer to capture both the essence and the nuance of the event or phenomenon under study—the key to effective description.

Observe this process in the passage below, which is taken from an observational study of singles' bars:

> We observed that people in the singles' bars had a habit of touching each other. It could be a hand or a shoulder, a pat on the head, a hand steadying a hand to light a cigarette, or an entire body touch. Touching happened not only in crowds but also when there was plenty of room to pass without having body contact.
>
> Touching was often a simple gesture to start a conversation. "What an attractive necklace you're wearing," one man said to a woman, while stroking her neck. "It must have taken you years to grow your hair that long," another man said as he ran his fingers through a woman's hair. The touching seemed to reinforce what they were saying and at the same time establish intimacy.
>
> Touching might be a sign of approval or a gesture of affection, or of course have sexual connotations. Touching might also be a pompous way of assuring oneself of being noticed.[9]

After the general observation that people in singles' bars "had a habit of touching each other," the authors provide a detailed description of the specific forms of touching—how it is done, what is said, and so on. Then they move to a slightly higher level of abstraction, and comment on the functions of touching—a sign of approval or affection, a sexual gesture, a way of being noticed. Thus, the reader is provided with both a description and an analysis of this particular behavior.

## NARRATION

As a rhetorical strategy, narration is a way of telling what happened. For this reason it is most identified with history. Indeed, history has its origins in storytelling—the earliest histories were epic accounts of the Greek wars. Even today, it is frequently commented that every good historian is a good storyteller, and "narrative history" is staunchly defended against those who would apply "scientific" concepts and methods to the writing of history.

The selection on the next page is taken from Oscar Handlin's book, *The Uprooted*. Handlin essentially "tells the story" of immigration, the

---

[8]Donald McQuade and Robert Atwan, *Thinking in Writing* (New York: Alfred A. Knopf, 1983), p. 280.

[9]Natalie Allon and Diane Fishel, "Singles' Bars as Examples of Urban Courting Patterns," in *Single Life*, ed. Peter J. Stein (New York: St. Martin's Press, 1981), p. 117.

"arduous transplantation" from the Old World to the New. Not unlike a story, his book is organized in terms of a chronological sequence, as is evident from the table of contents:

Note that some chapters adhere to a strict chronological sequence (especially Chapters 1, 2, 3, 4, and 12). Other chapters interrupt the chronology to analyze particular facets of the immigrant experience, such as economic survival, religion, and politics.

The narrative flavor of Handlin's account is evident in the following excerpt from Chapter 2, "The Crossing":

> Coming away from the village, the emigrant pushed toward a seaport. Surely in the beginning it was a task sufficiently difficult just to know the road. For guides there were only the remembered tales of pilgrims, of beggars, and of peddlers, the habitual wanderers of the peasant world. . . . Conveyances varied with conditions. On the continent, travel was most commodious by river or canal; but few poor folk could pay the heavy tolls. . . . In some places there were public stages. These too were out of reach, prohibitively expensive, meant for the gentry who alone, in more normal times, had occasion to use them. Here and there was a fortunate fellow with a cart. More rare was a beast to pull it; both would be sold at the destination. But not many peasants had been able to hold on to horse and wagon when all else in their world disappeared from around them. Mostly the emigrants relied on the power of their own legs and began the crossing with a long journey on foot.[10]

Note the sequencing of events as the emigrant leaves the village and pushes toward the seaport, beginning the long journey that ends in America. Also note the attention to detail: The only road map consisted of "remembered tales" of pilgrims, beggars, and peddlers; transportation was nonexistent or too expensive; most end up walking long distances to the points of disembarkation. These graphic details, arranged in chronological sequence, are what gives the reader a clear "mental picture" of what the crossing to America was like.

---

[10]Oscar Handlin, *The Uprooted* (New York: Grosset & Dunlap, 1951), p. 39.

## ILLUSTRATION

If there is a single, overriding purpose of social science, it is to *generalize* about the social universe. Yet generalization has its pitfalls. It is all too easy to spin out generalizations that are not adequately supported by the facts. And from the reader's standpoint, generalizations are often difficult to grasp, precisely because they are abstract. For both reasons, illustration is an indispensable rhetorical device. By citing specific examples, writers give substance to their generalizations. These examples also serve to clarify a writer's intentions and meaning. A good illustration, one might say, is worth a thousand words.

Here, too, an example is in order. In the passage below, Ruth Benedict, the anthropologist, is discussing what it means to "grow up" and to be "conditioned" to adult roles. As an illustration, she describes the process whereby children in our culture learn to eat according to adult schedules:

> It will make the point clearer if we consider one habit in our culture. . . . With the greatest clarity of purpose and economy of training we achieve our goal of conditioning everyone to eat three meals a day. The baby's training in regular food periods begins at birth and no crying of the child and no inconvenience to the mother is allowed to interfere. We gauge the child's physiological make-up and at first allow it food oftener than adults, but, because our goal is firmly set and our training consistent, before the child is two years old it has achieved the adult schedule. From the point of view of other cultures this is as startling as the fact of three-year-old babies perfectly at home in deep water is to us.[11]

This specific example helps to clarify and support what is meant by "cultural conditioning." Benedict furnishes more subtle examples as she develops her thesis further.

## COMPARISON-CONTRAST

Comparison-contrast is more than a rhetorical strategy. It is the essence of the scientific method itself. The classical experiment involves a comparison before and after some experimental condition has been altered. Whether through systematic research or less structured observation, social scientists are always looking for similarities and differences.

As a rhetorical device, comparison and contrast serves different purposes. One is to clarify a key term. In the example cited earlier, Wilson clarified the meaning of "sect" by placing it in opposition to "denomination." His classification of sects also involved comparisons and contrasts between different kinds of sects.

Second, comparisons are necessary to carry analysis to a higher level of generalization. For example, in a well-known study, anthropologist Marc Zborowski compared different groups in terms of their responses to pain.

---

[11]Ruth Benedict, "Continuities and Discontinuities in Cultural Conditioning," *Psychiatry*, **1** (1938), 154.

He found that, consistent with stereotype, "old Americans" were the most stoic of all groups. Not only did Italians and Jews exhibit a lower tolerance of pain, but even after a painkiller was administered, Jews continued to worry about the possible side effects of the medication. Through these comparisons, Zborowski was able to demonstrate differences among ethnic groups in their response to pain.[12] The very fact that groups were different suggests that pain is more than a physiological reaction, but a matter of cultural conditioning as well.

Third, comparisons and contrasts provide a frame of reference. It is not uncommon to hear bald statements like, "America is a racist country," to which someone is bound to retort, "Compared to what?" Only through comparisons and contrasts can we fully assess the significance of otherwise isolated facts or observations. For example, if we were to compare racist patterns in the United States with those in South Africa, we would come away with a better understanding of racism in both countries.

Indeed, this was precisely the purpose of George Fredrickson's historical study, *White Supremacy*. Here is a brief excerpt:

> The term "segregation" came into common use in both South Africa and the American South at about the same time—in the early years of the twentieth century. South African white supremacists may in fact have borrowed the term from their American counterparts. But a close examination of the two modes of legalized discrimination reveals some major differences in how they worked and in the functions they performed. Both, of course, were necessarily based on separatism; but the specific kinds of separation that were stressed and regarded as crucial for maintaining white privilege and furthering white interests were not the same. . . .[13]

Fredrickson's point is that despite obvious similarities, there are fundamental differences between segregation in America and apartheid in South Africa. In the case of South Africa, separation involves an extreme *territorial* division that relegates most blacks to remote and desolate "homelands." Pushed to the brink of starvation, men are forced to travel hundreds of miles to find work, for which they are paid subhuman wages. Comparatively, blacks in the United States are far more integrated into major social institutions. From a writing standpoint, the two cases cast each other in bold relief, enhancing our understanding of both.

## CAUSE-EFFECT

It is often held that causal analysis is the ultimate goal of all science. To establish the facts (description) is only a partial or preliminary step to explaining them (explanation). Indeed, as a rhetorical strategy, cause-effect

[12]Marc Zborowski, "Cultural Components in Responses to Pain," *Journal of Social Issues,* 8 (1953), 16–31.

[13]George M. Fredrickson, *White Supremacy: A Comparative Study in American and South African History* (New York: Oxford University Press, 1981), p. 241.

is probably the primary mode in social science writing. It is not that the other rhetorical strategies are used any less frequently, but rather they are used within the context of, or in conjunction with, a cause-effect mode.

For example, in his book *The Black Family in Slavery and Freedom*, Herbert Gutman explored the effects of slavery on the black family (an excerpt from this book is found in Chapter 9). Within this context, Gutman had to ascertain what the raw facts were about the condition of black families (description). To accomplish this, he employed slave narratives of various kinds (narration). Classification, comparison-contrast, and other rhetorical strategies were also employed in other parts of his study. However, the *primary* rhetorical mode—the one that was of overriding significance in terms of substance and organization—was cause-effect.[14]

Causal analysis may focus on either causes or effects, or both. For example, some economists have dealt with the causes of unemployment; others, with the effects; still others, with both causes and effects. Of course, dealing with both causes and effects within the same study is likely to become unwieldy. The reason is that causal analysis is never simple. Typically, there are multiple causes and multiple effects that must be sorted out. We also have to think about the relationship that exists among the various causal factors. They may operate more or less independently of each other. Thus, there may be a *convergence* of factors leading to some outcome—say, the Second World War. Or causal factors may be related to each other in a *causal chain*. For example, it might be held that widespread unemployment in the 1930s led to political unrest which undermined public confidence in elected officials, which culminated in Roosevelt's elevation to the presidency.

Whenever we deal with multiple causes, we must try to sort out the *sequence* of events or circumstances that lead to a given outcome. The sequence might be conceived as a movement from *proximate* causes to *ultimate* causes. For example, in the mid-1960s New York City was on the brink of bankruptcy. A proximate cause—the one highlighted in the mass media—was that the city's politicians busted the budget with "liberal spending programs." Another view, however, was put forward by Matthew Edel, an economist. Edel traced the city's fiscal crisis to changes in the global economy that resulted in a massive loss of industries and jobs in New York. This, in turn, sharply reduced the city's tax revenues at the same time that it increased expenditures for social welfare programs. Thus, the *ultimate* causes of the city's fiscal crisis were associated with sweeping changes in the international economy over which the city's politicians had little or no control.[15]

[14]Herbert Gutman, *The Black Family in Slavery and Freedom, 1750–1925* (New York: Pantheon Books, 1976).

[15]Matthew Edel, "The New York Crisis as Economic History," in *The Fiscal Crisis of American Cities*, eds. Roger E. Alcaly and David Mermelstein (New York: Random House, 1977).

Another way of sorting out the relationship among causal factors is in terms of their "explanatory significance"—that is, whether they are seen as having relatively great weight or relatively little weight. For example, social scientists with a Marxist perspective are often accused of placing too much emphasis on economic factors, and underestimating the operation of non-economic factors. The counterargument, however, is that economic factors are not the *only* factors that matter, but the most *important* ones, not only because they directly influence behavior, but also because they condition the effects of noneconomic factors as well.

These controversies underscore the importance of clear, logical writing. It is crucial that studies that posit cause-effect relations be unambiguous about what causal claims are being made, and what relationship exists among the various causal factors.

The example of causal explanation presented below deals with adolescent culture. Observe how the author, James Coleman, develops a causal chain from more remote, or ultimate, causes to more proximate ones, and then speculates about the effects of adolescent culture for the family system:

> Industrial society has spawned a peculiar phenomenon, most evident in America but emerging also in other Western societies: adolescent subcultures, with values and activities quite distinct from those of the adult society. . . . Industrialization, and the rapidity of change itself, has taken out of the hands of the parent the task of training his child, made the parent's skills obsolescent, and put him out of touch with the times—unable to understand, much less inculcate, the standards of a social order which has changed since he was young.
>
> By extending the period of training necessary for a child and by encompassing nearly the whole population, industrial society has made of high school a social system of adolescents. It includes, in the United States, almost all adolescents and more and more of the activities of the adolescent himself. . . .
>
> In effect, then, what our society has done is to set apart, in an institution of their own, adolescents for whom home is little more than a dormitory and whose world is made up of activities peculiar to their fellows. They have been given, as well, many of the instruments which can make them a functioning community: cars, freedom in dating, continual contact with the opposite sex, money and entertainment, like popular music and movies designed especially for them.[16]

The thrust of this passage concerns the sources or "causes" of adolescent culture. Its ultimate sources are in industrial society, which extends childhood and defines children and adults as occupying different spheres. The next link in the causal chain is the school system, which has been delegated many of the socializing functions that once were fulfilled by parents. Other factors—cars, popular culture, changes in sexual mores—

[16]James S. Coleman, "The Adolescent Subculture and Academic Achievement," *American Journal of Sociology*, 65 (1960), 337–38.

also contribute to the development of an adolescent culture that is more or less independent of parental control. The end result is that "home is little more than a dormitory."

Even in this brief excerpt, Coleman presents a sweeping causal analysis, beginning with the emergence of industrial society and ending with changes in the family system. The causal links are clearly spelled out. However, causal analysis is susceptible to a number of fallacies. Let us consider three of the most common ones.

1. *Inverting cause and effect.* This is the logical version of putting the cart before the horse. For example, a number of studies have found that black families where husband and wife are living together have more stable employment and higher incomes. From these facts, some analysts have concluded that a "weak family" is the cause for many of unemployment and poverty. Critics, however, have turned this proposition around, arguing that it is unemployment and poverty that cause families to break up in the first place. The implication here is that broken families are the effect, not the cause, of unemployment and poverty.

2. *Confusing correlation and cause.* Just because two factors vary together, this does not mean that one is the cause of the other. The correlation may be an accidental one. For example, it is known that the population of California has been increasing every year by about five hundred thousand people. It is also known that the California coastline has been disappearing into the Pacific Ocean at a rate of about nine inches every year. The unwary observer might conclude that the California coastline is sinking from the sheer weight of people. Obviously, however, it is not correct to infer a causal relationship since population increase and land erosion are totally unrelated events.[17]

A more serious example is suggested by a recent news story in the *New York Times*. A small town in Florida that was suffering from a mosquito infestation also reported an unusually high rate of AIDS. People speculated that the AIDS virus might be transmitted by mosquitoes. Upon investigation, however, it was found that there were no cases of AIDS among children under 10 or adults over 60. Obviously, if mosquitoes transmitted the AIDS virus then all age groups would be affected. Thus, the investigation dispelled fears that there was any causal connection between mosquitoes and AIDS.[18]

3. *Positing a causal relationship that turns out to be spurious.* A correlation between two factors may be a by-product of a third factor. For example, it would not be difficult to show a correlation between the number of storks in an area and the number of births in a given year. This hardly

[17]This example is taken from Lucy Horwitz and Lou Ferleger, *Statistics for Social Change* (Boston: South End Press, 1980), pp. 285–86.

[18]*New York Times*, January 8, 1988, p. B6.

proves that storks bring babies. What it does reflect is the fact that storks thrive in rural areas, and rural areas have higher birth rates than urban areas. Thus, we would say that the relationship between storks and babies is *spurious.*

To take a less frivolous example, it is known that drivers of small cars have a higher death rate than do drivers of large cars. However, automobile manufacturers contend that this does not constitute proof that small cars are more dangerous. They argue that small cars are more likely to be driven by young people who tend to be more reckless as drivers. In other words, the contention is that the relationship between car size and death rate is spurious, because it masks the effect of a third factor—the age of drivers. In the event that the automobile manufacturers were correct (and there is no reason to suppose that they are), then young drivers of large cars would be equally at risk.

## ARGUMENT

As we suggested in Chapter 1, social research is inherently argumentative, in that researchers must convince others of their conclusions. They do so on the basis of evidence and solid reasoning, and by anticipating objections likely to be raised by critics. As a rhetorical form, however, "argument" has a more restricted meaning. To quote McQuade and Atwan:

> In rhetoric, argument is a special form of discourse, one that attempts to convince an audience that a specific claim or proposition is true wholly because a supporting body of logically related statements is also true. In a well-constructed argument, once we establish the truth of statements A, B, and C, and so forth, then we can reasonably be expected to assent to the principal claim or assertion. In other words, the truth of a statement is entirely dependent on the previously acknowledged truth of the other statements.[19]

Like a trial lawyer pleading a case, the writer establishes certain facts (premises) which lead ultimately to a conclusion. Thus, argument conforms to the following thought pattern: If A, B, and C are correct, then X will follow. This leaves two possible sources of error that the writer must guard against: (1) the premises may not be correct, or (2) the premises may be true, but they may not necessarily lead to the stated conclusion. It requires clear thinking and sound reasoning to establish the linkages between premises and conclusions.

Consider the following excerpt from Charles Beard's pioneering study, *An Economic Interpretation of the Constitution,* first published in 1913. As the title itself suggests, Beard is advancing a bold interpretation of the Constitution, one that challenges the conventional view that our founding fathers drafted the Constitution in order to advance the ideals of life, liberty,

[19]Donald McQuade and Robert Atwan, *Thinking in Writing* (New York: Alfred A. Knopf, 1983), p. 417.

and the pursuit of happiness. Beard's argument is that the Constitution was basically an economic document, one that was conceived, drafted, and ratified by certain entrenched classes, and designed to protect their property interests. At the outset of his book, Beard presents his argument in capsule form:

> It will be admitted without controversy that the Constitution was the creation of a certain number of men, and it was opposed by a certain number of men. Now, if it were possible to have an economic biography of all those connected with its framing and adoption—perhaps about 160,000 men altogether—the materials for scientific analysis and classification would be available. Such an economic biography would include a list of the real and personal property owned by all of these men and their families: lands and houses, with incumbrances, money at interest, slaves, capital invested in shipping and manufacturing, and in state and continental securities.
>
> Suppose it could be shown from the classification of men who supported and opposed the Constitution that there was no line of property division at all; that is, that men owning substantially the same amounts of the same kinds of property were equally divided on the matter of adoption or rejection—it would then become apparent that the Constitution had no ascertainable relation to economic groups or classes, but was the product of some abstract causes remote from the chief business of life—gaining a livelihood.
>
> Suppose, on the other hand, that substantially all of the merchants, money lenders, security holders, manufacturers, shippers, capitalists, and financiers and their professional associates are to be found on one side in support of the Constitution and that substantially all of the major portion of the opposition came from the nonslaveholding farmers and the debtors—would it not be pretty conclusively demonstrated that our fundamental law was not the product of an abstraction known as "the whole people," but of a group of economic interests which must have expected beneficial results from its adoption?[20]

Observe the structure of Beard's argument. *If* we had the biographies of all 160,000 men who had a hand in the writing or ratification of the Constitution (premise 1), and *if* it were found that supporters and opponents of the Constitution were no different in terms of their social class (premise 2), *then* this would suggest that economics had nothing to do with the Constitution (the conclusion). If, on the other hand, most supporters were men of property (women could not vote), and most opponents were small farmers or debtors, would this not suggest the opposite conclusion? With this rhetorical question, Beard has set the stage for his study. The rest of the book may be seen as an attempt to substantiate his premises and to argue his conclusion regarding the economic basis of the Constitution.

It should be noted that Beard's thesis has its critics. One historian, Forrest McDonald, wrote a whole book in which he set out "to subject Beard's thesis to the most careful scrutiny," and "to discover whether the details are compatible with the broad outlines he sketched" (in other words, whether his premises were correct and whether they supported his con-

---

[20]Charles A. Beard, *An Economic Interpretation of the United States* (New York: Mac-Millan, 1968), pp. 16–17. Originally published in 1913.

clusions). McDonald collected data on the delegations to the Philadelphia conventions that ratified the Constitution, and found no support for Beard's assumption that there was a division between propertied elements, on the one hand, and small farmers and debtors, on the other. He concluded that "Beard's thesis is entirely incompatible with the facts."[21]

It goes without saying that McDonald's study also has its critics, and historians still debate the validity of Beard's thesis. Such is the nature of the intellectual enterprise. For every argument there is almost certain to be a counterargument, and no sooner is a debate resolved than it is opened up again. This only underscores the importance of good writing and cogent argument. We must write with the knowledge that our arguments will have to withstand the scrutiny of critics.

As a rhetorical strategy, argument lends itself to a number of fallacies:

*Faulty Generalization.* This refers to instances where the conclusions are not adequately supported by the evidence, precisely what McDonald meant when he wrote that Beard's "details were found to be incompatible with the broad outlines he sketched."[22]

*The Faulty Premise.* Not a few social theorists have propounded erudite theories whose only flaw is that the facts that they purport to explain are untrue. Again, this is what McDonald meant when he claimed that Beard's "facts did not substantiate his assumptions."[23] Facts are like the cornerstone of a building: if seriously flawed, the entire edifice may collapse.

*Begging the Question.* This is also called *circular argument.* It refers to instances where something is assumed as a premise and then stated as a conclusion. For example, Beard would have been guilty of circular reasoning had he declared that the wealthy voted for the Constitution because it served their economic interests, if the only evidence he offered for his assumption that the Constitution served the economic interests of the wealthy was that they voted for it. To avoid circular reasoning, Beard had to present independent evidence showing that the Constitution served the interests of the wealthy and that this perception governed how they voted.

*Evading the Issue.* Wittingly or unwittingly, writers sometimes gloss over a flaw or gap in their argument by shifting the focus to a vaguely related but not completely relevant point. In Beard's case he makes much of the fact that women, slaves, and people who did not meet property qualifications were denied the franchise, and therefore excluded from the process of ratifying the Constitution. To be sure, these facts call into question the extent of the new nation's commitment to democratic principles. But they do not by themselves prove that the groups in question would not have voted for ratification if they had been empowered to do so. Similarly, to

[21]Forrest McDonald, *We the People* (Chicago: University of Chicago Press, 1958), p. 357.
[22]Ibid., p. 400.
[23]Ibid.

show, as Beard does, that the founding fathers were all men of considerable wealth evades the issue of whether their politics were governed by narrow self-interest, or whether they were not genuinely devoted to the democratic ideals enshrined in the Constitution.

Hopefully, it will be easier to avoid these pitfalls by being aware of them. This is why it is important to be self-conscious as a writer. To be cognizant of the rhetorical strategies in your writing will also help you to write with greater clarity and conviction.

## SUGGESTIONS FOR WRITING AND THINKING

1.    Take a subject area—adolescent culture, for example—and show how the eight rhetorical strategies discussed in this chapter might lead to useful questions for probing the subject. For example:

      *Comparison-contrast:* How does adolescent culture in this country compare to adolescent culture in Western Europe?

      *Cause-effect:* What effects does adolescent culture have on the relationship between parents and children?

      Continue with respect to the remaining six rhetorical strategies: narration, description, illustration, definition, classification, and argument. Repeat this exercise using another subject area of your choice.

2.    The following passages are drawn from various studies, and delineate the main purpose or the overarching question that governs each study. For each, indicate the rhetorical strategy that is implied:

      In this paper, we attempt to describe the kind of idealism that characterizes the medical freshmen and to trace both the development of cynicism and the vicissitudes of that idealism in the course of the four years of medical training. [Howard S. Becker and Blanche Geer, "The Fate of Idealism in Medical School," *American Sociological Review,* 23 (1958), 50.]

      This essay is an attempt to interpret, from a sociological perspective, the effects of social class upon parent-child relationships. [Melvin L. Kohn, "Social Class and Parent-Child Relationships," *American Journal of Sociology,* 73 (January 1963), 471.]

      In this article, we offer a working definition of the garage sale, specifically how it can be distinguished from other sorts of informal sales, such as estate sales, tag sales or rummage sales. Next, we explain how we produced the ballpark figures of the number of garage sales and their revenues, and how the garage sale has been institutionalized, that is, how it has infiltrated the cultural mainstream. [Gretchen M. Herrmann and Stephen M. Soiffer, "For Fun and Profit: An Analysis of the American Garage Sale," *Urban Life,* 12 (January 1984), 397.]

      The main cause for our depressed industries is not foreign competition; nor are we becoming "a nation of hamburger stands." Our problem is slack demand

and an overvalued dollar. [Robert Z. Lawrence, "The Myth of U.S. Deindustrialization," *Challenge* (November-December 1983), 12.]

This paper attempts to specify some of the ways in which the modern family in the United States differs from its historical predecessor through a distinction between the public and private character of social institutions. [Barbara Laslett, "The Family as a Public and Private Institution: An Historical Perspective," in *The Family*, eds. Peter J. Stein, Judith Richman, and Natalie Hannon (Reading, Massachusetts: Addison-Wesley Publishing Company, 1977), p. 45.]

In summary, an attempt has been made to show that religious experiences, both diabolic and divine, can be analytically broken down into four general types and several further subtypes, on the basis of the configuration of relationships between the divine and human actor during any spiritual encounter. [Charles Y. Glock and Rodney Stark, *Religion and Science in Tension* (Chicago: Rand McNally, 1965), p. 64.]

This book tells the story of those east European Jews who, for several decades starting in the 1880s, undertook a massive migration to the United States. [Irving Howe, *World of Our Fathers* (New York: Harcourt Brace Jovanovich, 1976), p. xix.]

Current and emerging programs in bilingual-bicultural education represent a significant development in the evolution of the public school. . . . This chapter reports research on a bilingual-bicultural program in an elementary school with a high proportion of Mexican-American children. [Richard L. Warren, "Schooling, Biculturalism, and Ethnic Identity: A Case Study," in *Doing the Ethnography of Schooling,* ed. George Spindler (New York: Holt, Rinehart and Winston, 1982), p. 384.

# Chapter 5
# THE LOGICAL STRUCTURE OF SOCIAL SCIENCE WRITING

Not unlike a good story, good academic writing has a logical beginning, middle, and end. This is what gives shape or structure to an otherwise amorphous stream of words and ideas. In the social sciences this beginning, middle, and end tends to assume a more or less characteristic form. Generally speaking, the *logical beginning* consists of a statement of the research problem, or the questions or issues that are being addressed. The *logical middle* involves a marshalling of facts or data that pertain to the research problem. The *logical end* attempts a resolution of the original research problem, however tentative or incomplete it might be. This is also the place to assess the larger implications of the research for theory, future research, or social policy.

Our point is not that this model is or should be mechanically imposed on all social science writing. This would make for a deadly uniformity and stifle creative thought. Just as all stories should not begin with the stock phrase, "Once upon a time . . . ," it would be tedious, to say the least, if all social science papers began with the stock phrase, "The purpose of this paper is. . . ." Yet all writing has a purpose, whether or not it is stated explicitly, in bold type, or woven more subtly into a larger exposition. In the case of social science writing, there is typically an underlying structure centered around a search for answers to unresolved questions. Sometimes this structure is explicit; more often it is implicit. It will be of immense value to you, as students, to recognize this structure, both to sharpen your reading and comprehension of social science literature, and to help you write effectively when you are called upon to do so.

Thus, to say that all social science writing begins with questions, presents evidence, and reaches conclusions is not a narrow prescription on how to write a paper, but only a formula for calling attention to an underlying and often unstated logical structure. It may be helpful to think of this "structure" like that of a house, in the sense that every house has a foundation, a frame, and a roof, yet all houses do not look alike. By the same token, what is being proposed here is not a literary Levittown, but only an essential structure that will give shape and direction to social science writing, without restricting its content or hampering creative expression.

## A LOGICAL BEGINNING: QUESTIONS

Virtually all social science writing is defined by questions put forward by the writer, typically at the beginning of the work. These questions are an indispensable first step in the writing process in that they govern the organization and flow of the paper. To be clear about the questions is to be headed resolutely down a path leading to a set of conclusions. On the other hand, to be muddled about the questions, or to lose sight of them, is like being cut adrift on an open sea, buffeted in every direction, never sure where you will end up. Thus, if there is a first principle in social science writing, it is to be clear about what questions are being addressed.

Consider this from the point of view of the reader. Nothing is more frustrating than to be lost in someone else's intellectual muddle. A paper that fails to define its purpose, that drifts from one topic to the next, that "does not seem to go anywhere," is certain to frustrate the reader. If that reader happens to be your instructor, he or she is likely to strike back with notations scrawled in the margin criticizing the paper as "poorly organized," "incoherent," "lacking clear focus," "discursive," "muddled," or the like. Most instructors have developed a formidable arsenal of terms that express their frustration at having to wade through papers that, in one way or another, are poorly conceived or disorganized.

From the student's standpoint, too, writing such a paper must be a frustrating experience. After all, if you are unclear yourself as to the purpose or direction of your paper, how do you get from one sentence or paragraph to the next? Finding yourself hopelessly stalled, you may tell yourself that you are suffering from "writer's block." If this happens, we would suggest that you brainstorm and freewrite until you are able to forge ahead. Once you have generated some ideas and are in the process of shaping them, you can resolve your block by thinking through the purpose and objectives of the study.

Questions, then, carefully formulated and clearly stated, are the key—or at least one key—to effective writing. Indeed, if one surveys major works in the various social science disciplines, more often than not there is *one* overarching question that defines the main purpose or objective of the study. There may well be numerous secondary or subordinate questions, but these are typically subsumed under that single larger question that frames the study.

Sometimes, though by no means always, this overarching question is stated explicitly. For example, in Winthrop Jordan's history, *White Over Black,* the very first words that the reader encounters in the preface are as follows:

> This study attempts to answer a simple question: What were the attitudes of white men toward Negroes during the first two centuries of European and African settlement in what became the United States of America?[1]

This "simple question" is the prelude to a 600-page book based on prodigious research. Indeed, one prominent reviewer of *White Over Black* extolled Jordan for having "tackled one of the most abstruse, subtle, tangled, controversial and certainly one of the most important problems of American history."[2] It is worth repeating that this ambitious undertaking sprung from "one simple question." Nor did the fact that Jordan shaped his study around "one simple question" prevent him from carrying it out, as his reviewer said, "with imagination and insight."

In short, simple questions do not presuppose simple answers. What they do achieve is *clarity of purpose.* Let us return to the social science literature for two other examples of how leading writers go about formulating the overarching questions for their research and writing.

The psychologist Stanley Milgram sought to understand why people obey authority, even when this involves transgressing the normal rules of conduct, and inflicting great harm on others. At the outset of his article, he alludes to the biblical story in which Abraham is commanded by God to kill his son, and notes that in war, too, people are commanded to destroy the enemy. Milgram designed a series of psychological experiments that would allow him to probe this general phenomenon, and he framed his study as follows:

> In the more limited form possible in laboratory research, the question becomes: if an experimenter tells a subject to hurt another person, under what conditions will the subject go along with this instruction, and under what conditions will he refuse to obey?[3]

Having thus delineated the overarching question of his study, Milgram has set the stage for a systematic presentation of his findings.

As suggested earlier, the paradigmatic questions that govern research differ from discipline to discipline. As a psychologist, Milgram was concerned primarily with the psychological factors that explain obedience to authority. On the other hand, Emile Durkheim studied a phenomenon—suicide—that is usually regarded as a psychological phenomenon, but he

[1]Winthrop Jordan, *White Over Black* (Baltimore: Penguin Books, 1969), p. vii.

[2]C. Vann Woodward, *New York Times Book Review,* March 31, 1968, p. 6.

[3]Stanley Milgram, "Some Conditions of Obedience and Disobedience to Authority," *Human Relations,* 18, no. 1 (1965), 57.

studied it from a sociological perspective. Indeed, his book *Suicide* marks the beginning of modern sociology. The question behind Durkheim's study was not why this or that individual commits suicide; this, he conceded, was the province of psychology. Durkheim was struck by the fact that every society had a characteristic *rate* of suicide that hardly varied from one year to the next. He also observed that the suicide rate was higher for some groups than for others: for example, among Protestants as compared to Catholics, and among the unmarried as compared to the married. Durkheim called this "the social suicide rate," and the overarching purpose of his study was to understand why it is higher for some groups than for others.[4]

Our purpose in citing these studies has been to demonstrate how questions, and the pursuit of answers, govern research and writing in the social sciences. If the first step is the formulation of research *questions*, the next step is the collection and presentation of *evidence*.

## A LOGICAL MIDDLE: EVIDENCE

Who dunnit? This is the question that informs all Agatha Christie novels. As the novel unfolds, Hercule Poirot, her fictitious detective, relentlessly pursues every clue and collects shreds of evidence until they form a pattern that points, unmistakably, to the culprit and hence resolves the mystery.

The mission of social science, one might say, is to unravel the mysteries of the social world, and social scientists are engaged in a kind of detective work that involves the marshalling of evidence leading to a resolution of the original research question. The kind of evidence, and the ways in which it is collected, takes many forms. Social scientists have at their disposal a number of different research strategies and tools. Which strategy and which tools are applied in any particular instance depends on the questions that are being addressed.

To return to our earlier examples, the stated purpose of Winthrop Jordan's study—his "simple question"—concerned the nature of racism during the first two centuries that Europeans and Africans were together on American soil. How does a historian go about reconstructing social patterns that existed in the distant past? In Jordan's case, he used reports by travellers, personal diaries, private letters, newspapers, and early histories, as well as legislation and other kinds of official documents. From these varied sources Jordan sought to piece together the process of domination and oppression of "white over black."

If Stanley Milgram were a historian, he might have studied obedience and disobedience to authority within a specific historical context—for example, by conducting a comparative study of draftees and draft resisters

[4]Emile Durkheim, *Suicide* (Glencoe, Illinois: The Free Press, 1951).

during the Vietnam war. But Milgram is an experimental psychologist, and consistent with his training, he designed a series of experiments in which subjects were duped into believing that they were participating in a learning experiment, and were told to administer a memory test to a "learner" who was strapped into an "electric chair." The subject was instructed by the experimenter to administer electric shocks to the learner whenever he gave a wrong answer. Of course, the learner was a confederate in the experiment, and he played his role to the hilt—grunting and moaning and writhing with pain as the subjects dutifully turned up the voltage when instructed to do so. In the extreme position, labeled "Danger: Severe Shock," the learner demanded to be let out of the experiment, while the experimenter dispassionately instructed the subject to treat the absence of an answer as equivalent to a wrong answer, and to follow the usual shock procedure. In this way the experiment allowed Milgram to examine the process whereby people exhibit "blind obedience" to authority.

If Durkheim had been a psychologist, he might have sought to determine the psychological makeup of suicide victims, for example, by analyzing their suicide notes or by interviewing family members. Given his interest in the social suicide rate, however, Durkheim collected a mass of statistical data on the social characteristics of suicide victims. Were they more likely to be male or female? Old or young? Married or unmarried? Urban or rural? Protestant or Catholic or Jewish? From these empirical data Durkheim sought to identify the factors that groups with high or low suicide rates have in common.

As these examples suggest, there is a close logical connection between the questions that are posited and the evidence that is collected. This is worth stressing because students often err either by asking questions that cannot be answered with available evidence, or by collecting evidence that is not directly related to the stated objectives of their study.

## A LOGICAL END: ANSWERS

A paper without a conclusion is like a story without an end, or even more disconcerting, a joke without a punch line. Yet a common flaw of student papers is that they reach no conclusion. To be sure, they come to an end, but all too abruptly, without forewarning or logical preparation. Readers of such papers—your instructors—are left in a state of intellectual suspension as they read along and suddenly realize that they have come to the end of the paper. Once again, they retaliate with notations such as "lacks closure," "stops in midair," or an incredulous "Is this the end of your paper?"

When a paper lacks a conclusion, this is not necessarily because the student has run out of time, or energy, or even material. Rather, the problem may go back to the very conception of the paper. A student who has not formulated a clear topic, but is merely writing diffusely about a subject, will be hard pressed to find a graceful or logical way to end the paper. On the other hand, the student who begins with a clear statement of purpose, and who carefully formulates the questions that control the inquiry, will be compelled by the paper's internal logic to bring it to clear resolution.

Generally speaking, the conclusion ought to provide the best possible answer to the original questions on the basis of the evidence that has been marshalled in the body of the paper. However, the conclusion should be more than a summation. That is, it should go beyond the specific findings, and analyze some of the implications of these findings, whether for theory, research, or public policy.

Say, for example, that you did a study of the 1988 presidential election, with an eye to exploring voting patterns. The body of the paper might involve a detailed analysis of election returns, focusing on the social characteristics of areas where each candidate ran strong. Having thus waded through the data, the time is ripe to step back and to reassess the original question in light of what has been learned. What, in a nutshell, explains the election outcome? What overall conclusion is warranted by the evidence? Different implications of the findings might be explored. For example:

On the level of theory, what does the election reveal about the political values of the American people? The nature of electoral politics? The future of liberalism and conservatism?

On the level of research, are there any questions that are unresolved or suggested by the findings or analysis in the body of the paper? Insofar as the purpose of research is to push back the frontier of knowledge, it is certainly appropriate that a study end by taking stock of both what has been learned and what questions remain.

On the level of social policy, does the research have any implications concerning political strategy in future elections? The public financing of elections? The need to reform the electoral system?

These are the kinds of "larger questions" that might be explored in a concluding section of a paper on a presidential election. Obviously, the specific content that goes into a conclusion depends on the subject matter and the interests of the author. Our main point is that, as a matter of form, a good conclusion provides a sense of resolution to the original research question. However, it not only summarizes the main findings established in the body of the paper but also engages in some speculation or analysis about the implications or relevance of these findings for larger concerns.

Let us illustrate the operation of this principle by alluding again to the three studies discussed earlier in this chapter.

As a historical chronicle of racism in seventeenth- and eighteenth-century America, *White Over Black* does not come to a conclusion that can easily be encapsulated in a few sentences. The objective of Jordan's study was to provide a detailed account of the origins and development of racism on American soil. Its main thrust is to demonstrate how a nation that fought for its own freedom from colonial domination and that declared that "all men are created equal," could at the same time exclude blacks from its national covenant and justify slavery. Even those who opposed slavery rejected the idea of racial equality, and in his final chapter Jordan describes the campaign that developed among antislavery forces to "colonize" blacks to Africa or the Caribbean.

In the case of Milgram's study of obedience to authority, the conclusion was developed around one significant finding. Over half of Milgram's subjects were fully obedient to the experimenter's commands and delivered the maximum "shock." Milgram concluded that this finding had dire implications for the future. As he wrote:

> The results, as seen and felt in the laboratory, are to this author disturbing. They raise the possibility that human nature, or—more specifically—the kind of character produced in American democratic society, cannot be counted on to insulate its citizens from brutality and inhumane treatment at the direction of malevolent authority. . . . If in this study an anonymous experimenter could successfully command adults to subdue a fifty-year-old man, and force on him painful electric shocks against his protests, one can only wonder what government, with its vastly greater authority and prestige, can command of its subjects.[5]

Durkheim's evidence indicated that certain groups—for example, Catholics, rural dwellers, and married people—had relatively low rates of suicide. What did these groups have in common that might account for their relative immunity to suicide? The key factor, according to Durkheim, is that all three groups are marked by a relatively high degree of social integration. That is, the ties between the individual and the group tend to be strong. Compared to Protestantism, which stresses free will and individual responsibility, Catholicism is a more dogmatic and highly structured religion that defines a less ambiguous relationship between individual and church. Compared to the anonymity of urban life, rural dwellers tend to have more stable and enduring ties with family, neighbors, and community. Compared to those who live alone, married people are more likely to have kinship ties that give them a sense of purpose and responsibility to others. Durkheim postulated that people with strong social bonds are protected from feelings of isolation and despair that, in times of personal crisis, might otherwise lead them to suicide. Does this finding mean that too much freedom is a bad thing? This is the issue that Durkheim ponders in the closing pages of his book.

Perhaps the one abiding lesson in this chapter is that if you are clear about your questions, your research and writing will be guided by your search for answers. The content—that is, your purpose and argument—will motivate and direct your prose. If you concentrate on *what* you wish to say, you will have less trouble deciding *how* to say it.

[5]Milgram, "Some Conditions of Obedience and Disobedience to Authority," p. 75.

## ORGANIZATION

The schema of questions-evidence-answers corresponds to certain general principles for organizing papers. Specifically, there is a title and an introduction leading into the main body of the paper, which builds to a conclusion. Finally, there is a list of sources, usually at the end of the paper. Let us comment briefly on each of these organizational features.

### Title

All too often, students hand in papers without titles. Sometimes this may be a mere oversight. Usually it is a first sign of trouble, indicating that the paper lacks clear definition or focus. In this book we lay down very few unbending rules, but one is: Never hand in a paper without an appropriate title. The next question, of course, is, What makes a title "appropriate?"

An appropriate title is one that encapsulates the main thrust of the paper. It should be straightforward and concise. Social scientists usually avoid titles that use figurative language or that evoke images. Note the titles of the sample essays in Chapters 6 to 9 of this book:

"Teacher Expectations for the Disadvantaged"

"The Hustler"

"Emerging Sex-Role Attitudes, Expectations, and Strains Among College Women"

"Send Me Some of the Children's Hair"

These titles are straightforward, if not bland, with the exception of the last one which comes from Herbert Gutman's history of the black family. Perhaps reflecting their humanist traditions, historians are more likely than other social scientists to use evocative titles. In this instance, the title comes from a personal letter written by a slave to his wife, and is used to epitomize the desperate longing that slaves felt when they were separated from their children.

One further point. An appropriate title should be faithful to the contents of the paper. Do not promise more than you deliver.

### Introduction

The introduction should provide a clear statement of the problem that your paper addresses. Directly or indirectly, it should make the purpose clear. It should also include sufficient background material without overwhelming or distracting the reader with information that is tangential to the main thrust of the paper.

The introduction often includes a concise review of the previous literature on the topic. This should not be done ritualistically, however. The purpose of this review is to define your paper within the context of previous research or thought, and to set the stage for your own investigation. For students who do not yet have sufficient mastery of a subject area, this "review of the literature" might be limited to whatever related works you are familiar with and that stimulated your interest in the topic.

The introductory section should also define the limits of your study. Be explicit about what aspects of the subject you are treating and what aspects are "beyond the scope" of your paper. Identify and define key terms that are central to your paper, and provide appropriate examples or illustrations.

### Body of the Paper

The midsection of your paper is the exposition of the subject under study. If you have done original research, this would be the place to systematically report your findings. If you are writing about research that others have done, you will still need to marshall together relevant facts or ideas. Many student papers compare more than one work on a selected topic with an eye toward developing a point of view. In this case the synthesis of related sources constitutes the main body of the paper.

### Conclusion

A conclusion should evolve logically out of the prior sections of the paper. Even if you choose to have a separate heading labeled "Conclusions," it should not seem as if it were "tacked on" to the paper. As we cautioned in Chapter 2, do not depart from your focus or inject topics that constitute a whole new departure from the main body of the paper. You may, however, offer solutions to a problem or assess future trends, as long as this is a logical extension of the foregoing analysis.

While you should be careful not to raise new topics, you must also avoid merely repeating yourself. The conclusion affords an opportunity to step back and to reflect on the full import of whatever findings or observations were presented in the body of the paper. It should "stretch" the analysis presented in the body of the paper, but not to the point where the logical connection is broken.

### Sources

As we commented in Chapter 3, the accurate and appropriate use of source materials is essential to scientific or referential discourse. These references must be made accessible to the reader. A detailed discussion of how to incorporate source material into the body of your paper is presented in Chapter 12.

## SUGGESTIONS FOR WRITING AND THINKING

1.  At the end of Chapters 6 to 9 we provide annotated lists of studies in various social science disciplines. Read one of these articles, and ana-

lyze its structure in terms of the questions-evidence-answers schema. In a single paragraph, discuss the questions that govern the research; in a second paragraph, sum up the evidence; in a third paragraph, state the major conclusion.

*Chapter 6*
# THE EXPERIMENT

## INTRODUCTION

For the most part, social scientists are obliged to accept the world as they find it. The unique feature of the experiment is that social scientists actually manipulate the environment in order to test certain theories or assumptions. Just as the natural scientist conducts an experiment, say, to see what happens when an atom is split into smaller particles, the social scientist deliberately alters a social setting to see how human behavior is affected.

In the classical model of an experiment, the researcher begins with two groups that are initially identical in every respect. One of these, *the experimental group,* is then subjected to a "stimulus" by the researcher, while the second group, *the control group,* is not altered. The stimulus is then presumed to be the cause of whatever differences show up between the two groups at a later point in time.

For example, a number of experimental studies have been conducted in order to identify the conditions under which people will offer assistance to someone in need. One such experiment was called "Lady in Distress: A Flat Tire Study." The researchers concocted the following situation: A car with a flat tire was placed conspicuously on a street in a residential section of Los Angeles. In one instance (the control group) a woman stood helplessly by the car, which had a fully inflated tire leaning against it. In the other instance (the experimental group), the car was raised by a jack, and the woman stood by while a man changed the tire. The purpose of the experiment was to gauge whether helping behavior increased through the observation of other people being helpful. As it turned out, more people stopped when the woman was being helped by someone else than when she was stranded by herself. The authors concluded that the perception of someone else's altruistic behavior tends to elicit the same response on the part of the observer.[1]

Experiments are used more often in psychology than in the other social sciences. The reason is that psychologists are often preoccupied with problems that involve how individuals react to stimuli that can be produced or simulated in a laboratory under experimental conditions. For example, in Milgram's study of obedience to authority, discussed in Chapter 5, the researchers artificially contrived a situation where subjects were directed by some authority to inflict punishment on others, and their behavior could be observed and measured.

This is an example of a laboratory experiment. Other experiments occur "in the field," such as the Lady in Distress study described above. The sample essay in this chapter is also a field experiment, except that the experiment was carried out in a natural setting—an elementary school—rather than one contrived by the experimenter. In the experiment, two Harvard researchers wanted to test whether some students do poorly in school because their teachers have such low expectations of them that they neglect the children or underestimate their abilities. In other words, their hypothesis was that poor academic performance is the result of a self-fulfilling prophecy on the part of teachers who expect certain students—especially those of minority or lower-class backgrounds—to do poorly.[2]

The experiment was conducted in an elementary school in an economically and racially mixed neighborhood in San Francisco. At the beginning of the experiment, students were scored on a standard intelligence test. Teachers were then duped into believing that certain students were "potential spurters." In actuality, these students were chosen at random and were no different from the other students. The purpose of the experiment was to test whether students designated as "potential spurters" actually performed better because teachers had high expectations of them. The following is an excerpt from Rosenthal and Jacobson's study, as reported in *Scientific American*.

---

[1]James H. Bryan and Mary Ann Test, "Models and Helping: Naturalistic Studies in Aiding Behavior," *Journal of Personality and Social Psychology*, 6 (August 1967), 400–407.

[2]Robert Rosenthal and Lenore F. Jacobson, "Teacher Expectations for the Disadvantaged," *Scientific American*, 218 (April 1968), 19–23.

# Teacher Expectations for the Disadvantaged*

## Robert Rosenthal and Lenore F. Jacobson

*It is widely believed that poor children lag in school because they are members of a disadvantaged group. Experiments in a school suggest that they may also do so because that is what their teachers expect.*

[1]   One of the central problems of American society lies in the fact that certain children suffer a handicap in their education which then persists throughout life. The "disadvantaged" child is a Negro American, a Mexican American, a Puerto Rican or any other child who lives in conditions of poverty. He is a lower-class child who performs poorly in an educational system that is staffed almost entirely by middle-class teachers.

[2]   The reason usually given for the poor performance of the disadvantaged child is simply that the child is a member of a disadvantaged group. There may well be another reason. It is that the child does poorly in school because that is what is expected of him. In other words, his shortcomings may originate not in his different ethnic, cultural, and economic background but in his teachers' response to that background.

[3]   If there is any substance to this hypothesis, educators are confronted with some major questions. Have these children, who account for most of the academic failures in the U.S., shaped the expectations that their teachers have for them? Have the schools failed the children by anticipating their poor performance and thus in effect teaching them to fail? Are the massive public programs of educational assistance to such children reinforcing the assumption that they are likely to fail? Would the children do appreciably better if their teachers could be induced to expect more of them?

[4]   We have explored the effect of teacher expectations with experiments in which teachers were led to believe at the beginning of a school year that certain of their pupils could be expected to show considerable academic improvement during the year. The teachers thought the predictions were based on tests that had been administered to the student body toward the end of the preceding school year. In actuality the children designated as potential "spurters" had been chosen at random and not on the basis of testing. Nonetheless, intelligence tests given after the experiment had been in progress for several months indicated that on the whole the randomly chosen children had improved more than the rest.

[5]   The central concept behind our investigation was that of the "self-fulfilling prophecy." The essence of this concept is that one person's prediction of another person's behavior somehow comes to be realized. The prediction may, of course, be realized only in the per-

ception of the predictor. It is also possible, however, that the predictor's expectation is communicated to the other person, perhaps in quite subtle and unintended ways, and so has an influence on his actual behavior.

[6] An experimenter cannot be sure that he is dealing with a self-fulfilling prophecy until he has taken steps to make certain that a prediction is not based on behavior that has already been observed. If schoolchildren who perform poorly are those expected by their teachers to perform poorly, one cannot say in the normal school situation whether the teacher's expectation was the cause of the performance or whether she simply made an accurate prognosis based on her knowledge of past performance by the particular children involved. To test for the existence of self-fulfilling prophecy the experimenter must establish conditions in which an expectation is uncontaminated by the past behavior of the subject whose performance is being predicted.

[7] It is easy to establish such conditions in the psychological laboratory by presenting an experimenter with a group of laboratory animals and telling him what kind of behavior he can expect from them. One of us (Rosenthal) has carried out a number of experiments along this line using rats that were said to be either bright or dull. In one experiment 12 students in psychology were each given five laboratory rats of the same strain. Six of the students were told that their rats had been bred for brightness in running a maze; the other six students were told that their rats could be expected for genetic reasons to be poor at

running a maze. The assignment given the students was to teach the rats to run the maze.

[8] From the outset the rats believed to have the higher potential proved to be the better performers. The rats thought to be dull made poor progress and sometimes would not even budge from the starting position in the maze. A questionnaire given after the experiment showed that the students with the allegedly brighter rats ranked their subjects as brighter, more pleasant and more likable than did the students who had the allegedly duller rats. Asked about their methods of dealing with the rats, the students with the "bright" group turned out to have been friendlier, more enthusiastic and less talkative with the animals than the students with the "dull" group had been. The students with the "bright" rats also said they handled their animals more, as well as more gently, than the students expecting poor performances did.

[9] Our task was to establish similar conditions in a classroom situation. We wanted to create expectations that were based only on what teachers had been told, so that we could preclude the possibility of judgments based on previous observations of the children involved. It was with this objective that we set up our experiment in what we shall call Oak School, an elementary school in the South San Francisco Unified School District. To avoid the dangers of letting it be thought that some children could be expected to perform poorly we established only the expectation that certain pupils might show superior performance. Our experiments had the financial support of the National Science Foundation

and the cooperation of Paul Nielsen, the superintendent of the school district.

[10] Oak School is in an established and somewhat run-down section of a middle-sized city. The school draws some students from middle-class families but more from lower-class families. Included in the latter category are children from families receiving welfare payments, from low-income families and from Mexican-American families. The school has six grades, each organized into three classes—one for children performing at above-average levels of scholastic achievement, one for average children and one for those who are below average. There is also a kindergarten.

[11] At the beginning of the experiment in 1964 we told the teachers that further validation was needed for a new kind of test designed to predict academic blooming or intellectual gain in children. In actuality we used the Flanagan Tests of General Ability, a standard intelligence test that was fairly new and therefore unfamiliar to the teachers. It consists of two relatively independent subtests, one focusing more on verbal ability and the other more on reasoning ability. An example of a verbal item in the version of the test designed for children in kindergarten and first grade presents drawings of an article of clothing, a flower, an envelope, an apple and a glass of water; the children are asked to mark with a crayon "the thing that you can eat." In the reasoning subtest a typical item consists of drawings of five abstractions, such as four squares and a circle; the pupils are asked to cross out the one that differs from the others.

[12] We had special covers printed for the test; they bore the high-sounding title "Test of Inflected Acquisition." The teachers were told that the testing was part of an undertaking being carried out by investigators from Harvard University and that the test would be given several times in the future. The tests were to be sent to Harvard for scoring and for addition to the data being compiled for validation. In May, 1964, the teachers administered the test to all the children then in kindergarten and grades one through five. The children in sixth grade were not tested because they would be in junior high school the next year.

[13] Before Oak School opened the following September about 20 percent of the children were designated as potential academic spurters. There were about five such children in each classroom. The manner of conveying their names to the teachers was deliberately made rather casual: the subject was brought up at the end of the first staff meeting with the remark, "By the way, in case you're interested in who did what in those tests we're doing for Harvard. . . ."

[14] The names of the "spurters" had been chosen by means of a table of random numbers. The experimental treatment of the children involved nothing more than giving their names to their new teachers as children who could be expected to show unusual intellectual gains in the year ahead. The difference, then, between these children and the undesignated children who constituted a control group was entirely in the minds of the teachers.

[15] All the children were given the same test again four months after school had started, at the end of that school year and finally in May of the

following year. As the children progressed through the grades they were given tests of the appropriate level. The tests were designed for three grade levels: kindergarten and first grade, second and third grades and fourth through sixth grades.

[16] The results indicated strongly that children from whom teachers expected greater intellectual gains showed such gains. The gains, however, were not uniform across the grades. The tests given at the end of the first year showed the largest gains among children in the first and second grades. In the second year the greatest gains were among the children who had been in the fifth grade when the "spurters" were designated and who by the time of the final test were completing sixth grade.

[17] At the end of the academic year 1964–1965 the teachers were asked to describe the classroom behavior of their pupils. The children from whom intellectual growth was expected were described as having a better chance of being successful in later life and as being happier, more curious and more interesting than the other children. There was also a tendency for the designated children to be seen as more appealing, better adjusted and more affectionate, and as less in need of social approval. In short, the children for whom intellectual growth was expected became more alive and autonomous intellectually, or at least were so perceived by their teachers. These findings were particularly striking among the children in the first grade.

[18] An interesting contrast became apparent when teachers were asked to rate the undesignated children. Many of these children had also gained in I.Q. during the year. The more they gained, the less favorably they were rated.

[19] From these results it seems evident that when children who are expected to gain intellectually do gain, they may be benefited in other ways. As "personalities" they go up in the estimation of their teachers. The opposite is true of children who gain intellectually when improvement is not expected of them. They are looked on as showing undesirable behavior. It would seem that there are hazards in unpredicted intellectual growth.

[20] A closer examination revealed that the most unfavorable ratings were given to the children in low-ability classrooms who gained the most intellectually. When these "slow track" children were in the control group, where little intellectual gain was expected of them, they were rated more unfavorably by their teachers if they did show gains in I.Q. The more they gained, the more unfavorably they were rated. Even when the slow-track children were in the experimental group, where greater intellectual gains were expected of them, they were not rated as favorably with respect to their control-group peers as were the children of the high track and the medium track. Evidently it is likely to be difficult for a slow-track child, even if his I.Q. is rising, to be seen by his teacher as well adjusted and as a potentially successful student.

[21] How is one to account for the fact that the children who were expected to gain did gain? The first answer that comes to mind is that the teachers must have spent more time with them than with the children of whom nothing was said. This hypothesis seems to be wrong,

judging not only from some questions we asked the teachers about the time they spent with their pupils but also from the fact that in a given classroom the more the "spurters" gained in I.Q., the more the other children gained.

[22] Another bit of evidence that the hypothesis is wrong appears in the pattern of the test results. If teachers had talked to the designated children more, which would be the most likely way of investing more time in work with them, one might expect to see the largest gains in verbal intelligence. In actuality the largest gains were in reasoning intelligence.

[23] It would seem that the explanation we are seeking lies in a subtler feature of the interaction of the teacher and her pupils. Her tone of voice, facial expression, touch and posture may be the means by which—probably quite unwittingly— she communicates her expectations to the pupils. Such communication might help the child by changing his conception of himself, his anticipation of his own behavior, his motivation or his cognitive skills. This is an area in which further research is clearly needed.

[24] Why was the effect of teacher expectations most pronounced in the lower grades? It is difficult to be sure, but several hypotheses can be advanced. Younger children may be easier to change than older ones are. They are likely to have less well-established reputations in the school. It may be that they are more sensitive to the processes by which teachers communicate their expectations to pupils.

[25] It is also difficult to be certain why the older children showed the best performance in the follow-up year. Perhaps the younger children, who by then had different teachers, needed continued contact with the teachers who had influenced them in order to maintain their improved performance. The older children, who were harder to influence at first, may have been better able to maintain an improved performance autonomously once they had achieved it.

[26] In considering our results, particularly the substantial gains shown by the children in the control group, one must take into account the possibility that what is called the Hawthorne effect might have been involved. The name comes from the Western Electric Company's Hawthorne Works in Chicago. In the 1920's the plant was the scene of an intensive series of experiments designed to determine what effect various changes in working conditions would have on the performance of female workers. Some of the experiments, for example, involved changes in lighting. It soon became evident that the significant thing was not whether the worker had more or less light but merely that she was the subject of attention. Any changes that involved her, and even actions that she only thought were changes, were likely to improve her performance.

[27] In the Oak School experiment the fact that university researchers, supported by Federal funds, were interested in the school may have led to a general improvement of morale and effort on the part of the teachers. In any case, the possibility of a Hawthorne effect cannot be ruled out either in this experiment or in other studies of educational practices. Whenever a new educational practice is undertaken in a school, it cannot be demonstrated to have an

intrinsic effect unless it shows some excess of gain over what Hawthorne effects alone would yield. In our case a Hawthorne effect might account for the gains shown by the children in the control group, but it would not account for the greater gains made by the children in the experimental group.

[28] Our results suggest that yet another base line must be introduced when the intrinsic value of an educational innovation is being assessed. The question will be whether the venture is more effective (and cheaper) than the simple expedient of trying to change the expectations of the teacher. Most educational innovations will be found to cost more in both time and money than inducing teachers to expect more of "disadvantaged" children.

[29] For almost three years the nation's schools have had access to substantial Federal funds under the Elementary and Secondary Education Act, which President Johnson signed in April, 1965. Title I of the act is particularly directed at disadvantaged children. Most of the programs devised for using Title I funds focus on overcoming educational handicaps by acting on the child—through remedial instruction, cultural enrichment and the like. The premise seems to be that the deficiencies are all in the child and in the environment from which he comes.

[30] Our experiment rested on the premise that at least some of the deficiencies—and therefore at least some of the remedies—might be in the schools, and particularly in the attitudes of teachers toward disadvantaged children. In our experiment nothing was done directly for the child. There was no crash program to improve his reading ability, no extra time for tutoring, no program of trips to museums and art galleries. The only people affected directly were the teachers; the effect on the children was indirect.

[31] It is interesting to note that one "total push" program of the kind devised under Title I led in three years to a 10-point gain in I.Q. by 38 percent of the children and a 20-point gain by 12 percent. The gains were dramatic, but they did not even match the ones achieved by the control-group children in the first and second grades of Oak School. They were far smaller than the gains made by the children in our experimental group.

[32] Perhaps, then, more attention in educational research should be focused on the teacher. If it could be learned how she is able to bring about dramatic improvement in the performance of her pupils without formal changes in her methods of teaching, other teachers could be taught to do the same. If further research showed that it is possible to find teachers whose untrained educational style does for their pupils what our teachers did for the special children, the prospect would arise that a combination of sophisticated selection of teachers and suitable training of teachers would give all children a boost toward getting as much as they possibly can out of their schooling.

## CRITICAL ANALYSIS: CONTENT

Let us now analyze this sample essay in terms of the schema outlined in Chapter 5. What were the major *questions* that governed the study? What *evidence* was brought to bear on these questions? And what *conclusions* were finally reached? In other words, let us observe the "logical structure of social science writing" in practice. (To repeat, even though the schema of questions-evidence-conclusions can be detected in virtually all social science writing, it is not applied in rote fashion and does not result in a dull uniformity. That it takes varied and subtle forms will become apparent from the four sample essays in Chapters 6 to 9 of this book.)

### Questions

The authors waste no time in raising the main issue of their study. In the first paragraph they allude to the commonplace notion that minority children do poorly in school because they are culturally "disadvantaged." In the second paragraph they suggest an alternative explanation: that the problems of minority children may stem from the fact that teachers have low expectations of them. In a nutshell, this is the supposition or hypothesis that the authors wish to test, and that provides the background and rationale for their study. By the third paragraph the authors are prepared to elaborate on the central question and its implications for social policy:

> If there is any substance to this hypothesis, educators are confronted with some major questions. Have these children, who account for most of the academic failures in the U.S., shaped the expectations that teachers have for them? Have the schools failed the children by anticipating their poor performance and thus in effect teaching them to fail? Are the massive public programs of educational assistance to such children reinforcing the assumption that they are likely to fail? Would the children do appreciably better if their teachers could be induced to expect more of them?

These questions not only form the agenda for the research but they imply a format for organizing the remainder of the research report as well.

### Evidence

Having thus established the rationale and purpose of the study, the authors have set the stage to discuss their research procedures and to present their findings. First, they tell us why Oak School was chosen, how teachers were duped into believing that certain students were "potential spurters," and how students were periodically retested in order to measure any change that could be attributed to teacher expectations. The specific findings are reported in detail. However, there is one major finding—that teacher expectations are in fact associated with student performance—that is highlighted in the text and repeated at several intervals:

The results indicated strongly that children from whom teachers expected greater intellectual gains showed such gains. [paragraph 16]

The children from whom intellectual growth was expected were described as having a better chance of being successful in later life and as being happier, more curious and more interesting than the other children. [paragraph 17]

In short, the children for whom intellectual growth was expected became more alive and autonomous intellectually, or at least were so perceived by their teachers. These findings were particularly striking among the children in the first grade. [paragraph 17]

### Answers

In science, as in life, resolving one question often raises numerous others. The finding that students designated as potential spurters did in fact perform better resolved the empirical question, but raised a more fundamental issue: "How is one to account for the fact that the children who were expected to gain did gain?" [paragraph 21]. After discounting two possible interpretations, the authors come to the conclusion that the key factor has to do with the communication between teacher and student: "Her tone of voice, facial expression, touch and posture may be the means by which—probably quite unwittingly—she communicated her expectations to the pupils" [paragraph 23]. However, the authors indicate that this is a tentative conclusion, since they do not have the necessary data to substantiate it more fully.

In Chapter 5 we noted that the conclusion often goes beyond the specific issue under analysis, and assesses the larger implications of the study. In this case, Rosenthal and Jacobson weigh the policy implications of their findings. Instead of focusing educational reform on the children and the presumed disadvantages in their background, they argue, ". . . some of the deficiencies—and therefore at least some of the remedies—might be in the schools, and particularly in the attitudes of teachers toward disadvantaged children" [paragraph 30]. Conceding that their findings are suggestive but inconclusive, the authors urge future researchers to focus on the teacher, and in the closing paragraph, they suggest some directions that this research could take.

## CRITICAL ANALYSIS: COMPOSITION

In rhetorical terms, "Teacher Expectations for the Disadvantaged" is organized around a cause-effect analysis of a problem. Rosenthal and Jacobson are looking for a cause of the educational problems of disadvantaged children. The question that governs their study is not *whether* but *why* these problems exist, and their experiment is designed to test their hypothesis that teacher expectations are one cause of student failure.

### The Introduction (paragraphs 1 to 5)

The first paragraph of the essay fulfills the main requirements of a good introduction: It states the research problem, establishes its significance, and arouses our interest as readers. Note how the authors' choice of words conveys a sense of the importance of their research, beginning with the very first sentence: "One of the central problems of American society lies in the fact that certain children suffer a handicap in their education which then persists throughout life." This is provocative language. It engages the reader, and suggests that the problem is not only worthy of academic study, but warrants the concern of all civic-minded people.

The problems that disadvantaged children have in school are defined in the context of two possible explanations. The first, which reflects the conventional wisdom, is that the background of disadvantaged children deprives them of values and skills needed to excel in school. But, Rosenthal and Jacobson suggest, "there may well be another reason." With this transitional sentence, they put forward an alternative explanation which is stated as a hypothesis:

> It is that the child does poorly in school because that is what is expected of him. In other words, his shortcomings may originate not in his different ethnic, cultural, and economic background but in his teachers' response to that background. [paragraph 2]

This hypothesis functions as a thesis statement for the entire essay. It is the central idea that is repeated at appropriate junctures in the essay, and that controls the direction and the content of the writing. All of the data that is subsequently introduced is done so in order to test the validity of this thesis.

Paragraphs 1 to 5 comprise the full introduction to the essay. After elaborating on the thesis statement in the second and third paragraphs, the authors use paragraph 4 to provide a capsule summary of the experiment and its major findings, which bear out their hypothesis. Paragraph 5 then functions as a transition to the main body of the paper by identifying the key concept behind the investigation: the self-fulfilling prophecy.

### The Body Paragraphs (paragraphs 6 to 20)

For the most part the body of the paper consists of a step-by-step account of the experiment, followed by a detailed presentation of the findings. Thus, much of this section is descriptive and relies on careful reporting. Note the attention to detail:

> Oak School is in an established and somewhat run-down section of a middle-sized city. [paragraph 10]
>
> We had special covers printed for the test; they bore the high-sounding title "Test of Inflected Acquisition." [paragraph 12]
>
> The manner of conveying their names to the teachers was deliberately made rather casual: the subject was brought up at the end of the first staff meeting

with the remark, "By the way, in case you're interested in who did what in those tests we're doing for Harvard. . . ." [paragraph 13]

In paragraphs 16 to 20 the authors present the results, beginning with the transitional phrase, "The results indicated strongly that. . . ." These results, however, do not constitute the conclusion. Rather, they comprise the material on which the conclusion is based. As a bridge to the concluding section Rosenthal and Jacobson pose a question that calls for an interpretation of the data: "How is one to account for the fact that the children who were expected to gain did gain?" [paragraph 21].

### The Conclusion (paragraphs 21 to 32)

In addressing the question of why the "potential spurters" actually did better, Rosenthal and Jacobson first weigh the possibility that teachers spent more time with these students. The interpretation, however, is not supported by the data, and is readily dismissed. Why then discuss it at all? Rosenthal and Jacobson use it as a "straw man"—that is, an idea that is proposed in order to be knocked down, thus eliminating one possible interpretation and making their own appear more credible. At this point Rosenthal and Jacobson advance their own interpretation; namely, that through subtle cues teachers communicate their expectations to students. These expectations are then internalized, and influence how children perform in school.

Unfortunately, Rosenthal and Jacobson have no direct evidence to support this interpretation, since they have not observed the interaction between teachers and students. Indeed, this is one of the weaknesses of their study. Note how the authors deal with this problem in terms of their writing. First of all, they are somewhat tentative in stating their conclusion: "*It would seem that the explanation we are seeking* lies in a subtler feature of the interaction of the teacher and her pupils" [paragraph 23, italics added]. Secondly, in the closing paragraphs of the article the authors argue that there is a need for "further research," and indicate the directions this should take. Finally, they discuss the implications of their research assuming that they are ultimately proved correct. *If* future research bears them out, they write, then funds for educational assistance should go toward the "sophisticated selection" and "suitable training" of teachers. (Note that this issue, which is taken up in the very last paragraph, is not introduced as a new topic that departs from the paper. Rather it is presented as an issue of broader significance that is a logical extension of the research findings.)

## RHETORICAL STANCE: PERSUADING THE READER

As we stated in Chapter 4, the rhetorical stance is a manner of persuasion that involves the interaction of subject, audience, and voice. The writer's mastery of a subject is only a necessary first step. He or she must also develop a point of view about that subject, and communicate it effectively. Tone, sequence, and detail are all important elements in persuasive writing.

If we step back and look at "Teacher Expectations for the Disadvantaged" as a whole, we can see that Rosenthal and Jacobson have made their overarching purpose clear to their readers: They want to better understand why disadvantaged children fail in school. They have hypothesized a reason, conducted an experiment to test this hypothesis, and are prepared to defend their conclusions. The authors persuade their audience in the following ways:

1. They engage their readers by calling attention to a shared concern with a serious national problem: the education of disadvantaged children.

2. They elicit the trust of their readers by presenting an objective overview of the problem. By discussing the results of earlier learning experiments on rats, they demonstrate their knowledge of educational research and establish their authority to discuss the subject.

3. They convince their readers of the validity of their experiment by providing essential information about how they set up the experiment, and took precautions to prevent teachers from discovering its true purpose.

4. The authors strengthen their case by demonstrating that they have not jumped to a conclusion. In presenting their findings, the authors wrestle with conflicting interpretations, thus anticipating points that might be advanced by critics.

5. Finally, Rosenthal and Jacobson are very cautious in making their claims. They attempt to persuade their readers by finding a common ground from which to argue. They acknowledge the cause with which most people are familiar—the effect of social class and cultural influences—and instead of rejecting this explanation outright, they suggest that "there may well be" another explanation. They are careful to define teacher expectations as a "contributory cause"—that is, one cause among many. Note their language:

> Our experiment rested on the premise that *at least some of the deficiencies—and therefore at least some of the remedies*—might be in the schools, and particularly in the attitudes of teachers toward disadvantaged children. [paragraph 30, italics added]

> This note of caution inspires confidence. Rosenthal and Jacobson are careful not to overstate their case. Rather, they make a balanced and reasonable appeal.

## Language

The language of this essay is admirably clear and straightforward. It is neither overblown nor obscure. Although the original study was oriented to an audience of educational psychologists, this piece was published in a popular journal, *Scientific American*, and thus intended for a general but informed audience with some background or interest in science. The authors presuppose a basic understanding of the experimental model. However, in writing their essay, they had to make decisions about which terms needed to be defined. In some instances they assumed that their readers were familiar with specific terms or would understand them in context (for example, "hypothesis" [paragraph 3] and "control group" [paragraph 14]). In other instances they were careful to define their terms (for example, "self-fulfilling prophecy" [paragraph 5] and "the Hawthorne effect" [paragraph 26]).

Several other observations about language are worth noting:

> The authors use the first person plural (we) when describing the experiment, making their presentation of data seem more personal and less mechanistic.

> They use transitional phrases which function as markers of the direction of their discussion ("We have explained . . ."; "Our task was to . . ."; "The results indicated . . ."; "From these results it seems evident . . ."; "Our results suggest . . .").

> Through language, Rosenthal and Jacobson establish a tone that is serious, direct, and empathetic toward disadvantaged children. In one startling turn of phrase, they restate their thesis in a way that jolts the reader into confronting its full impact: "Have the *schools failed* the children by anticipating their poor performance and thus in effect *teaching them to fail?*" [paragraph 3, italics added]. This language is highly effective because it has inverted familiar words and meanings. Children have not simply failed; they have been taught to fail.

## SUGGESTIONS FOR WRITING AND THINKING

1.  This exercise is modeled after the "Lady in Distress" experiment described at the beginning of this chapter. This time *you* will be the person in distress, and the goal of the experiment will be to determine whether male or female bystanders are more likely to offer assistance.

    To carry out this experiment, it will be necessary to create a mock "distress situation." For example, you could drop a stack of books and school supplies in the corridor of your classroom building as unsuspecting subjects pass by. Repeat this twenty times, ten times when the bystander is male, and ten times when the bystander is female. The main observation is whether or not the bystander volunteers assistance. You might also want to record other aspects of verbal and nonverbal behavior. Do bystanders who offer assistance do so willingly or grudgingly? Do they express sympathy or remain silent? Do bystanders who refuse assistance pretend not to see what happened, or do they pretend they are too harried to stop?

    On the basis of these twenty trials, determine whether there are any systematic differences in the responses of male and female bystanders. By collating your results with other students in the class, you can increase your sample size and thus the reliability of your findings. In addition, you can determine whether results differ when the person in distress is male or female.

    Once the findings are established, you are ready to write up the results. Develop a context for presenting your research findings by discussing the purpose of the research, what you hope to learn, and why this is worth knowing. Like Rosenthal and Jacobson, describe the design of the research—where it was conducted, how you staged a mock distress situation, and so on. Finally, present your findings, and in a concluding section, discuss the implications of the research.

2. Read "The Experience of Living in Cities" by Stanley Milgram, published in *Science*, 167 (March 1970), 1461–68. This article reports the results of a series of experimental studies that attempt to determine how people in cities adapt to the overstimulation and stresses of urban life.

Analyze the article in terms of the questions-evidence-conclusions schema. Then analyze the article in terms of its rhetorical strategy. Discuss how the concept of "overload" helps to tie together the disparate empirical findings. What is Milgram's thesis? Where is it stated? Is his argument altogether persuasive? Why or why not?

## EXPERIMENTAL STUDIES ACROSS THE DISCIPLINES

### Economics

MOFFITT, ROBERT, "The Negative Income Tax: Would It Discourage Work?" *Monthly Labor Review*, 104 (April 1981), 23–27. This article summarizes the results of four field experiments that sought to test whether government cash transfer payments to the poor, in the form of a negative income tax, would discourage work effort among recipients.

### Political Science

COLOMBOTOS, JOHN, "Physicians and Medicare: A Before-After Study of the Effects of Legislation on Attitudes," *American Sociological Review*, 34 (June 1969), 314–18. When Medicare was first proposed, it was adamantly opposed by the organized medical profession. This study uses an experimental design to determine how individual physicians reacted in terms of their attitudes and behavior after the legislation was enacted.

### Experimental Psychology

BRANSFORD, JOHN D., and MARCIA K. JOHNSON, "Contextual Prerequisites for Understanding: Some Investigations of Comprehension and Recall," *Journal of Verbal Learning and Verbal Behavior*, II (1972), 717–26. Experiments show that comprehension and memory are enhanced if a reader or listener is able to put the information into a relevant context.

### *Social Psychology*

ROSENHAN, D. L., "On Being Sane in Insane Places," *Science*, 179 (January 1973), 250–58. Eight confederates in this experiment gained admission to psychiatric hospitals merely by complaining that they heard voices. Once labeled as schizophrenic, the pseudopatients had trouble overcoming this tag, proving that health care professionals have difficulty distinguishing the sane from the insane in psychiatric hospitals.

# Chapter 7
# OBSERVATION

## INTRODUCTION

All social scientists are "observers" of human society, although observation takes very different forms depending on the research methods that are employed. Since firsthand observation is not possible, historians must rely on documents to "observe" the past. Sociologists typically focus on contemporary society, but often need to observe patterns—for example, shifts in political opinion—that may not be visible to the naked eye. By drawing a sample and conducting interviews, survey researchers collect fragments of information which are then pieced together, much like a jigsaw puzzle, in order to construct the larger picture.

Still another approach involves direct, firsthand observation of people in their natural surroundings. Here the challenge for researchers is to immerse themselves as much as possible in the life of the community or group under observation. They become "participants," which happens, as one writer puts it, "when the heart of the observer is made to beat as the heart of any other member of the group under observation, rather than as that of a detached emissary from some distant laboratory."[1] Ideally, the participant observer is both a "detached emissary" and an empathetic insider, and writing based on participant observation should reflect both perspectives.

Howard Becker, who helped to pioneer the use of participant observation in sociology, describes the method as follows:

> The observer places himself in the life of the community so that he can see, over a period of time, what people ordinarily do as they go about their daily round of activity. He records his observations as soon as possible after making

[1]John Madge, *The Tools of Social Science* (Garden City, New York: Anchor, 1953), p. 137.

them. He notes the kinds of people who interact with one another, the content and consequences of the interaction, and how it is talked about and evaluated by the participants and others after the event. He tries to record this material as completely as possible by means of detailed accounts of actions, maps of the location of people as they act, and of course, verbatim transcriptions of conversation.[2]

Unlike the experimenter, who deliberately manipulates a setting in order to test for results, participant observers usually try to be as unobtrusive as possible, sometimes concealing their identity altogether.

Although participant observation is used to greater or lesser extent in all of the social sciences, its origins are in anthropology where it is still the prevalent research method. Franz Boas, the founder of academic anthropology, spent more than forty years studying the native peoples of the Pacific Northwest. Ever since, cultural anthropologists have used participant observation to develop an anthropological record of preliterate peoples in every corner of the planet.

A celebrated example is Margaret Mead's *Coming of Age in Samoa.* After years of living among the native people of the Samoan Islands, Mead reported that adolescents in Samoa were spared the intense anxiety and emotional conflict associated with adolescence in modern western societies. This conclusion, however, has been challenged by more recent investigators who also have done field work in the Samoan Islands. Over against Mead's image of an island paradise, these observers portray a society with a great deal of strife, and they specifically reject Mead's contention that adolescence is free of anxiety and conflict.[3]

This controversy points up one of the pitfalls almost inherent in the participant-observation approach: subjectivity and selectivity on the part of the observer. The danger is that field workers will see "what they want to see," and will unconsciously filter out observations that are inconsistent with their expectations or bias. Before rejecting participant observation as hopelessly subjective, however, remember that this is a problem that applies to all social research. Even the historian must select out which facts and observations to include in the historical record. The only recourse is to strive for objectivity, to muster as much evidence as possible, and to be clear and persuasive in the presentation of research findings. If other researchers come up with different conclusions, as in the case of Margaret Mead, then the issue is debated in books and journals and at academic conferences.

---

[2]Howard Becker, "Observation: Case Studies," *International Encyclopedia of the Social Sciences,* 11 (New York: The Macmillan Co. and The Free Press, 1968), p. 233.

[3]Margaret Mead, *Coming of Age in Samoa* (New York: W. Morrow &. Co., 1928). For a prominent critique of Mead's work, see Derek Freeman, *Margaret Mead and Samoa: The Making and Unmaking of an Anthropological Myth* (New York: Penguin, 1985). The controversy over Mead's work is itself the subject of a book by Lowell D. Holmes, *Quest for the Real Samoa* (South Hadley, Mass.: Bergin &. Garvey Publishers, 1986).

Although participant observation was pioneered by anthropologists engaged in the study of preliterate societies, social scientists subsequently applied the method to contemporary societies as well. In the 1940s and 1950s sociologists at the University of Chicago came to regard the city as "a mosaic of small worlds" that provided fertile ground for research by participant observers. The works they published had such titles as *The Hobo, The Gold Coast and the Slum, The Ghetto,* and *The Taxi Dance-Hall.*[4] More recently, urban ethnographers have provided rich accounts of various ethnic communities and subcultures. Two prominent examples are Herbert Gans's *Urban Villagers,* which is a study of an Italian community on Boston's North End, and Elliot Liebow's *Tally's Corner,* which is a study of streetcorner life in a ghetto in Washington, D.C.[5] There also have been countless studies of groups that stand outside the respectable mainstream—for example, prostitutes, pimps, and criminals. Still other studies—most notably by Erving Goffman and his followers—have focused on the routine aspects of everyday life, exploring such subjects as how people walk through doors or distance themselves in conversation. Indeed, there is hardly any sphere of social life that is not potential material for the participant observer.

This last comment has special relevance to you, as students. In effect, you are uncertified participant observers by virtue of living in distinctive neighborhoods or having access to such locales as student cafeterias, streetcorner hangouts, discos, and the like. Remember to make use of your insider experience when formulating topics for research papers.

In contrast to quantitative studies that are encumbered with numerical data and statistics, studies based on participant observation lend themselves to a more imaginative and vivid prose style. The challenge for the writer is to recreate the setting under observation as graphically as possible, in order to capture its essential character and to convey this even to readers who may have never experienced it firsthand.

Consider, for example, the opening paragraph from the following article "Rappin' in the Black Ghetto":

> "Rapping," "shucking," "jiving," "running it down," "gripping," "copping a plea," "signifying" and "sounding" are all part of the black ghetto idiom and describe different kinds of talking. Each has its own distinguishing features of form, style, and function; each is influenced by, and influences, the speaker, setting, and audience; and each sheds light on the black perspective and the black condition—on those orienting values and attitudes that will cause a

---

[4]Nels Anderson, *The Hobo* (Chicago: University of Chicago Press, 1923); Harvey Zorbaugh, *The Gold Coast and the Slum* (Chicago: University of Chicago Press, 1929); Louis Wirth, *The Ghetto* (Chicago: University of Chicago Press, 1928); Paul G. Cressey, *The Taxi Dance-Hall* (Chicago: University of Chicago Press, 1936).

[5]Herbert Gans, *Urban Villagers* (New York: The Free Press, 1982); Elliot Liebow, *Tally's Corner* (Boston: Little, Brown, 1967).

speaker to speak or perform in his own way within the social context of the black community.6

The author, Thomas Kochman, is a sociolinguist, and his study was based on field work that he conducted with the help of students and informants. The purpose of Kochman's study was not only to describe the "black ghetto idiom," but also to analyze its social and psychological functions. His article is peppered with actual quotes that illustrate different kinds of talking, and the thrust of his analysis can be gauged from the concluding paragraph:

> In conclusion, by blending style and verbal power, through rapping, sounding and running it down, the black ghetto male establishes his personality; through shucking, gripping and copping a plea, he shows his respect for power; through jiving and signifying he stirs up excitement. With all of the above, he hopes to manipulate and control people and situations to give himself a winning edge.7

The sample essay for this chapter fits squarely in the tradition of studies that seek to penetrate one of the small, self-contained "worlds" that lie outside the purview and experience of the average person. It is an ethnographic study of the poolroom hustler. The investigator, Ned Polsky, was a true participant-observer in that billiard playing had been his chief recreation for many years. As he discloses to the reader: "I have frequented poolrooms for over 20 years, and at one poolroom game, three-cushion billiards, am considered a far better than average player. In recent years I have played an average of more than six hours per week in various New York poolrooms, and played as much in the poolrooms of Chicago for most of the eight years I lived there."8 Polsky's other life was that of a doctoral student in the University of Chicago's Department of Sociology, where the field of urban ethnography had been pioneered. Polsky decided to make the poolroom hustler the subject of his dissertation. Clearly, he was in a unique position to describe the world of the hustler from an insider's point of view.

---

6Thomas Kochman, "Rappin' in the Black Ghetto," *Transaction*, 6 (February 1969), 26. For the original version on which the *Transaction* article was based, see "Toward an Ethnography of Black American Speech Behavior," in Thomas Kochman, *Rappin' and Stylin' Out* (Urbana: University of Illinois Press, 1972), pp. 241–64.

7Ibid., p. 34.

8Ned Polsky, *Hustlers, Beats, and Others* (Chicago: University of Chicago Press, 1985), p. 44.

# The Hustler*

## Ned Polsky

*Such a man spends all his life playing every day for small stakes. Give him every morning the money that he may gain during the day, on condition that he does not play—you will make him unhappy. It will perhaps be said that what he seeks is the amusement of play, not gain. Let him play then for nothing; he will lose interest and be wearied.*
—Blaise Pascal

*They talk about me not being on the legitimate. Why, lady, nobody's on the legit when it comes down to cases; you know that.*—Al Capone[1]

[1]  The poolroom hustler makes his living by betting against his opponents in different types of pool or billiard games, and as part of the playing and betting process he engages in various deceitful practices. The terms "hustler" for such a person and "hustling" for his occupation have been in poolroom argot for decades, antedating their application to prostitutes. Usually the hustler plays with his own money, but often he makes use of a "backer." In the latter event the standard arrangement is that the backer, in return for assuming all risk of loss, receives half of the hustler's winnings.

[2]  The hustler's offense in the eyes of many is not that he breaks misdemeanor laws against gambling (perhaps most Americans have done so at one time or another), but that he does so daily. Also—and again as a necessary and regular part of his daily work—he violates American

*Reprinted with permission of the publisher and author from Ned Polsky, *Hustlers, Beats, and Others.* Copyright © 1985 by University of Chicago Press. All rights reserved.

[1]The Pascal quotation is from *Pensées*, V. Al Capone's remark is quoted in Paul Sann, *The Lawless Decade* (New York: Crown Publishers, 1957), p. 214.

norms concerning (a) what is morally correct behavior toward one's fellow man and (b) what is a proper and fitting occupation. For one or another of these related reasons the hustler is stigmatized by respectable outsiders. The most knowledgeable of such outsiders see the hustler not merely as a gambler but as one who violates an ethic of fair dealing; they regard him as a criminal or quasi-criminal not because he gambles but because he systematically "victimizes" people. Somewhat less knowledgeable outsiders put down the hustler simply because gambling is his trade. Still less knowledgeable outsiders (perhaps the majority) regard hustlers as persons who, whatever they may actually do, certainly do not hold down visibly respectable jobs; therefore this group also stigmatizes hustlers—"poolroom bums" is the classic phrase—and believes that society would be better off without them. Hustling, to the degree that it is known to the larger society at all, is classed with that large group of social problems composed of morally deviant occupations.

[3]  However, in what follows I try to present hustlers and hustling on their own terms. The material below

avoids a "social problems" focus; to some extent, I deliberately reverse that focus. Insofar as I treat of social problems, they are not the problems posed by the hustler but for him; not the difficulties he creates for others, but the difficulties that others create for him as he pursues his career.

**[4]** This approach "from within" has partly dictated the organization of my materials. Some sections below are built around conceptual categories derived less from sociologists than from hustlers, in the hope that this may help the reader to see hustling more nearly as hustlers see it. The disadvantage for the scientifically-minded reader is that the underlying sociological framework may be obscured. Therefore I wish to point out that this framework is basically that of Everett Hughes's approach to occupational sociology.

**[5]** I try mainly to answer three types of questions: *(a) The work situation.* How is the hustler's work structured? What skills are required of him? With whom does he interact on the job? What does he want from them, and how does he try to get it? How do they make it easy or hard for him? *(b) Careers.* Who becomes a hustler? How? What job risks or contingencies does the hustler face? When and how? What is the nature of colleagueship in hustling? What are the measures of success and failure in the career? In what ways does aging affect the hustler's job skills or ability to handle other career problems? What leads to retirement? *(c) The external world.* What is the place of the hustler's work situation and career in the larger society? What changes in the structure of that society affect his work situation or career?

## PREVIOUS RESEARCH

**[6]** A bibliographic check reveals no decent research on poolroom hustling, sociological or otherwise. Apart from an occasional work of fiction in which hustling figures, there are merely a few impressionistic accounts in newspapers and popular magazines. With a couple of exceptions, each article is based on interviews with only one or two hustlers. No article analyzes hustling on any but the most superficial level or provides a well-rounded description. The fullest survey of the subject not only omits much that is vital, but contains numerous errors of fact and interpretation.[2]

**[7]** The desirability of a study of hustling first struck me upon hearing comments by people who saw the movie *The Hustler* (late 1961, re-released spring 1964). Audience members who are not poolroom habitués regard the movie as an

[2]Jack Olsen, "The Pool Hustlers," *Sports Illustrated,* Vol. 14 (March 20, 1961), pp. 71–77. Jack Richardson's "The Noblest Hustlers," [*Esquire,* Vol. IX (September, 1963), pp. 94, 96, 98] contains a few worthwhile observations, but it is sketchy, ill-balanced, and suffers much from editorial garbling, all of which makes it both confusing and misleading for the uninitiated. One article conveys quite well the lifestyle of a particular hustler: Dale Shaw, "Anatomy of a Pool Hustler," *Saga: The Magazine for Men,* Vol. 23 (November, 1961), pp. 52–55, 91–93. Useful historical data are in Edward John Vogeler's "The Passing of the Pool Shark," *American Mercury,* Vol. 8 (November, 1939), pp. 346–51. For hustling as viewed within the context of the history of pool in America, see Robert Coughlan's "Pool: Its Players and Its Sharks," *Life,* Vol. 31 (October 8, 1951), pp. 159 ff.; although Coughlan's account of the game's history contains errors and his specific consideration of hustling is brief (p. 166), the latter is accurate.

accurate portrait of the contemporary hustling "scene." The movie does indeed truly depict some social characteristics of pool and billiard hustlers and some basic techniques of hustling. But it neglects others of crucial importance. Moreover, the movie scarcely begins to take proper account of the social structure within which hustling techniques are used and which strongly affects their use. *The Hustler* is a reasonably good but highly selective reflection of the poolroom hustling scene as it existed not later than the mid-1930s. And as a guide to today's hustling scene—the terms on which it presents itself and on which the audience takes it—the movie is quite misleading.

## METHOD AND SAMPLE

[8]  My study of poolroom hustling extended over eight months. It proceeded by a combination of: (a) direct observation of hustlers as they hustled; (b) informal talks, sometimes hours long, with hustlers; (c) participant observation—as hustler's opponent, as hustler's backer, and as hustler. Since methods (b) and (c) drew heavily on my personal involvement with the poolroom world, indeed are inseparable from it, I summarize aspects of that involvement below.

[9]  Billiard playing is my chief recreation. I have frequented poolrooms for over 20 years, and at one poolroom game, three-cushion billiards, am considered a far better than average player. In recent years I have played an average of more than six hours per week in various New York poolrooms, and played as much in the poolrooms of Chicago for most of the eight years I lived there. In the course of traveling I

have played occasionally in the major rooms of other cities, such as the poolrooms on Market Street in San Francisco, West 25th Street in Cleveland, West Lexington in Baltimore, and the room on 4th and Main in Los Angeles.

[10]  My social background is different from that of the overwhelming majority of adult poolroom players. The latter are of lower-class origin. As with many American sports (e.g., baseball), pool and billiards are played by teenagers from all classes but only the players of lower-class background tend to continue far into adulthood. (And as far as poolroom games are concerned, even at the teenage level the lower class contributes a disproportionately large share of players.) But such differences—the fact that I went to college, do highbrow work, etc.— create no problems of acceptance. In most good-sized poolrooms the adult regulars usually include a few people like myself who are in the poolroom world but not of it. They are there because they like to play, and are readily accepted because they like to play.

[11]  The poolroom I play in most regularly is the principal "action room" in New York and perhaps in the country, the room in which heavy betting on games occurs most often; sometimes, particularly after 1:00 a.m., the hustlers in the room well outnumber the non-hustlers. Frequently I play hustlers for money (nearly always on a handicap basis) and occasionally I hustle some non-hustlers, undertaking the latter activity primarily to recoup losses on the former. I have been a backer for two hustlers.

[12]  I know six hustlers well, and during the eight months of the study I talked or played with over 50

more. . . . It seems safe to assume that the sample is at least representative of big-city hustlers. Also, it is probable that it includes the majority of part-time hustlers in New York, and certain that it includes a good majority of the full-time hustlers in New York.

## THE HUSTLER'S METHODS OF DECEPTION

[13] The structure of a gambling game determines what methods of deception, if any, may be used in it. In many games (dice, cards, etc.) one can deceive one's opponent by various techniques of cheating. Pool and billiard games are so structured that this method is virtually impossible. (Once in a great while, against a particularly unalert opponent, one can surreptitiously add a point or two to one's score—but such opportunity is rare, usually involves risk of discovery that is judged to be too great, and seldom means the difference between winning and losing anyway; so no player counts on it.) One's every move and play is completely visible, easily watched by one's opponent and by spectators; nor is it possible to achieve anything via previous tampering with the equipment.

[14] However, one structural feature of pool or billiards readily lends itself to deceit: on each shot, the difference between success and failure is a matter of a small fraction of an inch. In pool or billiards it is peculiarly easy, even for the average player, to miss one's shot deliberately and still look good (unlike, say, nearly all card games, where if one does not play one's cards correctly this is soon apparent). On all shots except the easiest ones, it is impossible to tell if a player is deliberately not trying his best.

[15] The hustler exploits this fact so as to deceive his opponent as to his (the hustler's) true level of skill (true "speed"). It is so easily exploited that, when playing good opponents, usually the better hustlers even disdain it, pocket nearly every shot they have (intentionally miss only some very difficult shots), and rely chiefly on related but subtler techniques of failure beyond the remotest suspicion of most players. For example, such a hustler may strike his cue ball hard and with too much spin ("english"), so that the spin is transferred to the object ball and the object ball goes into the pocket but jumps out again; or he may scratch (losing a point and his turn), either by "accidentally" caroming his cue ball into a pocket or by hitting his cue ball hard and with too much top-spin so that it jumps off the table; or, most commonly, he pockets his shot but, by striking his cue ball just a wee bit too hard or too softly or with too much or too little english, he leaves himself "safe" (ends up with his cue ball out of position, so that he hasn't another shot). In such ways the hustler feigns less competence than he has.

[16] Hustling, then, involves not merely the ability to play well, but the use of a kind of "short con." Sometimes the hustler doesn't need to employ any con to get his opponent to the table, sometimes he does; but he always employs it in attempting to keep his opponent there.

[17] The best hustler is not necessarily the best player among the hustlers. He has to be a very good player, true, but beyond a certain point his playing ability is not nearly so important as his skill at various kinds of conning. Also, he has to possess personality traits that make him "rocklike," able to exploit fully

his various skills—playing, conning, others—in the face of assorted pressures and temptations not to exploit them fully.

## JOB-RELATED SKILLS AND TRAITS

[18] Although the hallmarks of the good hustler are playing skill and the temperamental ability to consistently look poorer than he is, there are other skills and traits that aid him in hustling. Some are related to deceiving his opponent, some not.

[19] Chief of these is argumentative skill in arranging the terms of the match, the ability to "make a game." The prospective opponent, if he has seen the hustler play, may when approached claim that the hustler is too good for him or ask for too high a spot, i.e., one that is fair or even better. The hustler, like the salesman, is supposed to be familiar with standard objections and "propositions" for overcoming them.

[20] Another side of the ability to make a game reveals itself when the prospective opponent simply can't be argued out of demanding a spot that is unfair to the hustler, or can be convinced to play only if the hustler offers such a spot. At that point the hustler should of course refuse to play. There is often a temptation to do otherwise, not only because the hustler is proud of his skill but because action is his lifeblood (which is why he plays other hustlers when he can't find a hustle), and there may be no other action around. He must resist the temptation. In the good hustler's view, no matter how badly you want action, it is better not to play at all than to play when you are disadvantaged; otherwise you are just hustling yourself.

(But the hustler often will, albeit with much argument and the greatest reluctance, agree to give a fair spot if that's the only way he can get action.)

[21] The hustler, when faced, as he very often is, with an opponent who knows him as such, of course finds that his ability to make a game assumes greater importance than his ability to feign lack of skill. In such situations, indeed, his game-making ability is just as important as his actual playing ability.

[22] On the other hand, the hustler must have "heart" (courage). The *sine qua non* is that he is a good "money player," can play his best when heavy action is riding on the game (as many non-hustlers can't). Also, he is not supposed to let a bad break or distractions in the audience upset him. (He may pretend to get rattled on such occasions, but that's just part of his con.) Nor should the quality of his game deteriorate when, whether by miscalculation on his part or otherwise, he finds himself much further behind than he would like to be. Finally, if it is necessary to get action, he should not be afraid to tackle an opponent whom he knows to be just about as good as he is.

[23] A trait often working for the hustler is stamina. As a result of thousands of hours of play, all the right muscles are toughened up. He is used to playing many hours at a time, certainly much more used to it than the non-hustler is. This is valuable because sometimes, if the hustler works it right, he can make his opponent forget about quitting for such a "silly" reason as being tired, can extend their session through the night and into the next day. In such sessions it is most often in the last couple of hours, when the betting

per game is usually highest, that the hustler makes his biggest killing.

[24] Additional short-con techniques are sometimes used. One hustler, for example, entices opponents by the ancient device of pretending to be sloppy-drunk. Other techniques show more imagination. For example, a hustler preparing for a road trip mentioned to me that before leaving town he was going to buy a soldier's uniform: "I walk into a strange room in uniform and I've got it made. Everybody likes to grab a soldier."

[25] Finally, the hustler—the superior hustler at any rate—has enough flexibility and good sense to break the "rules" when the occasion demands it, will modify standard techniques when he encounters non-standard situations. An example: Once I entered a poolroom just as a hustler I know, X, was finishing a game with non-hustler Y. X beat Y soundly, by a higher margin than a hustler should beat anyone, and at that for only $3. Y went to the bathroom, whereupon I admonished X, "What's the matter with you? You know you're not allowed to win that big." X replied:

> Yeah, sure, but you see that mother-fucking S over there? [nodding discreetly in the direction of one of the spectators]. Well, about an hour ago when I came in he and Y were talking, and when S saw me he whispered something to Y. So I had a hunch he was giving him the wire [tipping him off] that I was pretty good. And then in his middle game it looked like Y was stalling a little [missing deliberately] to see what I would do, so then I was sure he got the wire on me. I had to beat him big so he'll think he knows my top speed. But naturally I didn't beat him as big as I *could* beat him. Now he'll come back cryin' for a spot and bigger action, and I'll nail him.

And he did nail him.

## THE HUSTLER AS CON MAN

[26] As several parts of this study illustrate in detail, hustling demands a continuous and complicated concern with how one is seen by others. Attention to this matter is an ineluctably pervasive requirement of the hustler's trade, and is beset with risks and contradictions. The hustler has not only the concerns that one ordinarily has about being esteemed for one's skills, but develops, in addition to and partly in conflict with such concerns, a complex set of special needs or desires about how others should evaluate him, reactions to their evaluations, and behaviors designed to manipulate such evaluating.

[27] The hustler is a certain kind of con man. And conning, by definition, involves extraordinary manipulation of other people's impressions of reality and especially of one's self, creating "false impressions."[3] If one compares the hustler with the more usual sorts of con men described by David Maurer in *The Big Con,* part of the hustler's specialness is seen to lie in this: the structural contexts within which he operates—the game, the setting of the game within the poolroom, the setting of the poolroom within the larger social structure—are not only more predetermined but more constraining.

---

[3]Of course, conning is only a matter of degree, in that all of us are concerned in many ways to manipulate others' impressions of us, and so one can, if one wishes, take the view that every man is at bottom a con man. This form of "disenchantment of the world" is central to Herman Melville's *The Confidence Man* (one of the bitterest novels in all of American literature) and to the sociological writings of Erving Goffman. Its principal corollary is the view expressed by hustlers, by other career criminals, and by Thorstein Veblen, that all businessmen are thieves.

Structures do not "work for" the poolroom hustler to anywhere near the extent that they often do for other con men, and hence he must involve himself in more personal ways with active, continuous conning.

[28] The point is not simply that the hustler can't find an ideal structural context, but that much less than the ordinary con man is he able to bend a structure toward the ideal or create one *ab ovo* (come up with an analogue of the con man's "store"). That is, the hustler is far less able to be a "producer" or "director" of ideal social "scenes." To a much greater extent he must work in poor settings, and to a correspondingly greater extent he must depend on being a continuously self-aware "actor."[4]

[29] The hustler needs to be continually concerned about evaluation of him by other persons. But the nature and degree of his concern vary with the particular kind of "others" that these persons represent. The victim or prospective victim, the hustler's orientation toward whom we have discussed at several points, is only one kind of other.

---

[4]The kinds of structural problems faced today by the pool or billiard hustler are by no means all endemic. Some are the result of recent social change.

On the other hand, such change does not create structural problems for all types of hustling. Today the golf hustler, for example, finds that with precious little "acting" he can (a) get heavy action from non-hustlers, (b) lose the good majority of the 18 holes and still clean up, and at the same time (c) not be suspected as a hustler. The structure of the game of golf itself, the peculiar structurally predetermined variations in the betting relationship as one makes the round of the course ("presses," etc.), and the present setting of the game within the larger society—all these combine to create a situation that is tailor-made for hustling. But that is another story.

Obviously the hustler must take cognizance of at least two additional types of significant others: outsiders and colleagues. . . .

## CONCLUSIONS

. . . Here I would like to point out certain other findings that seem to have no analogue in the literature of occupational sociology.

[30] *(1) The work situation.* We saw that the hustler must be not only a skilled player, but that he must be skilled at pretending *not* to have great playing skill. . . . As far as I know, this hustling reliance on competence at feigning incompetence is unique, and nowhere treated in the occupational literature. . . .

[31] *(2) Careers.* Certain occupational roles require youthfulness by definition (e.g., acting juvenile parts), and thus enforce unusually early retirement. In certain other occupations (airline pilots, for example) age-related career contingencies also force early retirement. It is common to cite competitive sports or games requiring high physical skills as examples of this type—but pool or billiard playing doesn't fit the pattern.

[32] *(3) The external world.* We saw that changes in American sporting life over the past three decades have severely damaged the hustler's work situation and career. These changes have reduced the number of places he can hustle in, the time-span in which he can stay unknown, the number of people he can hustle, and the average amount of money he can get from someone he hustles. Hustling is a dying trade.

[33] Whenever an occupational group faces a disappearance or

major decline of the market for its skills and a consequent inability to make ends meet, we conceptualize this situation as "technological unemployment." But this concept doesn't fit the situation of hustlers at all well. They suffer not from a shift in technology but from a shift in America's demographic structure, i.e., the decline of the bachelor subculture that populated poolrooms so heavily, and secondarily from a shift in fashion, i.e., the decline in the average amount of money bet on poolroom games. . . .

[34] A more general lesson of this essay is that sociology has unduly neglected the study of people who engage in sports or games for their livelihood. The sociological reason for this neglect is that sociology is compartmentalized into "fields" that tend to make such people, for all their visibility to the sociologist as citizen, invisible to him in his role as sociologist: such people are neglected by students of leisure because the latter are by definition concerned with sports involvement only in its impact on avocational life; and because sports involvement is for the very great majority of people strictly avocational, and those who earn a living at it constitute a minuscule fragment of the labor force, the study of the latter is neglected by occupational sociologists. Thus a largely unexplored area of social research consists of the people who work at what most of us play at.

## CRITICAL ANALYSIS: CONTENT

Polsky's study is an example of *qualitative* (as opposed to *quantitative*) research. That is, it is based on observational techniques that are less structured than those employed in experiments or surveys, and the analysis is not based on the enumeration of "hard" data, but rather attempts to reconstruct a social setting, the world of the hustler. Nevertheless, it is striking how well the schema of questions-evidence-answers fits both the research and writing.

### Questions

Stated in its broadest terms, the purpose of Polsky's study is to describe the world of the poolroom hustler to readers who probably never heard of a poolroom hustler, unless they happened to see Paul Newman's celebrated movie *The Hustler*. Furthermore, Polsky wants to describe it "from within," that is, from the vantage point of the participants themselves.

Is this approach different from that of a journalist or any other casual observer? Yes, in at least three respects. First of all, Polsky approaches his subject with greater discipline, making use of social science methods. Despite years of personal involvement in the world of poolroom hustling, he did not just write about it "off the top." On the contrary, once he decided to make this the focus of his dissertation, he went back into the field for over eight months, combining direct observation of hustlers, informal interviews, and finally participant observation in which he took on the role of the various actors—the hustler's opponent, the hustler's backer, and the hustler himself. This is a good example of how "controlled inquiry" differs from casual observation.

Secondly, as a social scientist Polsky must approach his subject with scientific objectivity. This does not mean that values play no role in his inquiry. On the contrary, the empathy that Polsky has for the poolroom hustler, and his own passion for billiards, are not only unavoidable, but actually useful if he is to present an insider's account. Objectivity in this instance involves a willingness to suspend moral judgment. As Polsky points out, the hustler tends to be stigmatized by "respectable outsiders" as morally deviant. Clearly, it is necessary to put aside this moral judgment if we are to understand hustlers and hustling in their own terms.

Third, Polsky adopts a more analytical stance toward his subject than one would expect from a journalist or a casual observer. He is preoccupied not only with the journalistic questions of "who, what, when, and where," but also with the more conceptual issue of how perceptions of reality are manipulated and exploited. Moreover, Polsky brings a body of theory and research to bear on his analysis of the poolroom hustler, making comparisons and exploring linkages to other work situations. Thus, in style and content this ethnographic study of the poolroom hustler is markedly different from what one would expect to find, say, in *Esquire* or *Playboy*.

Indeed, Polsky's overall approach is to treat hustling as any other occupation, and to ask the same kinds of questions that any occupational sociologist would ask. Thus, Polsky posits three sets of questions pertaining to (1) the work situation, (2) careers, and (3) the external world (see paragraph 5, which lists no fewer than fifteen questions under these three headings).

### Evidence

In ethnographic studies the presentation of evidence usually involves a detailed description of the social setting under observation. The problem, from the standpoint of writing, is how to select and arrange this material in order to achieve a reconstruction of the social setting that is meaningful, accurate, and effective. Polsky organizes his presentation around several subheadings:

The Hustler's Methods of Deception
Job-Related Skills and Traits
The Hustler as Con Man

Each of these subheadings denotes a particular facet of the hustling scene. Like parts of a jigsaw puzzle, they combine to produce a graphic whole.

What emerges is a profile of an unusual occupation where appearances define reality, and skill consists of *not* looking as good as you really are. The hustler must be more than an accomplished player. In order to entice opponents he has to be able to deceive them as to his true level of skill—for example, by putting so much spin on the ball that it "jumps" out of the pocket, or by pocketing his shot in such a way that his cue ball is out-of-position for the next shot. In this and other ways, the hustler manipulates appearances to his ultimate advantage. Time and again, Polsky restates and reformulates the notion that the hustler's playing abilities are not nearly as important as his skill at conning, and that the real challenge for a hustler is to look poorer than he really is. Thus, much of the "evidence" that Polsky presents consists of documenting the various methods of deception that constitute the "stuff" of a good hustler.

### Answers

Insofar as detailed description is the goal of ethnographic research, such studies do not always come to a tidy conclusion that goes beyond the ethnographic material itself. In the case of Polsky's study, the original questions—how the hustler's work is structured, what skills are required of him, and so on—are so specific that they are answered by the ethnographic detail in the body of the paper.

On the other hand, Polsky's essay is not completely descriptive. Consistent with his view of the hustler as a special kind of occupation, Polsky wishes to make a contribution to general occupational theory. He concludes that his findings "seem to have no analogue in the literature of occupational sociology," and conversely, that established principles of occupational sociology do not seem to apply to the hustler. Thus, Polsky not only succeeds in providing an insider's perspective of the "world" of the hustler, but uses this as a basis for reflecting on mainstream society as well.

## CRITICAL ANALYSIS: COMPOSITION

Although "The Hustler" treats a subject far removed from the "ivory tower" of the university, its author, Ned Polsky, brings the trained eye of the sociologist to observe and analyze the world of the poolroom. He asks the questions: *What* is a hustler and *how* does hustling function as work? Polsky is ultimately concerned not simply with describing the hustler but in *defining* him in his work setting. Thus, the principle rhetorical mode for organizing this essay is *definition*, that is, an extended definition of the hustler as worker and hustling as an occupation.

At the outset of his essay Polsky uses the terms "hustler" and "hustling" as they are used in common parlance. He then proceeds to discuss the attributes that distinguish the hustler from the general class of con men. Eventually, he identifies the most essential quality of the hustler—that he must be the "self-aware 'actor'" in a situation where he manipulates the way others see him.

These defining attributes are verified by detailed observation. In this way Polsky builds his definition through observation and inference. He is not a totally objective observer, however. He is also a participant who describes his personal observations in the poolroom, recounts the testimony of hustlers he has known, and recalls his own experience as player and hustler.

### The Introduction (paragraphs 1 to 5)

The essay is framed by two epigraphs or quotations: one by Al Capone, the notorious underworld gangster; the other by Blaise Pascal, the illustrious French philosopher. This startling juxtaposition in a sense mirrors Polsky's own straddling of two worlds: the ivory tower of academe and the "real world" of the poolroom. The specific content of these quotations also presages Polsky's own point of view: Hustling is more than "action." It is work, and like other kinds of work, skirts the edges of legitimacy.

In the introductory section Polsky begins to develop this perspective. The hustler's shadowy activities influence how others regard him, as well as how he regards himself and his "work." Paragraph 1 presents the simple definition: "The poolroom hustler makes his living by betting against his opponents in different types of pool or billiard games, and as part of the playing and betting process he engages in various deceitful practices."

The remainder of the introduction extends this definition by allowing readers to see the hustler from more than one vantage point. Thus, paragraph 2 presents the outsider's view of the hustler, which stigmatizes him to some extent, and influences his self-conception. Paragraph 3 then considers the insider's point of view, that is, how the hustler regards himself and the "difficulties that others create for him." Finally, paragraphs 4 and 5 introduce the sociologist's perspective, which sees hustling as having affinities with other occupations. Drawing on all these frameworks, with an unmistakable emphasis on the insider's point of view, Polsky generates research questions that will probe an aspect of the hustler that has not been considered: the hustler as worker in an admittedly unusual occupation.

### The Body Paragraphs (paragraphs 6 to 29)

The body of the essay fills out the definition of hustler. However, Polsky does not plunge into a description of the hustler's world. First he reviews the previous research (which is quite sparse) on this topic. Then he outlines his own research strategy, disclosing how he came to select his "sample." In effect, we follow him step by step from the library to the poolroom.

Finally, we encounter the hustler. Polsky gives us a detailed description of the hustler's "methods of deception," carefully placing his observations of the hustler's moves in the context of the game and its setting. For example, the structure of pool and billiard games makes certain techniques of cheating almost impossible, since "one's every move and play is completely visible, easily watched by one's opponent and by spectators" [paragraph 13]. Polsky then goes on to observe and catalogue the artifices that *are* possible within this game: the plays and "cons" that the hustler uses to deceive an opponent as to his "true speed."

These specific observations of hustling lead to a number of inferences about the nature of the hustler. In other words, Polsky moves from the concrete to the abstract. For example, after describing how the hustler operates, Polsky infers the "job-related skills and traits" needed to perform as a successful hustler: playing skill, argumentative skill, courage, patience, flexibility, and stamina.

Under another subheading, "The Hustler as Con Man," Polsky identifies *one essential characteristic* that distinguishes the hustler from other con men. His "con" depends upon his being a "continuing self-aware actor" in a more "constraining" and "predetermined" setting than those in which other con men operate. Since the hustler cannot manipulate the situation, he has to manipulate the way that he is seen by others.

### The Conclusion (paragraphs 30 to 34)

As Polsky brings his essay to a conclusion, he leaves the poolhall and adopts the persona of the sociologist. He analyzes the hustler's work in terms of "general occupational theory," and organizes this discussion around the three categories that he proposed at the outset of the study: the work situation, careers, and the external world.

In his final paragraph Polsky places his subject in an even larger framework: the implications for sociology in general. He comments on the blindness of his profession to groups who "work at what most of us play at," and implies a need to break out of established categories.

### RHETORICAL STANCE: PERSUADING THE READER

The author's primary means of persuasion is to bring his readers into the hustler's world. From a rhetorical standpoint, this is achieved primarily through Polsky's use of the first-person, "I." This is effective because it establishes a tone of immediacy (he is there, we are there). Polsky distances himself from those scornful outsiders, instead presenting himself as one who accepts the hustler on his own terms.

However, Polsky is also the scholar who persuades us by citing other authorities, and by being systematic in framing the research problem and presenting the findings. First he establishes his purpose—to view hustling as an occupation. Then he observes the hustler at work. And finally he infers what the hustler "is" by what he does and how he does it. Note that the

inferences or conclusions follow the actual observations. Through systematic analysis and attention to detail, Polsky establishes himself as a
credible observer, and is able to present a complex analysis without overwhelming the reader.

### Language

Like his point of view, Polsky's language reflects the academician/
hustler. Polsky skillfully weaves the argot, the almost secret vocabulary of
the hustler, into his categories of "methods and traits." Words, such as
"speed," "english," and "short con" punctuate the complicated descriptions of how the hustler deceives his opponents. Phrases such as the ability
to "make a game" or simply have the "heart" to play it are highly effective
because we can almost hear the hustler's banter.

In the end, however, the author returns to the language of the
sociologist as he concludes with references to "ideal social scenes." And
note his frequent allusions to hustling as an occupation (for example, paragraph 2: ". . . as a necessary and regular part of his daily work"; paragraph 5:
"How is the hustler's work structured?"; paragraph 19: "The hustler, like the
salesman . . ."). We stand back and try to understand the hustler, not by
removing him from the poolroom, but by contrasting him with other kinds
of con men. The sociologist's understanding of groups at work provides a
larger perspective of the hustler at work. The sociologist's vocabulary, kept
to a minimum, provides additional categories with which to analyze and
thereby understand the hustler.


## SUGGESTIONS FOR WRITING AND THINKING

1.  This exercise is modeled after Polsky's participant-observation study of
    the poolroom hustler. Instead of a poolroom, choose some other locale
    or hangout, preferably one that you know firsthand. Examples are: a
    video parlor, a disco, a streetcorner hangout, a ball park, or a student
    cafeteria. You can proceed in either of two ways:
    a.  Assume that you are describing this setting to someone who knows it
        only superficially. Your objective should be to provide a rich and
        detailed ethnographic description based on direct observation and
        interviews with participants. Specific details should be selected and
        organized to support some overall statement or interpretation that
        functions as a thesis statement. (For example, the local video parlor
        provides a harmless outlet for pent-up frustration and aggression. Or,
        to take the opposite tack, the video parlor is a refuge for alienated
        adolescents.)
    b.  Like Polsky, focus on a particular "actor" in a social setting (for exam-
        ple, a coach, a campus leader, or a charismatic person at a disco or
        hangout). Define his or her role within that context and the charac-

teristics that account for "success." Again, organize your essay around some overall statement or interpretation that functions as a thesis statement.

2. Read "The Fate of Idealism in Medical School" by Howard Becker and Blanche Geer, published in the *American Sociological Review*, vol. 23 (February 1958), pp. 50–56.

   Analyze the article in terms of the questions-evidence-conclusions schema. Then analyze it in terms of its rhetorical strategy. What thesis emerges about the fate of idealism in medical school? How do the authors trace the process whereby students modify their ideals during their student career? How is this reflected in the organization of the paper?

## OBSERVATIONAL STUDIES ACROSS THE DISCIPLINES

### Anthropology

GMELCH, GEORGE, "Baseball Magic," *Trans-action*, 8, no. 8 (June 1971), 39–41, 54. The author applies Malinowski's theory that magic flourishes in unpredictable situations, and describes the rituals, taboos, and fetishes that pervade baseball in the field, on the mound, and in the batter's box.

### Economics

TOBIN, JAMES, "The Economy of China: A Tourist's View," *Challenge*, 16, no. 1 (March/April 1973), 20–31. The author, a leading economist, was one of the first American scientists to travel to the People's Republic of China after the American-Chinese rapprochement in the early 1970s. This is his account of his travels.

### Political Science

BORGOS, SETH, "The ACORN Squatters' Campaign," *Social Policy*, 15, no. 1 (Summer 1984), 17–26. In 1982 a small army of 200 people, led by a cadre of political organizers, launched a squatters' campaign to lay claim to abandoned houses in a poor Philadelphia neighborhood. This is an eyewitness account by one of the leaders.

### Psychology

COLES, ROBERT, "The Moral Life of Children," *Educational Leadership*, 43, no. 4 (December 1985/January 1986), 19–25. Robert Coles, a prominent child psychiatrist, explores the moral life of children, based on observation of high school students in New Hampshire, Illinois, and Georgia.

## *Sociology*

THOMPSON, WILLIAM E., "Hanging Tongues: A Sociological Encounter with the Assembly Line," *Qualitative Sociology*, 6 (Fall 1983), 215–37. On the basis of nine weeks as a participant observer on an assembly line in a slaughter division of a large beef processing plant, the author analyzes how the workers coped with the danger, strain, and monotony of the assembly line, as well as the dehumanizing aspects of their jobs.

# Chapter 8
# THE INTERVIEW

## INTRODUCTION

Among the various research tools available to the social scientist, the interview is undoubtedly the one most often used in social research. In an interview the researcher, or a trained assistant, goes out and questions subjects in order to elicit information. Needless to say, there is great variation in terms of who gets interviewed, how they are interviewed, and for what purpose.

Generally speaking, interviewees (people selected for interviews) fall into two categories: influentials and ordinary people who belong to some group or population that is being studied. The first group—influentials—includes people in positions of status or authority, such as government officials, politicians, clergy, journalists, and other decision makers and opinion leaders. As a discipline political science takes special interest in such groups, and countless studies of influentials have been conducted using interviews as the primary source of data.

One such study sought to find out how leaders of different kinds stand on the issue of equality. Conducted by two political scientists, Sidney Verba and Gary Orren, the study was published under the title *Equality in America: The View from the Top*. The reason for studying leaders, according to the authors, is that "their views influence both the political establishment and the public at large."[1] Nine different types of leaders were interrogated in order to measure the extent to which they supported various government programs designed to reduce the gap between the haves and the have-nots. The researchers found large differences among different kinds of leaders. Support for these programs was relatively low among Republican, farm, and

[1]Sidney Verba and Gary R. Orren, *Equality in America: The View from the Top* (Cambridge: Harvard University Press, 1985), p. 53.

business leaders, and relatively high among Democrats, blacks, feminists, and intellectuals. Even among the more liberal groups, however, only a minority endorsed the idea that government should put a top limit on income. Thus, through the interview Verba and Orren were able to document "the view from the top" in precise detail.

Most studies based on interviews, however, use ordinary people as interviewees. Social scientists often need to know what "people" think on any number of topics, ranging from their favorite television program to their views on nuclear disarmament. In the study of influentials cited above, Verba and Orren also sampled the general public so that they could contrast the views of leaders with the public at large. Indeed, studies of the mass public are so common that they have virtually become a hallmark of modern social science.

Whether interviews are conducted with influentials or with ordinary people, researchers have to consider whether interviewees are altogether truthful, and whether their professed beliefs correspond to how they behave in actual situations. On the other hand, researchers have developed techniques to minimize dissembling on the part of interviewees. It is surprising how much people are willing to reveal about themselves, even on very personal matters. Whatever its limitations, the interview is still the best available tool for getting people to talk about themselves.

The need to know what people think has given rise to a whole field of *survey research*. The main feature of a survey is that it is based on a *sample* of a given population. The rationale for sampling is obvious. Since it is usually impossible or too costly to interview all members of a given population, we draw a sample that is a representative cross-section of that population. Representativeness is assured by selecting subjects according to some random procedure. For example, we could obtain a random sample of students at your college by taking every tenth name from the student directory. If the sample is truly representative, it allows the researcher to generalize findings based on the sample to the larger population from which the sample was drawn. Social scientists have perfected sampling techniques to the point that it is possible to predict the outcome of a national election with a high degree of accuracy based on samples of only 2,000 cases.

Many surveys, including most opinion polls, are based on *personal interviews*, conducted face-to-face or by telephone. Because the costs of personal interviews run very high, however, many surveys rely instead on *self-administered questionnaires*. In effect, subjects "interview" themselves by filling out the questionnaire and returning it to the researcher.

The form that questions take is also subject to variation. Most interviews and questionnaires are highly "structured," that is, subjects are offered a set of predetermined answer categories and forced to choose the one that best fits them. For example, a study of religious commitment among students might ask, "On the whole, how religious are you? Would you say very religious, fairly religious, or not too religious?" Studies that rely on structured questions are often criticized for pigeon-holing how people think. As an alternative, less restrictive, open-ended questions are sometimes used that allow subjects to answer in their own words. Thus, one might ask: "On the whole, how religious would you say you are?" This latter technique no doubt produces more varied, interesting, and authentic responses. The disadvantage of open-ended questions, however, is that they do not lend themselves to systematic analysis since responses cannot be easily compared to one another.

There is another genre of studies that employ less structured interviewing techniques, called *depth interviewing*. The point of these studies is *not* to classify and aggregate responses, but as the term suggests, to probe "in depth." Again, either influentials or ordinary people may serve as subjects.

For example, in his study *A Government of Strangers*, Hugh Heclo wanted to learn more about the relations between elected officials and appointed government bureaucrats. He conducted 200 interviews over a four-year period with present and past government executives. Heclo describes his sample as "an unassembled seminar with approximately 200 interviewees as the teachers and me as the student."[2] His modesty is somewhat misleading, however. After all, Heclo did not simply turn on his tape recorder, transcribe the interviews, and publish them as a book. Quite the contrary, he had to know what questions to ask. Then he had to develop a framework for analyzing the interview material. In fact, his book advances a general interpretation of the relation between elected officials and appointed government bureaucrats, and he uses quotations from his subjects only very selectively, to illustrate or document his analysis.

Ordinary people are also used as subjects for depth interviews. Compared to the highly structured questions used in surveys, depth interviews have the advantage of probing beyond the superficial responses elicited by such questions. Especially in psychological studies, depth interviews are useful for exploring the deeper feelings or motives underlying surface attitudes and behavior.

For example, the authors of *The Authoritarian Personality*, published in 1950, combined survey techniques and depth interviewing in order to explore the psychological roots of anti-Semitism. Surveys were used to tap the beliefs and attitudes that people have about Jews and other groups. Then in-depth interviews were used to probe "the deeper layers of the subject's personality."[3] Excerpts from two such interviews follow. The first

[2]Hugh Heclo, *A Government of Strangers* (Washington: The Brookings Institution, 1977), p. 1.

[3]T. W. Adorno and others, *The Authoritarian Personality* (New York: John Wiley & Sons, Inc., 1964), p. 17.

is with Mack, who typifies someone high on prejudice; the second with Larry, who is low on prejudice. The interviewer's questions are in parentheses.[4]

## MACK: A MAN HIGH ON PREJUDICE

This subject is a twenty-four-year-old college freshman who intends to study law and hopes eventually to become a corporation lawyer or a criminal lawyer. His grades are B − on the average. His brief sojourn in the Army was terminated by a medical discharge. He is a Methodist, as was his mother, but he does not attend services and says that religion is not important to him. His political party affiliation is, like his father's, Democratic. The subject is of Irish extraction and was born in San Francisco. Both of his parents were born in the United States.

> "My mother comes from an Irish-English-German background. I think of myself as Irish—perhaps because my father is definitely so, and proud of it. . . . I never met an Irishman I didn't like." (What about groups of people you dislike?) "Principally those I don't understand very well. Austrians, the Japanese I never cared for; Filipinos—I don't know—I'd just as soon leave them as have them. Up home there were Austrians and Poles, though I find the Polish people interesting. I have a little dislike for Jewish people. I don't think they are as courteous or as interested in humanity as they ought to be. And I resent that, though I have had few dealings with them. They accent the clannish and the material. It may be my imagination but it seems to me you can see their eyes light up when you hand them a coin. I avoid the Jewish clothiers because they have second-rate stuff. I have to be careful about how I dress. I mean, I buy things so seldom I have to be careful I get good things." (Can you tell that a person is a Jew?) "Sometimes, usually only after I get their ideas." (You mean there are certain ideas which characterize the Jews?) "Yes, to stick together, no matter what; to always be in a group; to have Jewish sororities and Jewish organizations. If a Jew fails in his business, he's helped to get started again. Their attention is directed very greatly toward wealth. Girls at the Jewish sorority house all have fur coats, expensive but no taste. Almost a superiority idea. I resent any show of superiority in people, and I try to keep it down myself. I like to talk with working people." (Do you think they would mingle more if they felt there was no prejudice against them?) "If they would mingle more, there would be more willingness to break down the barriers on the part of other people. Of course, they have always been downtrodden, but that's no reason for resentment."

## LARRY: A MAN LOW ON PREJUDICE

This subject is a twenty-eight-year-old college sophomore, a student of business administration, with a B − average. He is of "American" extraction and was born in Chicago. His father owns a café and bar as well as his own

_____
[4]Ibid., pp. 32–39.

home and some other real estate. Like his parents, the subject is a Methodist, though he seldom attends church. He is a Republican, again like his parents.

(What do you think about the minority problem in this country?) "I can say that I haven't any prejudices; I try not to." (Negroes?) "They should be given social equality, any job they are qualified for; should be able to live in any neighborhood, and so on. When I was young, I may have had prejudices, but since the war I've been reading about the whole world . . . I believe in life, liberty, and the pursuit of happiness for all . . . Racial and economic questions are at the root of the war. I don't believe in the suppression of anyone. I think the Japs are taken off the coast for undemocratic reasons. It's just that a lot of people wanted their farms and businesses. There was no democratic reason for it. The segregation of one nationality just leads to more segregation, and it gets worse. The discrimination toward Negroes is because they aren't understood and because they are physically different. Towards Jews it's because of their business ability—the fear that they'll take over business control of the country. There should be education in Negro history, for instance, the part Negroes have played in the development of the country; and education in the history of other minorities, too. How the Jews came to be persecuted, and why some of them are successful."

The researchers do not just present these case studies, but go on to analyze them in terms of broader issues. Here is a brief excerpt:

Mack rejects a variety of ethnic groups. And Larry, for his part is opposed to all such "prejudice." The first question for research, then, would be: Is it generally true that a person who rejects one minority group tends to reject all or most of them? Or, is it to be found more frequently that there is a tendency to have a special group against which most of the individual's hostility is directed? . . . Is the tendency, found in Mack but not in Larry, to make a rigid distinction between the ingroup and the outgroup, common in the population at large? Are Mack's ways of thinking about groups—rigid categories, always placing blame on the outgroup, and so forth—typical of ethnocentric individuals?[5]

These case studies point up both the advantages and limitations of depth interviewing. On the one hand, Mack and Larry are living examples of individuals who are high and low on prejudice. The reader sees them as whole people, and gets a sense of how their attitudes toward minorities reflect broader personality trends. On the other hand, we do not know to what extent Mack and Larry are typical or representative of the population at large. Indeed, this is why the authors of *The Authoritarian Personality* used in-depth interviews as a basis for generating ideas and questions that were then pursued through a general population survey.

Because surveys are so prevalent in the social sciences, we have chosen one for the sample essay in this chapter. The population under

[5]Ibid., p. 45.

study is the student body at Douglass College, a branch of Rutgers, the State University of New Jersey, that admits only women. The researcher, Ann Parelius, wanted to gauge the extent to which the new generation of college women have changed their "sex-role expectations"—that is, their conceptions of the appropriate roles of men and women with respect to family and career. In order to measure change, Parelius drew two samples, one in 1969, the other in 1973. Subjects were selected at random, and the research instrument was a self-administered questionnaire. When reading the results of this study, ask yourself how the women at your college would compare to the women at Douglass College in 1973.

# Emerging Sex-Role Attitudes, Expectations, and Strains Among College Women*

## Ann P. Parelius

*Questionnaire data are used to assess the attitudes of female college students toward various dimensions of their adult sex roles, their perceptions of men's attitudes toward women's roles, the degree to which these attitudes and perceptions have changed between 1969 and 1973, and the possibility that strains are arising with these changes. A marked shift toward feminism was found in the women's attitudes, but little change occurred in their perception of men as relatively conservative. Strains may be developing as more women adopt attitudes which they believe men reject.*

[1]  In spite of general agreement that sex-role attitudes and expectations are changing, little is actually known about the specific dimensions, extent, or consequences of this change. A perusal of the sex-role literature suggests several themes. First, sex-role behavior, as measured by women's participation in the workforce, has changed radically over the last few decades. Second, although some sex-role attitudes have apparently shifted, others, such as those toward women working while their children are still young, have remained remarkably stable (Mason and Bumpass, 1973). Third, many women have experienced considerable anxiety as they have been caught between conflicting normative definitions of appropriate sex-role behavior (Horner,

*Reprinted by permission of the author and the National Council on Family Relations from Ann P. Parelius, "Emerging Sex-Role Attitudes, Expectations, and Strains Among College Women," *Journal of Marriage and the Family*, 37 (February 1975), 146–53.

1969). Fourth, at least part of this anxiety has been traced to the relatively persistent belief that men want only "extremely nurturant and traditional" females (Steinmann and Fox, 1969; and Rapoport et al., 1970).

[2] The sex-role literature from which these themes are drawn is limited in several respects, however. Most of the currently available studies were done too early to tap the influence of the Women's Liberation Movement. Few studies have documented change with longitudinal data, and much of the research has focused on populations least likely to evidence changes in sex-role orientations (Millman, 1971). Consequently, both the extent to which sex-role expectations are changing and the degree to which such changes are generating strain may be grossly underestimated.

## THE PRESENT STUDY

[3] This study assesses women's attitudes toward various dimensions of their adult sex roles, their perceptions of men's attitudes toward women's roles, the degree to which these attitudes and perceptions have changed over the last four years, and the possibility that strains are arising with these changes. The subjects were students attending Douglass College, a state-supported women's college in New Jersey. As a women's college, Douglass was especially sensitive to the Women's Liberation Movement, offering numerous courses and activities related to women's issues. These students, exposed to the Movement while still relatively free to experiment with new life-styles and identities, should reflect generously

the impact of changing sex-role attitudes and perceptions.[1]

### The Sample

[4] Two independent random samples of the entire student body were selected, one in 1969, and another in 1973. The first sample consisted of 175 women; 147 (84 percent) returned completed questionnaires. The second sample consisted of 250 women; 200 (80 percent) returned completed questionnaires.

### The Instrument

[5] The instrument consisted of a Likert-type questionnaire. The items were short "descriptions of various women," each expressing either a "feminist" or a "traditional" orientation toward sex-role behavior. Traditional orientations suggest that a woman's primary purpose is to marry, bear children, and spend most of her time in the home doing housework and childrearing tasks. Feminist orientations stress equality between the sexes, encouraging women to develop talents and pursue careers. Within marriage, feminist orientations give both partners an equal share of financial and domestic responsibilities.

[6] Each subject read the descriptions and indicated whether or not she was "just like" the women described in each. The women then went over the same items and indicated whether or not men would "want to marry a woman" like the one described. The answer to each question was given on a five-point scale with "yes" and "no" marking the extremes. Examples of the descriptions can be seen in Table 1.

[1]We will not be able to attribute attitudinal change specifically to exposure to the Women's Liberation Movement. We are merely arguing that this particular sample is likely to be in the forefront of those evolving new gender-role expectations.

**Table 1.** Percent Giving Feminist Responses and Percent Believing that Men Would Want to Marry a Feminist, 1969 and 1973

| Descriptive Item | Feminist Responses | | Belief that Men Would Want to Marry a Feminist | |
|---|---|---|---|---|
| | 1969 | 1973 | 1969 | 1973 |
| Work and Finances | % | % | % | % |
| Believes that a wife's career is of equal importance to her husband's. | 49 | 81 | 20 | 31 |
| Believes that both spouses should contribute equally to the financial support of the family. | 37 | 65 | 27 | 45 |
| Intends to work all her adult life. | 29 | 60 | 15 | 32 |
| Division of Labor in the Home | | | | |
| Does not expect to do all the household tasks herself.* | 56 | 83 | 18 | 24 |
| Expects her husband to help with the housework. | 47 | 77 | 14 | 28 |
| Expects her husband to do 50% of all household and childrearing tasks. | 17 | 43 | 10 | 10 |
| Marital and Maternal Role Supremacy | | | | |
| Does not think the most important thing for a woman is to be a good wife and mother.* | 31 | 62 | 8 | 9 |
| Would marry only if it did not interfere with her career. | 10 | 22 | 8 | 13 |
| Would forego children if they would interfere with her career. | 17 | 28 | 7 | 8 |
| | (N = 147) | (N = 200) | (N = 147) | (N = 200) |

*These questions were actually phrased in the affirmative; a negative answer was considered to be a feminist response.

### Analysis

[7] The nine items selected for analysis covered three central issues: (1) women's work patterns and financial responsibilities, (2) the division of labor in the home, and (3) the importance of marital and maternal roles relative to other goals a woman might have. For purposes of analysis, the responses in the two boxes at either end of each scale were combined. The responses were then classified as either "feminist" or "traditional." A response was defined as "feminist" if the subject indicated that she was "just like" the woman in a "feminist" description or "not like" the woman in a "traditional" description. All other responses were defined as "traditional." The perceptual data were treated in a similar manner. Subjects who indicated that men "would want to marry" a woman "just like" the one in a feminist description or that men "would not" want to marry a woman "just like" the one in a traditional description were regarded as perceiving men as accepting of feminism. All other subjects were regarded as perceiving men to be rejecting of feminism.

## FINDINGS

### Sex-Role Orientations, 1969 and 1973

[8] The first two columns of Table 1 indicate the sex-role orientations of the two samples. Looking first at the women of 1969, it is evident that on all but three items, only a minority gave feminist responses. On the remaining items, believing that "a wife's career is of equal importance to her husband's," not expecting to "do all household tasks alone," and expecting husband's "help with the housework," approximately half of the sample gave feminist responses. The women were especially conservative on the two items involving a choice between occupational success and the traditional roles of wife and mother. Only 17 percent "would forego children" for the sake of occupational success, and only 10 percent "would marry only if it did not interfere" with their careers. The item suggesting a fifty-fifty division of labor also evoked only 17 percent in feminist responses.

[9] Turning to the women of 1973, we see that the percentages giving feminist responses increased by approximately 30 points on seven of the nine items. The two items positing a choice between occupational success and familial roles showed much smaller shifts, only about 10 percentage points each.

[10] These data suggest that a substantial shift toward feminism occurred between 1969 and 1973. The 1973 sample was more strongly oriented toward occupational activity and more supportive of equal rights and duties for both sexes than the 1969 sample. Only a minority of either sample would forego marriage or motherhood in order to maximize occupational success, but a much greater percentage of the 1973 sample denied that marriage and motherhood were a woman's most important goals. The 1973 women also took their economic responsibilities more seriously and expected help if not absolute equality in the division of labor in the home.

### Perception of Male Attitudes, 1969 and 1973

[11] Turning to the last two columns of Table 1 and looking first at the 1969 sample, it is clear that few women believed that men wanted to marry feminists. This was particularly true when questions of marital and maternal role supremacy were involved. Fewer than 10 percent of the women believed that men would want to marry women who expressed feminist views on any of the three items relevant to this issue. Men were perceived as most willing to accept feminism in the area of work and finances, especially when it involved a wife contributing equally to the financial support of the family. On this item, 27 percent of the women believed that men would want to marry women with feminist perspectives.

[12] Turning to 1973, we find that few major changes occurred in the women's perception of men's attitudes. Only four items showed a shift of 10 percentage points or more, with the 1973 sample perceiving men to be more ready to marry feminists in all four cases. The greatest and most consistent change occurred in the area of work and finances, where all three items shifted towards greater perceived acceptance of feminism.

[13] These data suggest that the women in both samples tended to view men as basically traditional in

their sex-role orientations. Men were perceived as most likely to accept feminism when it involved women sharing the financial responsibilities normally shouldered by the man alone. Men were seen as less accepting of feminism when it involved recognizing their wives' careers as of equal importance to their own, accepting a wife's working all her adult life, or assuming household responsibilities. Men were seen as most conservative on issues of marital and maternal role supremacy, where women's occupational interests might challenge their primary commitment to home and family.

[14] Comparing the women's own sex-role orientations to their perception of men, it is clear that in both samples women were much more likely to express feminist perspectives than they were to believe that men wanted women with these perspectives. This tendency is particularly strong in the 1973 sample. Thus, many of the women sampled probably had attitudes which they believed men would reject in a potential spouse. . . .

## SUMMARY AND CONCLUSIONS

[15] A comparison of the two samples indicated that sizeable shifts toward feminism occurred between 1969 and 1973. These shifts appeared among women who were attending college during this period as well as among those who were just entering as freshmen. Attitudes toward work, financial responsibilities, and the division of labor in the home showed the greatest amount of change. By 1973, a majority of those sampled believed

that their careers were of equal importance to their husbands' and that they should share equally in the financial support of their families. They also expected to work all of their adult lives and to have substantial help from their husbands with household chores. Attitudes toward the importance of marital and maternal roles changed also, but to a lesser degree. Although the majority of women in the 1973 sample denied that "the most important thing for a woman is to be a good wife and mother," few would sacrifice marriage or motherhood for occupational success. The far-reaching changes observed in the women's attitudes and expectations were not accompanied by equal shifts in their perceptions of men's willingness to marry feminist women. . . .

[16] The combined effect of the shifts in the women's own attitudes and the relative stability of their perception of men was to increase the proportion of women holding views which they did not believe men would accept in a wife. Since most of these women were still interested in marriage and motherhood, many were probably experiencing considerable anxiety about their futures.

[17] These findings suggest several conclusions about emerging trends in sex-role definitions. First, it is clear that these definitions are shifting rapidly, at least among some segments of our population. Young women, such as those studied here, are rejecting the economic dependence and unalleviated household responsibilities of the traditional wife-mother role. Yet, these women remain basically positive about both marriage and motherhood. They reject neither men nor children. Their

goals imply a restructuring of the family, but not its dissolution.

[18] We do not yet know the extent to which new sex-role definitions are being accepted by various segments of American society nor the various forms in which these new definitions can be found. Research is needed on individuals at all stages of the life cycle, on both sexes, and all racial and ethnic groups. But in addition, research is needed on the behavioral consequences of changing sex-role orientations. Attitudes are not necessarily expressed in behavior (Teevan, 1972) and attitudinal shifts which occur on campus sometimes revert to previous patterns once students leave the college environment. This is especially true when attitudes are not widely supported by individuals' reference groups and peers. It is possible, therefore, that these women will leave college to live relatively traditional lives.

[19] It is more likely, however, that these women will lead lives that differ from the traditional pattern. First, behavior has already begun to change. The median age at first marriage is rising, the birth rate is declining and women are pressing for equality. Second, there is considerable social support available now for women who are adopting feminist perspectives. Women's centers, communes, consciousness-raising groups, literature, and organizations extoll the virtues of feminist lifestyles and provide some of the structure within which these lifestyles might be realized. With such support, attitude shifts which occur at college can become remarkably stable (Newcomb, 1967). Third, women seem ready to maintain feminist attitudes in spite of perceived male rejection of these attitudes.

[20] Research is needed in order to determine what proportions of American women are in fact experiencing strain and anxiety as sex-role definitions change. What is the effect of such strains on other dimensions of women's lives? If many women wish to marry in spite of having attitudes which they believe men reject, how do they expect to resolve this dilemma? Will young women increasingly put off marriage, waiting for a man who they regard as "exceptional" to appear? Will young women become increasingly hesitant to commit themselves to marriage at all? And what about men? Research is desperately needed on male sex-role attitudes and expectations. If male attitudes are changing in the same direction and as rapidly as those of females, new patterns of family life will surely emerge. This would take time, of course, and will be delayed if women stereotype men as more conservative than they actually are. If male attitudes are remaining rigidly traditional, or if they are lagging substantially behind female attitudes, however, increased marital instability and strain between the sexes may result. In the long run, though, this strain will dissipate. Research (cf. Axelson, 1963, and Meier, 1972) has already shown that the husbands of working wives and the sons of working mothers are more positive toward sexual equality than are the spouses and children of traditional women. In time, with increasing numbers of wives and mothers entering the workforce, most men and women will stand together as spouses and parents, but also as equals.

## REFERENCES

Axelson, Leland
1963    "The marital adjustment and role definitions of husbands of working and nonworking wives." *Journal of Marriage and the Family,* 25 (2):189–195.

Festinger, Leon
1957    *The Theory of Cognitive Dissonance.* New York: Harper and Row.

Horner, Matina
1969    "Fail: bright women." *Psychology Today,* 3 (6):36–41.

Mason, Karen Oppenheim and Larry L. Bumpass
1973    "Women's sex-role attitudes in the United States, 1970." Revision of a paper presented at the annual meetings of the American Sociological Association (August, 1973).

Meier, Harold C.
1972    "Mother-centeredness and college youths' attitudes toward social equality for women: some empirical findings." *Journal of Marriage and the Family,* 34 (1): 115–121.

Millman, Marcia
1971    "Observations on sex-role research." *Journal of Marriage and the Family,* 33 (4): 772–776.

Newcomb, Theodore M. et al.
1967    *Persistence and Change: Benington College and its Students After Twenty-Five Years.* New York: Wiley.

Rapaport, Alan F., David Payne, and Anne Steinmann
1970    "Perceptual differences between married and single college women for the concepts of self, ideal woman, and man's ideal women." *Journal of Marriage and the Family,* 32 (3): 441–442.

Steinmann, Anne and David J. Fox
1969    "Specific areas of agreement and conflict in women's self-perception and their perception of men's ideal woman in two South American communities and an urban community in the United States." *Journal of Marriage and the Family,* 31 (2):281–289.

Teevan, James J., Jr.
1972    "Reference groups and premarital sexual behavior." *Journal of Marriage and the Family,* 34 (2):283–291.

## CRITICAL ANALYSIS: CONTENT

Parelius frames her study against the background of the conventional wisdom with respect to the women's liberation movement. She concedes that there is "general agreement" that sex-role attitudes and expectations are changing, but as a social scientist she wants to scrutinize these changes more closely, and to reach a clearer and more precise understanding of the nature, extent, and consequences of these changes.

### Questions

After a review of the social science literature on changing sex roles, Parelius offers a clear statement of purpose for her own study:

This study assesses women's attitudes toward various dimensions of their adult sex roles, their perceptions of men's attitudes toward women's roles, the degree to which these attitudes and perceptions have changed over the last four years, and the possibility that strains are arising with these changes. [paragraph 3]

Implicitly, this statement of purpose contains a series of questions:

1. How does the present generation of college women view adult sex roles?
2. How do they perceive men's attitudes toward "the new woman"?
3. To what extent have these attitudes and perceptions changed over the last four years?
4. Are the changes in women's self-definitions producing "strains" in their relations with men?

### Evidence

Parelius attempts to answer these questions through a survey of women at Douglass College. To measure change she sent questionnaires to a representative sample of women in 1969 and then repeated this in 1973. In her analysis she compares responses on a series of questions pertaining to women's role. The survey produced two basic findings:

1. The percentage of women giving "feminist responses" to questions regarding gender, family, and work increased dramatically between 1969 and 1973. For example, in 1969 only 49 percent of the women said that a wife's career is of equal importance to her husband's, but by 1973 the figure had increased to 81 percent. All nine items showed similar increases in feminist sentiment.

2. On the other hand, perceptions of male attitudes had hardly changed between 1969 and 1973. For example, in both years less than 10 percent of the women thought men would want to marry a woman who did not think the most important thing for a woman is to be a good wife and mother. Yet the percentage of women who rejected this traditional definition of women's role doubled from 31 to 62 percent. Thus, even as women became more feminist they continued to believe that men would not want to marry women with their feminist orientations. Put another way, increasing numbers of women hold views that they do not believe men would accept in a wife.

### Answers

Parelius is struck by the fact that "women seem ready to maintain feminist attitudes in spite of perceived male rejection of these attitudes" [paragraph 19]. Since these women typically also want to get married, they are left with a high degree of "role strain." Having carried the analysis to this crucial point, Parelius raises a number of questions that go an interpretive step beyond the actual findings. What, she asks, are the behavioral consequences of changing attitudes? Once these students leave college, will they revert to traditional sex roles, especially as they confront the prospect or reality of marriage? Parelius speculates that it is becoming easier to maintain feminist attitudes since marriage and childbearing are occurring later, and there are more institutional supports for feminist attitudes than there used to be. Still, she argues, role strain is a topic on which research is badly needed. How widespread is role strain? What effect does it have? Will some women avoid marriage, or be unable to find husbands? And what about men? Are attitudes changing? If not, can we expect increased marital instability? Parelius brings her paper to closure with this cluster of questions. In the final two sentences, she offers a tentative answer, speculating that role strain may diminish over time since it has been shown that the husband and sons of working women tend to be more positive toward sexual equality.

## CRITICAL ANALYSIS: COMPOSITION

As already indicated, Parelius's article on sex-role attitudes of college women focuses on *change*, specifically a change that she believes has been influenced by the women's liberation movement and the increased participation of women in the workplace. Any study that looks for change has comparison-contrast built into its design. "What it was like before" is compared to "What it is like now." This comparison-contrast approach, then, becomes the principal rhetorical mode.

### The Introduction (paragraphs 1 to 3)

Like other writers we have cited, Parelius begins by presenting a common or popular assumption: that sex-role attitudes are changing. In this case, however, she does not take issue with the conventional wisdom. Rather, she argues that there is a need to collect "hard data," not to prove that sex-role attitudes are changing, but to gauge the extent and consequences of this change. Note that her statement of purpose is contained in her very first sentence.

Consistent with the conventions of much academic writing, the first two paragraphs allude to previous research. In her review of the literature, Parelius identifies several themes that will be central to her own study. Paragraph 2 then indicates some ways in which previous studies have been inadequate, thus establishing another rationale for her study.

Paragraph 3 is the transition paragraph that introduces and describes the study. Here she outlines four facets of the research problem that will govern the presentation of the evidence in the body of her paper: (1) attitudes toward sex-roles; (2) perceptions of men's attitudes toward sex-roles; (3) changes in these attitudes over four years; (4) possible strains arising with these changes.

## The Body Paragraphs (paragraphs 4 to 14)

The body paragraphs of this article present the details of the survey under a series of headings and subheadings:

"The Sample" (the population surveyed)
"The Instrument" (the questionnaire)
"Findings" (observations based on the responses)
"Summary and Conclusions" (an overall statement about the findings)

The heading "Findings" has two subheadings which not only organize the presentation but also highlight the key comparisons:

"Sex-Role Orientations, 1969 and 1973" (changes in what women think)
"Perception of Male Attitudes, 1969 and 1973" (changes in what women believe men think)

To make matters more complicated, these two changes are then analyzed in relation to each other. To deal with this complexity, a tight organizational format is needed.

Below is a paragraph outline of the "Findings" section. Note that (1) the two subheadings are parallel in construction, and (2) each paragraph begins with a general statement or topic sentence that unifies the various facts and observations within the paragraph.

I. Sex-Role Orientations, 1969 and 1973
  A. Attitudes of women toward sex roles in 1969
    1. General statement: "Looking first at the women of 1969, it is evident that . . . only a minority gave feminist responses."
    2. Specific observations substantiating general statement
  B. Attitudes of women toward sex roles in 1973
    1. General statement: "Turning to the women of 1973, we see that the percentages giving feminist responses increased . . ."
    2. Specific observations substantiating general statement
  C. General statement comparing the two samples: "These data suggest that a substantial shift toward feminism occurred between 1969 and 1973."

II. Perception of Male Attitudes, 1969 and 1973
  A. Women's perception of male attitudes in 1969: ". . . looking first at the 1969 sample, it is clear that few women believed that men wanted to marry feminists."
  B. Women's perceptions of male attitudes in 1973: "Turning to 1973, we find that few major changes occurred in the women's perception of men's attitudes."
  C. General statement comparing the two samples: "These data suggest that the women in both samples tended to view men as basically traditional. . . ."

III. Summary Statement and Inference: Comparing Women's Sex-Role Orientations to their Perceptions of Men ("Thus many of the women sampled [in 1973] probably had attitudes which they believed men would reject in a potential spouse.")

The method for organizing the final comparison is whole-subject by whole-subject rather than point by point. In other words, women's attitudes on the whole are compared to women's perceptions of men's attitudes on the whole.

Note that paragraph 14 functions as a transition and begins to compare the two subsections. It concludes with a general but pointed observation that is then further developed in the conclusion: ". . . many of the women sampled probably had attitudes which they believed men would reject in a potential spouse."

The final heading is "Summary and Conclusions." To be precise, the first two paragraphs (15 and 16) constitute a summary, while the next four paragraphs (17 to 20) constitute the conclusion. Note the transitional sentence: "These findings suggest several conclusions."

### The Conclusion (paragraphs 17 to 20)

The conclusion goes beyond a restatement of the findings. Parelius is clearly interested in looking at the overall picture. Sex-role definitions are shifting rapidly in some segments of the population. However, the values that young women reject are qualified by the values they continue to hold. This general observation leads to an equally broad inference about what these values mean for the family as an institution: "Their goals imply a restructuring of the family, but not its dissolution" [paragraph 17].

In the remainder of the conclusion, Parelius explores the implications of her findings for the family and for American society as a whole. Like much scholarly writing, this article ends with some suggestions for further research.

## RHETORICAL STANCE: PERSUADING THE READER

Clarity is a goal for all writing, one not easily achieved when writing is based on quantitative research. All too often the data are ambiguous, confusing, and even contradictory. The challenge for the researcher-writer is to sift through the data, discerning patterns that are clear and consistent, and as a next step, to organize this material into a cogent argument. Like Parelius, you will need to begin with the "raw data," making connections between categories and forming generalizations out of these connections.

For example, Parelius often deals with clusters of items at a time (as in paragraph 12: "Turning to 1973, we find that few major changes occurred in the women's perception of men's attitudes. Only four items showed a shift . . ."). Her aim is always to locate trends that will help to answer the primary research question: How are women's sex-role expectations changing, and are such changes generating strain?

### Organization

A simple device for achieving clarity is the use of headings and subheadings—the social scientist's trademark. The headings divide the discussion into discrete sections that function as signposts for the reader. Under the major heading "Findings," for example, the subheadings highlight the two categories that are to be compared and contrasted. This visual distinction is useful in helping the reader to grasp the difference between categories.

Another device for clarifying the data in terms of the argument is a clear hierarchy of ideas. In this case Parelius moves from specific observations of patterns in the responses to general inferences about what these patterns might mean, always in terms of the research question and hypothesis. Note the increasing generalization as we move through the essay:

> Comparisons between 1969 and 1973 indicate a substantial shift toward feminist conceptions of sex-roles.
>
> There is no comparable shift, however, in women's perceptions of men's sex-role orientations.
>
> As a result, many of the women embrace roles which they believe men would reject in a potential spouse.
>
> Since most of these women are still interested in marriage and motherhood, presumably many are experiencing intense anxiety about their futures.
>
> Since women increasingly want equality as well as marriage and motherhood, this may lead to a restructuring of the family.

Each of these statements grows out of the previous one, leading to the conclusion that changes in sex-role attitudes among women are producing anxiety in women, as well as strain between the sexes.

In rhetorical terms this is an example of cause-effect analysis. The causal factor is that women have different attitudes than they believe men have. The effect is role strain.

### Language

This article was written for a professional journal and conforms to the conventions of academic writing: an abstract precedes the article; distinct sections describe the research design, sum up the findings, and argue the conclusions; appropriate tables present the raw data. Yet the actual writing is relatively free of jargon. Given the intended audience (professional social scientists), Parelius cannot be faulted for assuming familiarity with such terms as "sex roles," "division of labor," and "longitudinal data." However, she is careful to define the two terms that are at the heart of her study: "traditional" and "feminist":

> Traditional orientations suggest that a woman's primary purpose is to marry, bear children, and spend most of her time in the home doing housework and childrearing tasks. Feminist orientations stress equality between the sexes, encouraging women to develop talents and pursue careers. Within marriage, feminist orientations give both partners an equal share of financial and domestic responsibilities. [paragraph 5]

Precisely because "traditional" and "feminist" are popular terms and subject to many meanings, Parelius did well to define exactly how they would be employed within the context of her study.

As we suggested earlier, quantitative studies do not lend themselves to a rich and imaginative prose style. The paramount goal is clarity. In this case Parelius is skillful at communicating her findings to her audience within the scientific community.

## SUGGESTIONS FOR WRITING AND THINKING

1.  Conduct in-depth interviews with two female students, one of whom might be described as a "feminist," the other as "traditional" with respect to women's role. On the basis of the issues raised in Parelius's article, explore their sex-role attitudes. You might also explore the experiences and emotions that accompany these attitudes.

    When writing up your interviews, first develop a context or framework for presenting your interview material. For example, like Parelius, you might discuss recent changes in the prevailing definition regarding women's role. Then state the rationale for doing in-depth interviews. That is, indicate why these are worth doing and what you hope to learn. In the introduction to your paper, you should either present a hypothesis or suggest the major finding that emerges from the interviews. In other words, you need a clear thesis statement that organizes the presentation. Finally, introduce your subjects and present your findings.

    This last step—the presentation of findings—can be executed in at least two different ways. Like the interviews with Mack and Larry in this chapter, you might simply present an edited version of the interview. By "edited version," we mean that you should improve the readability of the interview—for example, by deleting unnecessary repetition, unfruitful digressions, or answers that run on too long. Once you have presented the interviews themselves, develop your analysis of the results, leading to one or more conclusions.

    As an alternative to an edited transcription, develop one or more themes that are suggested by the interview, and that focus on areas of similarity or difference between your two subjects. For example, you could focus on the sexual division of labor in the household. Do your subjects think that women should be responsible for most of the household tasks? How would they deal with an uncompromising male? Weave relevant quotations from your interviews into the text, in order to highlight, illustrate, and document the particular forms that "feminist" and "traditional" attitudes take, as represented by your two subjects.

2.  This exercise involves a survey of sex-role attitudes among women at your college. The questionnaire should consist of the ten items in Table 1 of Parelius's study. These can be framed as questions. (For example: Do you think that a wife's career is of equal importance to her hus-

band's?) To simplify matters, do not ask interviewees about their perceptions of men.

If this exercise is conducted as a class project, then each student should interview ten undergraduate women. At the next class, collate the results. That is, tally up the number of students who gave "feminist" responses to each question, and compute the percentage. Now create a table modeled after the one in Parelius's article, showing the percentages who gave a feminist response to each question in Parelius's 1969 sample, her 1973 sample, and your current sample. The table should be constructed as follows:

| | Feminist Responses | | |
|---|---|---|---|
| | Douglass | | My College |
| Sex-Role Attitudes | 1969 | 1973 | Today |
| A wife's career is as important as her husband's | 49% | 81% | |
| Both spouses should contribute equally to the financial support of the family | 37 | 65 | |
| Etc. | | | |

Now you are ready to "write up the results." In doing so, you should first develop a context for your study. For example, you could argue a need to update Parelius's findings, since they are somewhat dated. Or you might say that you wish to contrast the level of feminist sentiment at your college with what Parelius found at Douglass College in 1973. (What is your initial hunch—that your college will be even more feminist than Douglass College or less so? Why?)

Present your findings as they relate to the questions raised at the outset of your study. Discuss areas of similarity and difference between Parelius's findings and your own. Do you think that differences exist because women at your college are different from those that attended Douglass College? Or do you think that differences exist because times have changed? Bring your paper to a logical conclusion.

3. This exercise is identical to the previous one, except that males at your college will be interviewed instead of females. In some cases you will have to reword the question. (For example: Do *you* expect to do 50 percent of all household and childrearing tasks?) Questions 3, 8, and 9 should either be deleted or rephrased. After you have tallied the results and constructed a table modeled after the one in Parelius's article, develop your analysis of the findings.

4. Read "What Professors Think about Student Protest and Manners, Morals, Politics and Chaos on the Campus," by Seymour Martin Lipset and Everett Carl Ladd, Jr., published in *Psychology Today*, 4 (November 1970), pp. 49ff. The article is based on surveys of faculty and student

opinion that were conducted in 1969 at the height of the student activism on the nation's campuses.

Analyze the article in terms of the questions-evidence-answers schema. Then analyze the article in terms of its rhetorical strategy. What is the authors' thesis regarding faculty opinion and student activism? How do the authors organize the presentation of their findings? Is the article persuasive?

## INTERVIEW STUDIES ACROSS THE DISCIPLINES

### Anthropology

ZAVELLA, PATRICIA, "Abnormal Intimacy: The Varying Work Networks of Chicana Cannery Workers," *Feminist Studies*, 11 (Fall 1983), 541–47. On the basis of in-depth interviews with Chicana women employed in canneries in Santa Clara Valley, California, the author explores the nature of work networks and how they operate within women's private lives.

### Economics

HORVATH, FRANCIS W., "Work At Home: New Findings From the Current Population Survey," *Monthly Labor Review*, 109 (November 1986), 31–35. The article summarizes the results of a recent government survey that found that more than 8 million Americans worked at home in 1985. The most common category was services, ranging from consulting to child care.

### History

STAHL WEINBERG, SYDNEY, "The World of Our Mothers: Family, Work, and Education in the Lives of Jewish Immigrant Women," *Frontiers*, VII, no. 1 (1983), 71–79. This article is based on oral histories with forty immigrant Jewish women who arrived in this country between 1901 and 1924. The focus of the interviews was on family, work, and education, and the role that each played in the adjustment to life in America.

### Political Science

LANE, ROBERT E., "The Fear of Equality," *American Political Science Review*, 53 (1959), 35–51. On the basis of interviews with working-class men in New Haven, the author explores how people who themselves have low status rationalize inequality, and actually fear a more egalitarian society.

### Psychology

BART, PAULINE B., "Mother Portnoy's Complaints," *Trans-action*, 8 (November-December 1970), 69–74. The author conducted intensive interviews with twenty clinically depressed middle-aged women in psychiatric hospitals. A common pattern was that these women adhered to an exaggerated version of "supermother," and as their children reached maturity, had great trouble dealing with maternal role loss.

### Sociology

HIRSCHI, TRAVIS, and RODNEY STARK, "Hellfire and Delinquency," *Social Problems*, 17 (Fall 1969), 202–13. On the basis of a survey of over 4000 junior- and senior-high school students in a California community, the authors found that religious devotion, including fears of "hellfire and damnation," seemed to have little effect as a deterrent to delinquency.

# Chapter 9
# THE DOCUMENT

## INTRODUCTION

Compared to those who study contemporary society, social scientists who study the past are at a distinct disadvantage since they cannot go out and directly observe the event or phenomenon under study. Thus, when Ned Polsky decided to do research on the poolroom hustler, he had to go no farther than the local poolrooms a few miles from the University of Chicago. In contrast, consider the dilemma of the historian who wishes to trace the origins of billiards. Where would he or she "go" for data on billiard playing as it existed centuries ago? Invariably, the historian's quest for data ends up in an archive or some other repository of old books and historical documents.

Indeed, sport historians have unearthed documents that shed considerable light on the history of billiards.[1] Probably it originated in classical times. At least this is what Shakespeare assumed when he wrote *Anthony and Cleopatra* in 1607. In the play he has Cleopatra, who is bored by Anthony's absence, saying to her attendant, "Let us to billiards." Some historians, however, place the origins of billiards in fifteenth-century France; by the seventeenth century it had become Louis XI's favorite pastime. Of course, these isolated facts convey few of the nuances of the kind that Polsky captured through direct observation. However, with resourcefulness and luck the historian might turn up eyewitness accounts like the

---

[1] A recent volume lists nearly 600 sources on billiards alone. See Robert R. Craven, *Billiards, Bowling, Table Tennis, Pinball, and Video Games: A Bibliographical Guide* (Westport, Conn.: Greenwood Press, 1983). Ned Polsky also provides a historical analysis of billiards in *Hustlers, Beats, and Others* (Chicago: University of Chicago Press, 1985), chap. 1.

one below, written by an English general in 1890. Note the striking similarities to Polsky's account:

> It [billiards] was played principally in public houses, and the players were not always those who belonged to the respectable class. These men studied the game for the sole purpose of being able to win money from the unwary. The rooms were dirty, and drinking was considered a necessary accompaniment of the game. . . .[2]

Clearly, the inability to engage in direct observation is not an insurmountable obstacle to studying the past. Instead historians rely on *documents* to write and rewrite the historical record. According to one famous dictum, "Pas de documents, pas d'histoire" ("Without documents, there is no history").[3]

Indeed, as a discipline history begins with the first written records about five thousand years ago. To be sure, human life existed for millennia before that, but this time span is usually conceived of as "prehistory" and delegated to archaeology and anthropology. Not until humankind left written records do we have the essential documentary material for writing history.[4]

Documents can be divided into two general categories: *personal documents* and *records.* Personal documents include first-person accounts such as diaries, letters, and autobiographies. For example, in their classical study, *The Polish Peasant in Europe and America,* Thomas and Znaniecki relied almost exclusively on letters between Polish immigrants in America and their relatives in Poland. The letters provided rich documentary evidence of the painful adjustment that immigrants went through, and particularly the strains that existed between immigrant parents and their American-born children.[5]

Personal documents have also provided valuable raw material for the relatively new field of family history. For example, in *Cradle of the Middle Class* Mary Ryan studied the impact of industrialization on the family system by doing research on families in Oneida County, New York, between 1790 and 1865. Among the various sources that she turned up in local libraries and historical societies were five diaries and more than a dozen collections of family correspondence. These personal documents yielded rich documentary evidence of changes in the family system as the local

---

[2]Original source: Dr. W. Pole, *Handbook of Games* (London: George Bell, 1890). Quoted in Vernon Bartlett, *The Past of Pastimes* (Hamden, Conn.: Archon Books, 1969), pp. 130–31.

[3]John Madge, *The Tools of Social Science* (Garden City, N.Y.: Anchor, 1965), p. 75.

[4]Donald V. Gawronski, *History: Meaning and Method* (Glencoe, Illinois: Scott, Foresman, 1969), p. 4.

[5]William I. Thomas and Florian Znaniecki, *The Polish Peasant in Europe and America* (New York: Alfred A. Knopf, 1927).

economy shifted from agriculture to industry, producing an urban middle class.[6]

The limitations of personal documents are perhaps obvious. Inasmuch as they reflect the values, points of view, or idiosyncracies of their authors, they are inherently subjective. This is less a drawback, however, when subjective states of mind (such as feelings or attitudes) are themselves the object of historical inquiry, as they were in Thomas and Znaniecki's study of Polish immigrants. Besides, personal documents rarely constitute the only source of data. Typically they are used in conjunction with other, less subjective data, often for purposes of illustration.

As an example, let us return to Mary Ryan's *Cradle of the Middle Class.* Ryan uses a variety of sources—old books, magazines, church sermons, and literature—to show that nineteenth-century women had powerful bonds to one another. She brings her analysis to this critical juncture:

> . . . it is clear that female bonds laced through the everyday life of the middle class and formed a denser social and emotional network than ties between the sexes.

In this context, and in the very next sentence, Ryan introduces a diary to document her claim that women were more bound to each other than to men:

> The fullest diurnal account of the private world of females is Lavinia Johnson's diary, written in small hand, filling more than eight hundred pages, and detailing less than two years in the life of a middle-class woman. During that period in the late 1850s Mrs. Johnson rarely even mentioned members of the opposite sex. She seemed to have totally discarded the possibility of communicating with her husband and seldom referred to her son James, who had migrated to New York City. . . . The daily life of Lavinia Johnson transpired in an almost perfectly segregated female culture.[7]

In the next paragraph Ryan substantiates her claim that women's experience was largely restricted to the domestic sphere by quoting from the diary itself:

> "What a wilderness would this world be without my children, I should have none to love, nor anybody to take care of me. Father is a trouble to himself as he is to me."[8]

Whether one can generalize on the basis of personal documents is always problematic. As Ryan comments, "it would be a mistake to indict the marriages of the nineteenth-century middle class on this limited and extreme evidence. . . ."[9] Nevertheless, the life material garnered from per-

---

[6]Mary Ryan, *Cradle of the Middle Class* (New York: Cambridge University Press, 1981).
[7]Ibid., p. 196.
[8]Ibid., p. 197.
[9]Ibid., p. 196.

sonal documents can provide corroborating evidence for generalizations established on the basis of other, more objective sources.

The second category of documents is records. One characteristic of the modern nation-state is that it produces an immense volume of official records—proceedings of legislatures, courts, and government agencies, not to speak of the executive branch of government. It has become customary for retiring presidents to establish libraries to house the mounds of records and documents produced during their tenure of office, and these materials provide political scientists and future historians with infinite possibilities for research. Sociologists and economists, too, have come to rely on statistical information routinely collected by the Department of Commerce, which conducts the decennial Census, and the Bureau of Labor Statistics, which churns out an endless stream of statistics on the economy and the labor force. With the passage of time, these data assume historical significance as well, and future historians will have access to a vast body of empirical data that simply did not exist until recently. This is not an unmixed blessing, however. As two leading historians have commented: "We are overwhelmed by mountains of evidence; it accumulates faster than even computers can record it, and we still have to process the material from the computers."[10]

Many nongovernmental organizations also produce records that are potentially useful in social science research. In *Cradle of the Middle Class* Ryan makes extensive use of records of churches and businesses. To quote from her bibliographical note:

> Utica's churches housed a plentitude of useful documents, including membership lists, proceedings of church trials, and records of benevolent societies. My research strategy also identified an array of serial records that were especially susceptible to social-historical analysis—among them annual city directories, sixteen volumes of wills, credit records for more than six hundred local businesses, and the employment records of the New York Mills Company.[11]

Newspapers and magazines, also used extensively in Ryan's study, constitute an on-going record of events, though obviously this record is refracted through the lens of editors and journalists, and reflects their values and perceptions. Nevertheless, newspapers and magazines are a valuable resource, widely used in historical research.

All the above documents, including the personal documents discussed earlier, are examples of *primary sources*, in that they are original records based on direct observation. Insofar as possible, historians use primary sources to write history. The works they produce are then considered *secondary sources*.

---

[10]Henry Steele Commager and Raymond Henry Muessig, *The Study and Teaching of History* (Columbus, Ohio: Charles E. Merrill Publishing Co., 1980), p. 46.

[11]Ryan, *Cradle of the Middle Class*, p. 293.

As this term implies, secondary sources are one step removed from the original source. For this reason it is extremely important that writers cite the source of material that is being incorporated into secondary works. Not only do these citations give credit where it is due, but they also allow readers to track down the original source of material used in secondary works. Readers may simply wish to "see for themselves"—that is, to assess the validity of the original source. Or they may wish to go to the original source for further information. To fail to cite the original source in effect cuts information off from its source, thus truncating the research process as well.

Insofar as history is a cumulative enterprise whereby historians build upon the work of their predecessors, it is certainly valid to use secondary as well as primary sources. In doing so, however, there is a danger of repeating the misconceptions and errors of previous researchers, or at the least, merely regurgitating what has already been established by others, thus failing to advance the frontier of knowledge. For this reason historians who break new ground and turn up new data are accorded a certain respect, in that they are adding new information to the historical record, possibly leading to new or deeper understanding. On the other hand, few of the major issues that divide historians into opposing camps are likely to be resolved with new data. Debate turns not on points of fact but on differences of interpretation. As Arthur Schlesinger once observed: ". . . almost all important questions are important precisely because they are *not* susceptible to quantitative answers."[12]

Generally speaking, undergraduate research papers are based on secondary sources. Rarely are students expected to go out and turn up new sources of data, though at times you may be asked to write a paper on the basis of specific primary source materials, such as copies of the Federalist Papers, old newspapers, or a collection of manuscripts. More often, however, students are asked to compile or synthesize information and ideas from works by established writers. This is not to say there is no room for creative thought. For the professional and student alike, the challenge is to arrive at a new synthesis—one that will advance an original interpretation of known facts and bring fresh insight to familiar problems.

## DOCUMENTS AND THE PROBLEM OF OBJECTIVITY

No less than other social scientists, historians who work with documents have to grapple with the problem of objectivity—that is, the subtle ways in which values impinge upon and potentially compromise objectivity. According to one formula, which reigned in the nineteenth century and is still embraced by many historians, the task of the historian, as encapsulated in the German phrase, *wie es eigentlich gewesen*, is "simply to show how it

---

[12]Arthur Schlesinger, "The Humanist Looks at Empirical Social Research," *American Sociological Review*, 27 (1962), 770.

really was." The historian, it is argued, should first ascertain the facts, and only afterwards draw conclusions from them. "Hard fact" is separated from interpretation and speculation, thus assuring "objectivity."

This view has come under attack, most notably by Edward Carr in a provocative book entitled *What Is History?* Carr argues that it is a "preposterous fallacy" to think that facts exist objectively and independently of interpretation. The problem is that the historian is "necessarily subjective" in choosing which facts, from the myriad of facts available, to include in the historical record. Carr draws an analogy to fish in a vast ocean:

> . . . what the historian catches will depend partly on chance, but mainly on what part of the ocean he chooses to fish in and what tackle he chooses to use—these two factors being, of course, determined by the kind of fish he wishes to catch. By and large, the historian will get the kind of facts he wants. History means interpretation.[13]

The facts that the historian retrieves, furthermore, are not self-explaining, but must be placed within an interpretative context. As Carr puts it: "The facts speak only when the historian calls upon them: it is he who decides to which facts to give the floor, and in what order or context."[14]

Thus, not only will different historians select different facts but the same facts lend themselves to different interpretations, depending upon the point of view of the writer and the context in which these facts are placed. Therefore, it should come as no surprise, for example, that northern and southern historians have written sharply divergent accounts of how the Civil War "really was." Or that historians in the 1980s, reflecting a different consciousness in the wake of the civil rights revolution, have challenged earlier accounts of the Civil War. Consider the following assessment of how the Reconstruction era is viewed differently by contemporary historians as compared to what historians wrote half a century earlier:

> . . . instead of emphasizing the loss to slave-holders we emphasize the victory for Negro slaves; instead of deploring the establishment of military rule in the South we are astonished that the civil authority was so speedily restored and that the South was back in the Union—and even running it—within a few years. Instead of lamenting the fate of Jefferson Davis, languishing in prison for over a year, we note that after the greatest civil war of the century not one rebel lost his life, not one was proscribed, except briefly. . . . We re-examine these in the light of recent developments in the position of the Negro in American life, and ask whether the Radical program might not have set the Negro question on the way to solution instead of leaving it for us to grapple with a century later.[15]

As this example suggests, historians inescapably see the past through the eyes of the present. Indeed, this is why history needs always to be rewritten in the light of new concerns and understandings.

---

[13]Edward Carr, *What Is History?* (New York: Vintage, 1961), p. 26.

[14]Ibid., p. 9.

[15]Commager and Muessig, *The Study and Teaching of History*, p. 60.

Does this mean that history is irreparably subjective, and that one historian's view is as good as the next? No, argues Carr. Just as facts cannot be divorced from interpretation, neither can interpretations be advanced irrespective of the facts. The obligation of the historian, Carr writes, is "to bring into the picture all known or knowable facts relevant, in one sense or another, to the theme on which he is engaged and to the interpretation proposed."[16] Without credible evidence, an interpretation will not be convincing and withstand the critical scrutiny of other historians.

The close relationship that exists between fact and interpretation has implications for writing as well. Carr scoffs at the commonplace notion that the historian first collects all of the facts and then writes up the findings. Instead, he posits a model, not unlike the one proposed in Chapter 2, whereby reading, writing, and thinking are interrelated and overlapping:

> For myself, as soon as I have got going on a few of what I take to be the capital sources, the itch becomes too strong and I begin to write—not necessarily at the beginning, but somewhere, anywhere. Thereafter, reading and writing go on simultaneously. The writing is added to, subtracted from, re-shaped, cancelled, as I go on reading. The reading is guided and directed and made fruitful by the writing: the more I write, the more I know what I am looking for, the better I understand the significance and relevance of what I find.[17]

In short, facts and interpretation are molded to each other, and much of this is done in the actual process of writing.

## THE INTERPLAY OF WRITING AND THINKING: A CASE STUDY

The sample essay for this chapter illustrates the interrelationship between facts and interpretation. It is an excerpt from the first chapter of a book by Herbert Gutman entitled *The Black Family in Slavery and Freedom, 1750–1925.*[18] In his preface Gutman provides the reader with unusual detail about the evolution of his ideas and writing. This is worth our attention because it points up the ways in which research, thinking, and writing are interrelated within the context of scholarly organizations that provide researcher-writers with feedback and criticism.

Gutman's research was originally stimulated by the controversy surrounding the publication of a report by Daniel Moynihan, then assistant to President Johnson, on *The Negro Family in America: A Case for National Action.*[19] Moynihan contended that many of the problems that beset black

---

[16]Carr, *What Is History?*, p. 32.

[17]Ibid., p. 33.

[18]Herbert Gutman, *The Black Family in Slavery and Freedom* (New York: Pantheon, 1976), pp. 3–11.

[19]Daniel P. Moynihan, *The Negro Family: The Case for National Action*, in Lee Rainwater and William C. Yancey, *The Moynihan Report and the Politics of Controversy* (Cambridge: MIT Press, 1967), pp. 39–124.

Americans, such as poverty and unemployment, stemmed from a weak family system, indicated by the high incidence of out-of-wedlock births and female-headed households. Citing a number of "authoritative sources," Moynihan further argued that the fragility of the black family could be traced to slavery. This claim affronted Gutman's sense of history, and he set out to test the validity of the proposition that "slavery destroyed the black family."

Undoubtedly, documentary evidence could be found either to support or refute this proposition. Take literary accounts, for example. In *Uncle Tom's Cabin* Harriet Beecher Stowe presents images of black families suffused with warmth and affection despite the abuses of the slave system. But another contemporary, Fanny Kemble, wrote a journal portraying a slave system so oppressive that it stripped slave families of "tenderness" and "spiritual grace."[20] Thus, documentary evidence, selected at will by the historian, could not resolve the issue since, then as now, one could find evidence of both "strong" and "weak" families. A more systematic approach was needed.

As a first step, Gutman, together with Lawrence Glasco, did a study of the black community of Buffalo, New York, between 1855 and 1875. They reasoned that if the thesis that "slavery destroyed the black family" were correct, then broken families should have been common among urban blacks around the time of slavery. To test whether this was the case, Gutman and Glasco examined the New York State manuscript census schedules that, unlike the federal census, contained information about household relationships. Their basic finding was that virtually all Afro-American households during the period under examination were "double-headed, kin-related households," meaning that they consisted of two parents raising their children.

Gutman and Glasco wrote papers that they delivered in 1968 at two academic conferences: The Wisconsin Conference on the History of American Political and Social Behavior, and the Yale Conference on Nineteenth-Century Cities. One may be tempted to scoff at the pretentious titles of these conferences, but their purpose is to bring together scholars who share similar research interests and to provide a forum for the presentation of new research. According to Gutman, the papers were well received, but critics worried about the "typicality" of Afro-Americans from Buffalo. Could the finding that Buffalo families showed no signs of disorganization be generalized to other regions? Gutman held off publishing his findings, and launched another study in which he examined the households of southern blacks, both urban and rural, in 1880 and 1885, based on population censuses carried out by the Freedmen's Bureau. These findings corroborated the Buffalo studies. Gutman presented two more papers at the 1969 meetings of the Association for the Study of Negro Life and History and the 1970

[20]Robert William Fogel and G. R. Elton, *Which Road to the Past* (New Haven: Yale University Press, 1983), p. 45.

meetings of the Organization of American Historians. These papers were subsequently published in academic journals.

Gutman then extended his research in two ways. First, he examined black households in New York City in 1905 and 1925. Again, the statistical evidence showed that most families were intact. Secondly, Gutman became concerned that most of his findings were based on quantitative data. A number of leading scholars in the field argued that Gutman's data showed that the black family survived under slavery, but did not explain how and why this was so. With this in mind, Gutman turned to "the voluminous Freedmen's Bureau records and the vast literary record left by other northern and southern whites" to find qualitative evidence that "might help *explain* what the quantitative data *described*."[21]

In the sample excerpt that follows, Gutman employs both personal documents and records. Note how he skillfully uses records to establish the fact that most blacks left slavery with their families intact, and supplements this with personal documents that convey the emotional intensity and depth of family relationships. If records constitute the bare bones of history, then it is the personal document that puts flesh on the historical skeleton.

[21]Gutman, *The Black Family in Slavery and Freedom*, p. xx. [Italics added.]

# Send Me Some of the Children's Hair*
## *Herbert Gutman*

---

*It is difficult to get a clear picture of the family relations of slaves, between the Southern apologist and his picture of cabin life, with idyllic devotion and careless toil, and that of the abolitionist with his tale of family disruption and cruelty, adultery, and illegitimate mulattoes.*
—W. E. B. Du Bois (1909)

*Can a people . . . live and develop over three hundred years simply by reacting? Are American Negroes simply the creation of white men, or have they at least helped to create themselves out of what they found around them?*—Ralph Ellison (1964)

---

[1] This is a book about ordinary black men, women, and children mostly before the general emancipation but after that time, too—a study of enslaved Afro-Americans, their children, and their grandchildren, how they adapted to enslavement by developing distinctive domestic arrangements and kin networks that nurtured a new Afro-American culture, and how these, in turn, formed the social basis of developing Afro-American

*Reprinted by permission of the publisher from Herbert Gutman, *The Black Family in Slavery and Freedom, 1750–1925* (New York: Pantheon Books, 1976), pp. 3–11.

communities, which prepared slaves to deal with legal freedom. This book is also about poor Americans, non-whites who spent a good portion of their American experience enslaved. It is therefore concerned with a special aspect of American labor history: those men and women who labored first in bondage and then mostly as half-free rural workers. . . .

**[2]** This is not a study of well-known Americans but seeks to understand men like Laura Spicer's ex-slave husband and the South Carolina ex-slave Sam Rosemon and women like the early-nineteenth-century slave mother Hannah Grover and the mid-nineteenth-century slave wife and mother Sarah Boon. Only bits and pieces of their individual histories survive, fragmentary clues about who these four people were and what they believed. Our concern is with what sustained and nurtured their beliefs and behavior. Nothing more.

**[3]** These four persons were not related to one another, and their separate slave lives spanned the full century between the War for Independence and the general emancipation. Each revealed a strong attachment to a family. Hannah Grover, known earlier as Hannah Van Buskerk, wrote her son Cato on June 3, 1805. "I long to see you in my old age," the slave woman began:

> Now my dear son I pray you to come and see your dear old Mother—Or send me twenty dollar and I will come and see you in Philadelphia—And if you cant come to see your old Mother pray send me a letter and tell me where you live what family you have and what you do for a living—I am a poor old servant I long for freedom. . . . I love you Cato—you love your Mother—You are my only son.

A postscript added: "If you have any love for your poor old Mother pray come or send to me My dear son I love you with all my heart." She had not seen Cato since 1785.

**[4]** Sarah Boon's husband was a free black carpenter, and she lived on her owner's farm near Raleigh, North Carolina. She and her husband had their troubles. Although it pained her to learn of his "bad health" in 1850, she would not accept his denial that he had lived with another woman: "When the subject was broach before you and that worman eather of you mad no reply."

> [L]et it be eather way. My Dear Husband I frealy forgive. I have no doubt that you will find it in the end that I was rite. I wish it to be banished from our memoreys and it neve be thought of again and let us take a new start and join on together as we have binn doing for many years. Miss Marian has given t[o] me great concorlation but before that I was hardely able to creep [sleep?] I hope you will concider my fealings and give me sentiments of your mind in ancer to this letter

She urged him to work nearer to her home; "witch would be a great prise to me than all the money you could make." A "little son" had apparently been sold, and she awaited word about him, promising to tell him when she heard. Her letter ended:

> I wish you to rite me word when you are rite you coming out. I do not thing it is rite for me for sutch a long absence from me if I cant come to join you. [You] can come to me. we are all well as to health. I feel very loanesome be sertin to answer this letter as soon as you get it. I have nothing more at present, onley I remain your Affectnate Wife untill Death.[1]

---

[1] Robert S. Starobin, ed., *Blacks in Bondage: Letters from American Slaves* (1974), 87–92, 105.

[5] Sam Rosemon and Laura Spicer's slave husband also were deeply attached to their families. Like Hannah Grover and Sarah Boon, they had been separated from them. But their letters were written just after the emancipation. Rosemon sought his South Carolina parents, and Spicer, who had remarried, grieved over an earlier forced separation from his slave wife and children. Rosemon had made it to Pittsburgh from South Carolina and sent a letter asking the Greenville, South Carolina, Freedmen's Bureau about his parents Caroline and Robert Rosemon:

> To the freedmen Bureau in Greenville, S.C.
> Dear freinds the deep crants of rivous ceprate ous but i hope in God for hours prasous agine and injoying the same injoyment That we did before the war begun and i am tolbile know but much trubbel in mind and i hope my truble Will not Be all Ways this Ways. . . .
> [I] inquire for Caline then inquire for marther live at Fane Ranson and Harriett that live at doct Gant and if you heir from tham let me know if you Plese soon Writ to Pittsburg Pa to Carpenters No 28
> Robard Rosemon that lived in Andison Destrect my farther and Carline my mother i remien your refractorate son
> *Sam Rosemon*[2]

[2]J. H. Croushore, D. M. Potter, eds., John deForest, *A Union Officer in the Reconstruction* (1948), 343. Sam Rosemon's letter can be "translated" as follows:

To The Greenville, South Carolina, Freedmen's Bureau:

Dear Friends. Although deep rivers separate us, I hope to God that we can enjoy ourselves as we did before the Civil War. I am well but very much troubled. I seek information about my mother Caroline and about Harriet, who lived at Dr. Gants, and about my father Robert Rosemon, who lived in the Anderson district. If you hear from them, please write to me at 28 Carpenter Street, Pittsburgh, Pa. Your stubborn and unmanageable son

SAM ROSEMON.

Sometime before the Civil War, Laura Spicer and her children were sold from their husband and father. They considered coming together again after the emancipation, but Spicer had remarried. Letters passed between them. "I read your letters over and over again," Spicer once wrote. "I keep them always in my pocket. If you are married, I don't ever want to see you again." Another letter revealed his turmoil, and he pressed Laura to find a husband:

> I would much rather you would get married to some good man, for every time I gits a letter from you it tears me all to pieces. The reason why I have not written you before, in a long time, is because your letters disturbed me so very much. You know I love my children. I treats them good as a Father can treat his children; and I do a good deal of it for you. I am sorry to hear that Lewellyn, my poor little son, have had such bad health. I would come and see you but I know you could not bear it. I want to see and I don't want to see you. I love you just as well as I did the last day I saw you, and it will not do for you and I to meet. I am married, and my wife have two children, and if you and I meets it would make a very dissatisfied family.
> Send me some of the children's hair in a separate paper with their names on the paper. Will you please git married, as long as I am married. My dear, you know the Lord knows both of our hearts. You know it never was our wishes to be separated from each other, and it never was our fault. Oh, I can see you so plain, at any-time, I had rather anything to had happened to me most than ever to have been parted from you and the children. As I am, I do not know which I love best, you or Anna. If I was to die, today or tomorrow, I do not think I would die satisfied till you tell me you will try and marry some good, smart man that will take care of you and the children; and do it because you love me; and not because I think more of the wife I have got than I do of you.
> The woman is not born that feels as near to me as you do. You feel this day like myself. Tell them they must re-

member they have a good father and one that cares for them and one that thinks about them every day—My very heart did ache when reading your very kind and interesting letter. Laura I do not think I have change any at all since I saw you last.—I think of you and my children every day of my life.

Laura I do love you the same. My love to you *never* have failed. Laura, truly, I have got another wife, and I am very sorry, that I am. You feels and seems to me as much like my dear loving wife, as you ever did Laura. You know my treatment to a wife and you know how I am about my children. You know I am one man that do love my children. . . .[3]

[6] These few letters are quite unusual historical documents. Some may have been written by an amanuensis. Most adult slaves and former slaves, of course, could not write. But the letters' importance does not rest upon whether they were a common form of slave expression. They were not. What is important is their relationship to the beliefs and behavior of other slaves who left no such historical records. Women like Hannah Grover and men like Laura Spicer's slave husband were not unusual Afro-Americans. Their letters were individual expressions of an adaptive and changing slave culture that had developed in the century preceding the general emancipation.

[7] This study of the Afro-American family reaches back into the eighteenth century and moves forward to the Harlem tenements of 1925, but its chief focus is on the Afro-American family in the decades just before emancipation and in the few years following it. The novelist Albion W. Tourgee wrote in 1888, "Much

has been written of the slave and something of the freedman, but thus far no one has been able to weld the new life to the old."[4] The evidence in this study deals mostly with some of the important relationships between these two critical moments in the Afro-American experience. It unfolds a very different story from that found in the pages of E. Franklin Frazier's pioneering study *The Negro Family in the United States* (1939) and in nearly all other standard works on this important subject that rest heavily upon this influential book.

[8] The recovery of records of viable Afro-American families and kin networks during and after slavery makes it possible to begin a long overdue examination of how there developed among black Americans a culture shaped by the special ways in which they adapted first to the harshness of initial enslavement, then to the severe dislocations associated with the physical transfer of hundreds of thousands of Upper South slaves to the Lower South between 1790 and 1860, and later to legal freedom in the rural and urban South and in the urban North prior to 1930. The sociologist T. B. Bottomore reminds us that "the family transmits values which are determined elsewhere; it is an agent, not a principal."[5] But for it to be an "agent," there must be links between generations of different families. Without them, it is difficult for a culture to be transmitted over time, and members of developing social classes cannot adapt to changing

---

[3]H. L. Swint, ed., *Dear Ones at Home: Letters from the Contraband Camps* (1966), 123–24, 242–43.

[4]Albion W. Tourgee, "The South as a Field for Fiction," *Forum,* VI (December 1888), 408–10.

[5]T. B. Bottomore, *Sociology: A Guide to Problems and Literature* (1971), 181.

external circumstances. That is so for slaves and nonslaves.

**[9]** The family condition and familial beliefs of some Virginia, North Carolina, Mississippi, Louisiana, Tennessee and Kentucky Afro-Americans between 1863 and 1866—*the last slave generation*—are examined first. Who these ex-slaves were and the types of families they lived in between 1863 and 1866 pose questions about who they had been in the half century preceding the general emancipation and who they would become in the half century following it. Evidence about them in 1865 provides important clues to who their slave grandparents had been in 1815 (before the rapid spread of slavery from the Upper to the Lower South) and who their grandchildren would be in 1915 (at the beginning of the twentieth-century migration of rural southern blacks to northern cities). The emancipation freed the slaves not only of their owners but also of the constraints that had limited their ability to act upon their slave beliefs, and their behavior during and shortly after the Civil War reveals aspects of that earlier belief system otherwise difficult for the historian to discern. Early-twentieth-century historians and social scientists suggested such continuities, but either their racial beliefs or the flawed sociohistorical "models" they used to explain lower-class behavior over time led them to stress "continuities" that had no relationship at all to the behavior of ordinary ex-slaves.[6]

[6]See, for examples, Walter L. Fleming, *Civil War and Reconstruction in Alabama* (1905), 271, 381, 523, 763–64; Arthur W. Calhoun, *Social History of the American Family*, III (1917–9), 58–59; Edward B. Reuter, *The American Race Problem* (1938), 204; Francis Simkins and Robert Woody, *South Carolina During Reconstruction* (1932), 331, 359–60.

**[10]** No one better illustrates this misdirected emphasis than the sociologist E. Franklin Frazier. Frazier, of course, was not a racist and vigorously combatted the racial scholarship that dominated early-twentieth-century historical and social-science writings. But he underestimated the adaptive capacities of slaves and ex-slaves and therefore wrote that their families, "at best an accommodation to the slave order, went to pieces in the general breakup of the plantation system." He had the ex-slave laborer and field hand in mind when he asked:

> What authority was there to take the place of the master's in regulating sex relations and maintaining the permanency of marital ties? Where could the Negro father look for sanctions of his authority in family relations which had scarcely existed in the past? Were the affectional bonds between mother and child and the solidarity of feeling and sentiment between man and wife strong enough to withstand the disorganizing effects of freedom? In the absence of family traditions and public opinion, what restraint was there upon individual impulses unleashed in these disordered times? To what extent during slavery had the members of slave families developed common interests and common purposes capable of supporting the more or less loose ties of sympathy between those of the same blood or household?

The "crisis" accompanying emancipation "tended to destroy all traditional ways of thinking." "Promiscuous sexual relations and constant changing of partners became the rule" among "demoralized blacks," and the rest hardly fared better. "When the yoke of slavery was lifted," he wrote, "the drifting masses were left without any restraint upon their vagrant impulses and wild desires. The old intimacy between master and slave, upon which the moral order of the slave regime had rested, was destroyed forever." Frazier's influential writings paradoxically fed the racist scholarship he attacked. Frazier's error was not that he exaggerated the social crisis accompanying emancipation but his belief that the "moral order of the slave regime . . . rested" on "the old intimacy between master and slave."[7] Some slaves experienced such intimacies, but neither the beliefs and behavior of most slaves nor their familial arrangements depended upon so fragile a bond. The familial condition of the typical ex-slave differed greatly from that emphasized by Frazier and so many others. That is illustrated in the pages which follow. Why the typical ex-slave family was composed of a poor husband, his wife, and their children and what that meant are the subject of the rest of Part One of this book.

[11] No slave family was protected in the law, but upon their emancipation most Virginia ex-slave families had two parents, and most older couples had lived together in long-lasting unions. That is made clear in Union Army population censuses of Montgomery (1866), Princess Anne (1866), and York (1865) county blacks and in Freedmen's Bureau 1866 marriage registers for Louisa, Nelson, Rockbridge, and Goochland county blacks, the only such documents found in the Virginia Freedmen's Bureau manuscript records.[8] The three population censuses describe the composition of 1870 black households in which two or more members had

either blood or marriage ties, and the four marriage registers record the renewal of 2817 slave marriages. [12] Although the blacks in these seven counties had experienced slavery in very different ways, the typical Virginia ex-slave family had at its head a male ex-slave who had been either a common laborer or a field hand. Whether these slaves had lived in plantation or farm counties or in counties with few or many slave residents did not matter. Neither did the diverse ways in which the Civil War had affected these places. Despite their many different slave experiences, these blacks shared a common occupational status. They were very poor. A small number of men had artisan skills, mostly carpenters, blacksmiths, and shoemakers, and hardly any had higher status. A few were servants, but in Montgomery, York, Goochland, and Louisa counties between 85 and 91 percent of all occupations were recorded as farmer, farm laborer, and laborer. The three population censuses show that most Montgomery, York, and Princess Anne families, composed mostly of poor ex-slaves, had adapted to and absorbed the shocks of enslavement, war, emancipation, and migration. Relatively few Montgomery blacks—no more than 12 percent—lived as "single" persons. The rest were members of immediate families. Nearly two-thirds of the 1866 Princess Anne blacks had

---

[7]E. Franklin Frazier, *Negro Family in Chicago* (1932), 33–34; *id., Negro Family in the United States* (1939), 89, 95–98; *id., Negro in the United States* (1949), 313, 627.

[8]Montgomery County, Virginia, manuscript census, 1866, volume 137; York

County, Virginia, manuscript census, 1865, volume 511; Princess Anne County, Virginia, manuscript census, 1866, volume 511; Rockbridge County, Virginia, Marriage Register, volume 271; Nelson County, Virginia, Marriage Register, volume 283; Goochland County, Virginia, Marriage Register, volume 236; Louisa County, Virginia, Marriage Register, volume 280; Virginia Freedmen's Bureau Mss., Record Group 105, National Archives.

**Table 1**  Composition of Black Households with Two or More Residents, Montgomery, York, and Princess Anne Counties, Virginia, 1865–1866

| Type of household | Montgomery County | York County | Princess Anne County |
|---|---|---|---|
| Husband-wife | 18% | 26% | 17% |
| Husband-wife-children | 54 | 53 | 62 |
| Father-children | 5 | 5 | 4 |
| Mother-children | 23 | 16 | 17 |
| Number | 498 | 997 | 375 |

lived in that county fewer than four years. No significant differences existed between long-time residents and migrants. The same percentage in each group lived in families. The York census was sufficiently detailed to reveal that few blacks—less than one in twenty—lived alone, and that the typical household was of modest size. Only 7 of the 997 York households with two or more residents had ten or more persons in it. The largest had fourteen. About one in six had between six and nine residents; more than four in five had between two and five residents.

[13] Equally important, most Montgomery, York, and Princess Anne households with two or more residents had in them either a husband and wife or two parents and their children (Table 1). The more mobile York and Princess Anne blacks had fewer single-parent households than the Montgomery blacks. More significantly, the uniformity in household composition among these ex-slaves in three distinct social settings and the fact that more than three-fourths of the households contained either a father or a husband cast doubt on conventional assertions that slavery had shattered the immediate slave family and made the two-parent household uncommon among poor, rural blacks fresh to legal freedom.

## CRITICAL ANALYSIS: CONTENT

Gutman's study is a stunning example of the use of primary source materials to challenge the "received wisdom" contained in countless secondary works. Gutman characterized his study in more modest terms: "It unfolds a very different story from that found in the pages of E. Franklin Frazier's pioneering study *The Negro Family in the United States* (1939) and in nearly all other standard works on this important subject that rest heavily upon this influential book" [paragraph 7].

The overriding question governing Gutman's research is whether the problems that beset black families today—such as high rates of broken marriages and out-of-wedlock births—can be traced to the adverse effects that slavery had on the family system.

Gutman begins his book with heartrending personal accounts drawn from diaries and letters that testify to the intense familial bonds of their authors. These accounts suggest the possibility that blacks left slavery with powerful family traditions. The key question, however, is how typical are they? Gutman asserts that "women like Hannah Grove and men like Laura Spicer's slave husband were not unusual Afro-Americans" [paragraph 6]. This statement marks the transition from his introduction, which relies on personal documents, to a more systematic analysis of data on the household structure of ex-slaves at the time of their emancipation. Gutman must now prove that Hannah Grove and Laura Spicer's husband, and the family values they personify, were in fact typical of slave culture prior to emancipation.

To do this, Gutman employs population censuses conducted by the Union Army in three counties of Virginia in 1865 and 1866. These data show that most ex-slave families had two parents, and that most older couples had lived together in long-lasting unions. In short, despite the notorious abuses of slavery, more than three-fourths of the households had both parents present. The female-headed household that was the focus of Moynihan's report was the exception, not the rule.

Gutman's concluding statement from the analysis developed in these opening pages of his book is that the findings "cast doubt on conventional assertions that slavery had shattered the immediate slave family and made the two-parent household uncommon among poor, rural blacks fresh to legal freedom" [paragraph 13]. This is a matter of simple empirical fact, easily demonstrated in just a few pages. The rest of Part I of *The Black Family in Slavery and Freedom* attempts to *explain* "why the typical ex-slave family was composed of a poor husband, his wife, and their children and what that meant" [paragraph 10]. This is done through a meticulous study of slave families and kin networks, and how they adapted to the stresses that slavery placed on the family system.

Part II of his study then examines the experience of the descendants of slaves in the late nineteenth and early twentieth centuries. Gutman's data indicate that even as late as 1925, most blacks living in New York City lived in husband-wife families. These historical findings cast new and different light on the crisis that afflicts many black families today. By showing that the crisis cannot be blamed on slavery, or on a defective cultural pattern rooted in slavery, Gutman shifts the attention to conditions of poverty and unemployment that prevail in the nation's ghettos today, and that make it difficult for young blacks to form and maintain families. The moral implications of Gutman's study is that it is *our* crimes, not the crimes of our forefathers, that are responsible for the continuing plight of black America.

## CRITICAL ANALYSIS: COMPOSITION

At first it seems as though Gutman intends to narrate a story of the black family during and after slavery, allowing his subjects to speak for themselves through their letters and diaries. Note the almost storybook beginning:

"This is a book about ordinary black men, women, and children mostly before the general emancipation but after that time, too . . . [paragraph 1]. Gradually, however, the author makes it clear that he is doing more than telling an engaging story. He wants to establish the historical validity of his narrative, and this brings him to a search for systematic data proving that blacks left slavery with powerful family traditions. He also wants to explain how it was that the family was able to survive the abuses of a slave system.

Thus, the rhetorical strategy for this study combines narration and cause-effect. The analysis is causal in that Gutman's overall purpose is to document the effects of slavery on the family system. Within this context, the diaries and letters function as a kind of narrative of how slavery was experienced by black families.

## The Introduction (paragraphs 1 to 2)

The skeptical tone of this essay, which challenges the commonplace assumption that slavery destroyed the black family, is established by the two epigraphs, both by prominent black writers. In different ways DuBois and Ellison suggest that black history should be viewed not through the lens of white society, but from the point of view of blacks themselves. Though Gutman is white, his methods allow him to reconstruct black family history as it was experienced and shaped by blacks. This is the significance of his extensive use of letters and diaries.

The first two paragraphs describe the overall purposes of his study. Paragraph 1 begins with one long, complex, and abstract sentence that seems to mirror the long chain of causation that is the focus of Gutman's study: how enslaved Afro-Americans and their children and grandchildren "adapted to enslavement by developing distinctive domestic arrangements and kin networks that nurtured a new Afro-American culture, and how these, in turn, formed the basis of developing Afro-American communities, which prepared slaves to deal with legal freedom." Paragraph 2 develops this theme by focusing on specific individuals who typify the black experience under slavery. In this way Gutman makes the subject more concrete and personal.

## The Body Paragraphs (paragraphs 3 to 12)

Paragraphs 3 to 11, which constitute the body of this chapter, begin to tell the story of the black family, and to bring into focus Gutman's interpretation of the effects of slavery on the family system.

Paragraphs 3, 4, and 5 present excerpts from letters and diaries—graphic evidence of powerful family bonds. Paragraph 6 then asserts that these letters were "expressions of an adaptive and changing slave culture." In paragraphs 7 to 10, Gutman steps back from this direct testimony and returns to the point raised in the opening paragraph: the need "to begin a long overdue examination" of how blacks adapted their family system to the stresses of slavery and the dislocations associated with emancipation.

Gutman's perspective brings him into conflict with previous scholars who contended that slavery destroyed the black family. Gutman is especially critical of Franklin Frazier, the black sociologist who wrote an influential book called *The Black Family in the United States*. Frazier argued that slavery prevented blacks from developing autonomous, self-regulating families, and that emancipation threw the already weak family into total crisis. Part of Gutman's tack in casting doubt on Frazier's study is to quote passages that today read more like racist fantasy than social science. For example, Frazier wrote: "When the yoke of slavery was lifted, the drifting masses were left without any restraint upon their vagrant impulses and wild desires." Gutman is careful to say that Frazier was not himself a racist, but that his writings "paradoxically fed the racist scholarship he attacked" [paragraph 10]. His error, according to Gutman, was that he "underestimated the adaptive capacities of slaves and ex-slaves" [paragraph 10]. By quoting extensively from Frazier, and documenting the argument that he intends to refute, Gutman has established a rationale for his study, and prepares the reader to grasp the import of his findings.

### The Conclusion (paragraph 13)

In paragraph 12 Gutman presents evidence from public records that substantiate the image conveyed by the letters and diaries; namely, that most ex-slave households conformed to the conventional model of husband, wife, and children. On this basis he reaches his conclusion: the facts "cast doubt on conventional assertions that slavery had shattered the immediate slave family . . ." [paragraph 13]. This thesis statement, which comes near the end of Gutman's first chapter, is a prelude to the rest of his book, which seeks to explore the specific adaptations that allowed the family to survive the stresses of slavery and emancipation.

## RHETORICAL STANCE: PERSUADING THE READER

As a scholar, Gutman wants to make a contribution to the historical record. As a writer, he wants to interest readers in the central argument of his book, and to arouse their curiosity about the voluminous material presented as evidence for this argument. Certainly this is the effect of the evocative title of his first chapter: "Send Me Some of the Children's Hair," which is taken from one of the letters. It is a highly effective title for several reasons. First, it reflects Gutman's determination to let blacks "tell their own story." Also, it conveys a sense of the desperate longing of parents who had been cruelly separated from their own children. Finally, it suggests the major thesis of the book: that blacks had powerful family traditions, even in slavery.

Thus, Gutman simultaneously addresses his readers on two planes: the affective and the intellectual. He stirs their interest in black family history by making them privy to the actual personal correspondence of slaves. And he interprets this history, gaining the readers' confidence by presenting himself as a disciplined scholar, obliged to substantiate his claims with hard evidence. Although he wishes to explore his subject from an insider's point of view, he is also the detached observer who must verify his claims.

Gutman's voice of reason is evident in several ways. Since he is challenging the received wisdom, he is careful to present a substantial exposition of the opposing point of view (paragraphs 9 to 11). Not only does he challenge Frazier's overall conclusions, but he also identifies the "fatal flaw" in his argument: "Frazier's error was not that he exaggerated the social crisis accompanying emancipation but his belief that the 'moral order of the slave regime . . . rested' on 'the old intimacy between master and slave'" [paragraph 10].

Gutman's tone is also fair and precise. He is careful to say that Frazier was "of course, not a racist and vigorously combatted the racial scholarship that dominated early-twentieth-century historical and social-science writings" [paragraph 10]. On the other hand, Gutman is modest in advancing his own claims: His findings "cast doubt" on previous scholarship. He does not pretend to have all the answers. There is yet room for debate.

### Language

The language of this chapter is relatively jargon-free. Yet Gutman also makes his scholarly intentions clear. Note the way in which the deceptively simple first sentence referring to "ordinary black men, women, and children" opens up onto a long and somewhat abstruse depiction of the complex changes that the black family underwent during and after slavery. This sentence reflects both the simple question that governs the research and the complex ramifications of answering it fully. Gutman reiterates his simple purpose in paragraph 2: "Our concern is with what sustained and nurtured their beliefs and behavior. Nothing more." Yet he is compelled to use abstract terms, such as "kin networks" and "domestic arrangements" in constructing his answer. Of course, these terms are part of a shared vocabulary among social scientists about how families and communities are organized.

For the most part, however, Gutman's analysis is presented in unembellished prose, designed to capture the nuances of the black experience during and after slavery: the "harshness" of enslavement; the "severe" dislocations accompanying emancipation; and the adjustment of blacks "fresh" to legal freedom.

### SUGGESTIONS FOR WRITING AND THINKING

1. Turn up some old letters or perhaps a diary from a grandparent or some other family member. On the basis of these documents, develop an analysis around a general theme or concept, such as sex-role

expectations, the crisis of adolescence, or some other topic that is suggested by the available documents. Be sure to incorporate specific quotations into your text to illustrate or document your analysis.

2. Your college library has copies of old newspapers or magazines on microfilm. Figure out what year your mother or father was the same age that you are now. Then identify some area of interest—for example, sports, fashion, or popular music—and use the relevant newspapers to develop a comparison between your parent's era and yours. Make use of feature articles, stories, or even advertisements that provide documentary evidence to support your conclusions.

## DOCUMENTARY STUDIES ACROSS THE DISCIPLINES

### Anthropology

HANDLER, RICHARD, and DANIEL A. SEGAL, "Hierarchies of Choice: The Social Construction of Rank in Jane Austen," *American Ethnologist*, 12 (November 1985), 691–706. On the basis of Jane Austen's novels, the authors develop an analysis of social hierarchy in early nineteenth-century England.

### Economics

McGEE, JOHN S., "Predatory Price Cutting: The Standard Oil (N.J.) Case," *Journal of Law and Economics*, I (October 1958), 137–69. The author uses court records to challenge one of the great legends of American capitalism—that John Rockefeller and the Standard Oil Company used predatory price cutting to drive out competition.

### History

SHAMMAS, CAROLE, "The Domestic Environment in Early Modern England and America," *Journal of Social History*, 14 (Fall 1980), 3–24. The author uses probate inventories, which list the personal property of recently deceased people, to analyze changes in "the domestic environment" between the sixteenth and eighteenth centuries, with respect to household possessions, the family meal, and patterns of consumption.

### Political Science

BRANDS, JR., H. W., "Decisions on American Armed Intervention: Lebanon, Dominican Republic, and Grenada," *Political Science Quarterly*, 102, no. 4 (1987), 607–24. The author relies heavily on presidential papers and other official records to analyze the decision-making process that led to armed intervention in Lebanon in 1958, the Dominican Republic in 1965, and Grenada in 1983.

### *Psychology*

LOEWENBERG, PETER, "The Psychohistorical Origins of the Nazi Youth Cohort," *American Historical Review*, 76 (December 1971), 1457–1502. The author applies psychological concepts to argue that the childhood traumas experienced by a generation of Germans who were children or adolescents during World War II predisposed many of them to become ardent followers of Naziism.

### *Sociology*

ARONSON, SIDNEY H., "The Sociology of the Bicycle," *Social Forces*, XXX (1952), 305–12. This article uses old books and popular magazines to document the moral controversy and social conflict that accompanied the introduction of the bicycle into American cities during the late nineteenth century, and the impact that the bicycle had on such disparate areas of social life as the economy, the military, women's attire, and leisure-time activities.

# Part III
# THE FORMS OF ACADEMIC WRITING

---

## Chapter 10
# THE SUMMARY

---

The summary is a basic form of writing about research. Its chief aim is to identify the controlling idea of a work and to condense the information and arguments used to develop that idea. Strictly speaking, the summary precludes analysis, interpretation, and evaluation. Rather, it constitutes a straightforward distillation of a book, article, or report. The scope of the summary depends upon your purpose and audience. For example, if you are taking notes in preparation for a term paper, and you wish to generate a bibliography that will help you to remember the essential point of each source that you have read or scanned, then your summary can be brief. It might consist of a few sentences or even phrases that indicate the central idea and its relevance for your own work.

Suppose that you are not writing a term paper, but are sharing your library research as part of a class project or reporting on assigned readings. In this case, you are informing others who are not familiar with a work. Ideally, your summary should convey enough information to grasp the author's purpose and argument without overwhelming your audience with too much detail.

Finally, suppose you are asked to present a formal summary of a work or a number of works on a particular subject. If you are given such an assignment, be sure you are clear about the length, format, and level of detail that is expected in your presentation. Whatever its length or scope, however, the key to writing a good summary is to be comprehensive, yet concise.

How is it possible to be comprehensive and concise at the same time? The "trick" is to capture the main thrust of a work—to distill it down to its bare essentials. Obviously, a great deal of material is left out. At the least, however, a good summary will report the author's main conclusion, and the most important evidence supporting this conclusion.

In this chapter, we present the basic forms of summary that appear in professional publications: the annotation, the abstract, the report, and the review. As will be seen, these forms differ mainly in length and scope. As students, you may also be asked to develop an annotated bibliography on a particular subject, to write an abstract of a paper (yours or someone else's), to present a report, or to review a book or a body of material. Thus, the examples presented below can serve as models for your own writing.

One additional point. The ability to distill a large body of material to its "bare essentials" is a basic skill that applies to listening, reading, and thinking, as well as to writing. This skill also comes into play in an exam situation where you are expected to state the main point of a reading, and there is not enough time to go into great detail. Therefore, insofar as writing different kinds of summaries helps you to master this skill, it may make you a better listener, reader, and thinker, as well as a better writer.

## THE ANNOTATION

Annotations are usually encountered as part of an *annotated bibliography* where each work is accompanied with an explanatory note describing the work. By definition, an annotation is brief, usually not more than a few sentences. A good annotation indicates the author's thesis, method, and major findings or conclusions. In some instances it may mention the author's intended audience, or other salient details.

Here are two sample annotations. The first one refers to Herbert Gutman's book on the black family which we excerpted in Chapter 9:

> Gutman, Herbert G. *The Black Family in Slavery and Freedom, 1750–1925.* 1976. Pantheon Books.
>
> The author utilizes slave narratives, plantation records and census tracts to document the continued existence of a strong, universal family structure in both slave and postslave society.[1]

Thus, in one carefully crafted sentence this writer has provided a capsule summary of Gutman's entire book, at least to the extent of indicating the research materials on which the study was based ("slave narratives, plantation records and census tracts"), and the author's thesis ("the continued existence of a strong, universal family structure in both slave and postslave society").

---

[1]This is an annotation of a review published in *Book Review Digest,* 1976–77.

Here is a slightly more detailed annotation of a study of parental aid to married children:

Adams, Bert N. "Structural Factors Affecting Parental Aid to Married Children." *Journal of Marriage and the Family*, 1964, 26 (3), pp. 327–331.
Examines the effect of residence, length of child's marriage, occupational level, and the sex of the child upon parental aid. The findings reveal that receiving aid is greatest during the young couple's first ten years of marriage. Financial help is given more frequently to middle-class children than to those in the working class. In addition, in both classes, the wife's parents help more often than do the husband's parents.[2]

This annotation lists the factors that were explored as "predictors" of parental aid, and then summarizes the principal findings.

As is clear from the preceding examples, annotations vary in style and scope. However, most annotations have the following characteristics:

- Bibliographic details.
- A comprehensive sentence that states the overriding purpose or thesis of the study.
- Description of research questions, method, and sources of data.
- Key phrases from the original text that alert readers to essential ideas and research questions.

As we mentioned earlier, you are most likely to encounter the annotation when you consult a reference volume, such as the *Social Science Index*. Under some circumstances you may be asked to write annotations yourself. Some instructors routinely ask students to hand in an annotated bibliography before writing their term papers. Even if you are not required to do this, you might find it a useful step, since writing annotations forces you to condense a large body of material, and to identify and think about the key points in your reading. For the same reasons, writing annotations is a useful device in preparing for exams.

## THE ABSTRACT

Compared to an annotation, an abstract is a more fully developed summary, usually about 100 to 200 words in length. Many professional journals require authors to provide abstracts that are printed at the beginning of an article. In addition, each of the social sciences publishes a monthly journal (*Anthropological Abstracts, Psychological Abstracts*, and so on) that provides abstracts of articles published in major journals within the discipline and related fields (see Appendix A). The function of these abstracts is to allow readers and researchers to keep abreast of recent developments in

---

[2]Diana K. Harris, *The Sociology of Aging: An Annotated Bibliography and Sourcebook* (New York: Garland Publishing, Inc., 1985), pp. 117–18.

their fields, and to efficiently locate studies related to their particular interests.

Generally speaking, the abstract follows the standard divisions of the research paper: statement of the problem, research objectives, method, results and conclusions. Here is the abstract that was published with Parelius's article "Emerging Sex-Role Attitudes, Expectations, and Strains Among College Women" (see Chapter 8):

Questionnaire data are used to assess the attitudes of female college students toward various dimensions of their adult sex roles, their perceptions of men's attitudes toward women's roles, the degree to which these attitudes and perceptions have changed between 1969 and 1973, and the possibility that strains are arising with these changes. A marked shift toward feminism was found in the women's attitudes, but little change occurred in their perception of men as relatively conservative. Strains may be developing as more women adopt attitudes which they believe men reject.[3]

Studies that do not conform to a rigorous scientific model are abstracted in terms of whatever divisions are inherent in the work itself. Here is the abstract of Ned Polsky's article on "The Hustler" (see Chapter 7) published in *Sociological Abstracts:*

Polsky, Ned, "The Hustler," *Social Problems,* 1964, 12, 1, 3–15.

A study of the poolroom hustler (one who participates in a game of pool engineered through skills of deception to be a "sure thing"). Methods used were: (1) participant observation of hustlers & personal involvement with the poolroom world; & (2) extended informal talks with hustlers. . . . The poolroom situation is so structured that ordinary methods of cheating are obviated but deceit is possible by feigning near-misses while sustaining the impression of keeping good form. The hustler relies on his ability to "con" another player into a game & to keep his opponent playing successively; hence the margin of gain through betting on each game must be sufficiently small to sustain the other player's interest. The hustler never shows his true skill and restrains himself from making many difficult shots & occasionally permits his opponent to win. . . . The hustler's main skills consist of good salesmanship; the ability to function efficiently despite distractions or heavy "action"; & stamina. . . . The hustler's context of action is constraining & he must involve himself in personal ways through active "conning"; he must work in poor settings & must depend "on being a continuously self-aware 'actor.'"[4]

This is a long abstract, approximately 400 words in its entirety. Like the article, the abstract presents a considerable amount of detail. Note, however, that the abstract organizes this detail by referring to the major division of the study: methods of observation; the "modes" of poolroom betting; the hustler's "main skills"; the hustler's work "context."

Thus, the abstract is like the annotation except that it includes some-

---

[3]Ann P. Parelius, "Emerging Sex-Role Attitudes, Expectations, and Strains Among College Women," *Journal of Marriage and the Family,* 37 (February 1975), 146.

[4]*Sociological Abstracts,* XIII, no. 1 (1965), 75.

what more detail, especially detail that is essential to the author's thesis. In the case of Parelius, we are given the two major findings and the overall conclusion. In the case of Polsky, we are presented with what the hustler does, how he must act, the boundaries of the game, and the environment in which he must function, all related to the "art of deception."

As a student, you may be asked to abstract a number of books and articles so that your instructor can determine that you have read and understood assignments. In writing an abstract:

- Begin with a statement of the work's purpose or thesis.
- Allude to the major divisions or organizing principles of the work.
- Write a coherent paragraph summarizing the contents. For the most part this should be in your own words, although it is a good idea to incorporate key terms or phrases from the original source. These should be enclosed in quotation marks.

## THE REPORT

The report is the most extensive form of summary. Basically, there are two kinds of reports. The first presents a full-fledged account of an investigation, a meeting, or perhaps a legislative proceeding. The second kind of report synthesizes a variety of sources. Thus, unlike the annotation or abstract, the report is based on more than one source. It also differs from the research paper in that its aim is to summarize rather than to evaluate, interpret, or advance an original point of view.

As an example, let us take a report on legislative and judicial efforts to control drunk drivers, published in *The Urban Lawyer*. The original report was thirteen pages long, and therefore we are printing an abstract of this report which appeared in *Sage Urban Studies Abstracts*.

Pearl, L. D. The Party's Over: Controlling Drunk Drivers. *The Urban Lawyer*, 17 (4) 812–826, Fall, 1985.

President Reagan appointed a Presidential Commission on Drunk Driving in April, 1982, and in so doing noted that out of 50,000 highway deaths in 1981, drunk drivers were involved in 25,000; in addition, some 750,000 injuries were attributed to drunk drivers. In recent years, the war against drunk drivers has escalated considerably; two of the more interesting developments, the author finds, are as follows: (1) Several courts have held social hosts liable for serving liquor to minors who, after drinking, kill or injure other persons or themselves on the highway. Two courts have imposed liability on a social host for serving liquor to an adult. (2) Congress has developed financial incentives to encourage states to raise their minimum legal drinking age to 21; this approach having failed, though, for the most part, Congress has exchanged the proverbial carrot for the stick: cutting federal highway funds to those states which fail to take the desired action. The author examines policy and legal issues raised by such efforts.[5]

[5]*Sage Urban Studies Abstracts,* 142 (May 1986), entry 396.

The abstract, like the full report, begins by citing statistics that point up the magnitude of the problem of drunk driving. It then goes on to document relevant court decisions and Congressional actions. Thus, the report synthesizes a number of different sources and provides a useful, up-to-date compilation of available material relevant to the escalating "war against drunk driving."

As students, you may be asked to prepare a similar report on the basis of government publications, newspaper accounts, or other sources. Or you may be asked to present a report of a book or a series of articles on a common subject. As with all the summary forms described above, your report should begin with an overview. If your report deals with a single book, this overview should indicate its purpose or thesis. If the report synthesizes the contents of more than one work, then the introduction should include a statement about the issue that connects them. The remainder of the report would then discuss each work in terms of that initial statement.

For example, in a class assignment one student had the following unifying statement in his introductory paragraph: "There are a number of studies that demonstrate the usefulness of the developmental approach to learning in trying to understand the influence of television on young children." He then went on to discuss specific studies in relation to this common topic.

## THE REVIEW

Thus far, we have defined the summary as a condensation or synthesis of sources that is presented with little or no commentary. The writer of the summary remains in the background. However, the summary is often part of a longer essay in which the writer goes on to analyze the work and to assess its strengths and weaknesses. The book *report* becomes a *review* when it evaluates as well as summarizes.

Here is an excerpt from a review of Herbert Gutman's book *The Black Family in Slavery and Freedom:*

> HERBERT G. GUTMAN. *The Black Family in Slavery and Freedom, 1750–1925.* New York: Pantheon Books, 1976. Pp. xxviii, 664.
>
> Herbert G. Gutman's book has received much publicity in the news media as well as in long reviews, both laudatory and critical. Challenging traditional theories of black family disorganization and "pathology," Gutman contends that even centuries of slavery and injustice failed to weaken the remarkable "adaptive capacities" of Afro-Americans. At least until the 1920s, he argues, blacks managed to preserve cultural traditions, family continuities, and the "double-headed kin related household."
>
> The first eight of Gutman's ten long chapters deal with the black family in slavery, and his central evidence consists of plantation records, a few surviving county census schedules, and Freedmen's Bureau records, especially of

validated marriages. Whatever the faults of Gutman's study, this information is invaluable—in the place of a few observers' impressions, one is now confronted with *some* information about the lives of tens of thousands of largely illiterate and unskilled Americans, the ancestors of living Americans. This evidence, often interpreted with skill and imagination, dramatically reinforces the key theme of the best recent works on American Negro slavery: that the worst barbarities of human bondage could coexist with a kind of accommodation between black and white cultures. The controversial point is whether the relative autonomy and perseverance of black family life was a wholly independent force, as Gutman maintains, immune from white-determined rules of the game, rules pragmatically chosen to ensure the stability of the slave regime.

Gutman is not always sensitive to the limitations and ambiguity of his evidence. . . .[6]

Like the one-sentence annotation that we examined earlier, the first two paragraphs of this review provide a summary of Gutman's book. At the end of the second paragraph, however, the reviewer identifies a "controversial point." This marks the transition from summary to analysis. The reviewer begins by critically assessing Gutman's evidence on this controversial issue, leading to an extended discussion (not reprinted here) in which the reviewer advances his own point of view on the issues raised by Gutman's book.

Typically, the student-reviewer does not have the skill or confidence to challenge the findings or conclusions of a professional social scientist. Thus, most students *report* on books rather than review them. However, any thoughtful reader can pose questions regarding the logic or applicability of a particular work, or assess its merits or shortcomings. Our purpose in the next chapter is to show you what it means to adopt "a critical perspective."

## SUGGESTIONS FOR WRITING AND THINKING

1. On the basis of your general knowledge and interests, formulate a topic for a social science paper. Develop an annotated bibliography of at least five sources that relate to this topic. Appendix A, "Selective Reference Works in the Social Sciences," will help you in your library search.

2. Chapter 6 included a study by Rosenthal and Jacobson entitled "Teacher Expectations for the Disadvantaged." Write an annotation, an abstract, and a longer review (1 to 2 pages) of this article.

3. Repeat the above exercise for Polsky's study of "The Poolroom Hustler," reprinted in Chapter 7.

---

[6]The reviewer is David Brion Davis, *American Historical Review*, 82 (June 1977), 744–45.

# Chapter 11
# THE CRITICAL PAPER

The aim of the critical paper is to clarify, dispute, or otherwise analyze a text by another writer. Thus, a critical paper (or "critique," as it is sometimes called) goes beyond summarizing a work's content to interpreting or criticizing its central findings or ideas. A critical paper may also explore the implications or usefulness of these findings or ideas for other concerns, not necessarily those considered by the author.

As we noted in Chapter 3, a "critical stance" does not necessarily involve a negative attitude or judgment. When you adopt a critical perspective, you examine an author's claims. Instead of passively absorbing what the author has written, you are, in a sense, entering into a written dialogue with the author, searching for new meanings and relevance.

Students often feel unequipped to enter into such a dialogue with a professional social scientist. To be sure, the average undergraduate does not have the background to evaluate the validity of data put forward in professional publications. Nevertheless, even with limited background and knowledge, there is a great deal that students *can* do, and it is the purpose of this chapter to provide some guidelines and principles that will be useful when you are called upon to write a critical paper.

There are two kinds of critical papers that are commonly assigned in social science courses. The first asks students to develop a *critical interpretation* of one or more works. The second involves an original *application of a concept*—usually to a situation that the student has observed firsthand. We address these separately in the pages that follow.

## THE CRITICAL INTERPRETATION

Criticism begins with a responsive reading. At the least, you should jot down notes in the margin in response to passages that you see as persuasive, provocative, or problematic. Where appropriate, you should also record more extensive comments on note cards. After your initial reading, review your notes and the text once again. At this point you might find it useful to brainstorm or freewrite in order to generate some preliminary ideas. Make sure that you have grasped the author's argument on its own terms before you launch into a full-fledged critique.

In developing this critique, it is not enough to summarize a work, and then to declare your admiration or skepticism. You need to specify exactly what passages or ideas you are responding to, and explain your response in a coherent discussion.

### Probing the Work

The key to developing a critical interpretation is knowing how to probe a work—that is, knowing what questions to ask about it. Let us distinguish among three kinds of questions: those pertaining to summary, to analysis, and to application.

*Summary.* The first step in writing a critical interpretation is to accurately represent its contents. In doing this, keep in mind the discussion presented in Chapter 5 on the logical structure of social science writing. You may want to apply the schema of questions-evidence-answers, much as we did to the sample essays in Chapters 6 to 9 of this book. Specifically:

1. What is the author's stated purpose in writing the article or book? Do not overlook the preface of a book which is often revealing of an author's intentions.
2. What is the main issue being explored? Are there opposing points of view on this issue?
3. What is the central question that governs the work?
4. What methods or sources of data are used in addressing the central question?
5. What are the principal findings?
6. What conclusion does the author come to? How are the findings linked to the conclusion?
7. Does the author take issue with findings or conclusions put forward by other writers?

This is not intended as a checklist of questions that you should cover in serial order. Even if you do not explicitly incorporate them into your paper, however, these are questions that you should be clear about before launching into your critique. They will sharpen your understanding of the text, and lay the groundwork for more critical evaluation.

*Analysis.* A second set of questions makes the transition from summary to analysis, and probes the work in terms of its internal logic. To do this effectively, you need to examine how an argument is developed and substantiated. Try also to identify assumptions that are not stated explicitly, and thus are not part of your summary. The following questions are often useful:

1. Are there any flaws in the reasoning? What are the premises, and do you agree with them? Assuming that you agree with the premises, do you think they lead to the conclusion as stated? Has the author evaded any important issues?
2. What assumptions or unstated claims underlie the argument? Do you think that the author has overstated the argument—that is, is it fully supported by the data presented?
3. If a causal argument is presented, do you accept the author's identification of cause and effect, or is this a case of spurious causation (see Chapter 4)? Is there confusion between correlation and cause?

Students often have difficulty grasping what is meant by "assumptions," "unstated claims," and "spurious causation." Consider the following passage from Thomas Sowell's *Ethnic America*:

> With many generations of discouragement of initiative and with little incentive to work any more than necessary to escape punishment, slaves developed foot-dragging, work-evading patterns that were to remain as a cultural legacy long after slavery itself disappeared. Duplicity and theft were also pervasive patterns among antebellum slaves, and these too remained long after slavery ended.[1]

Is Sowell correct in assuming that under slavery blacks developed "foot-dragging, work-evading patterns?" Except for a few perfunctory citations to other studies, he provides no direct evidence to support this key assumption. Secondly, even if it is true that slaves did develop poor work habits, what evidence is there to support Sowell's assumption that this became "a cultural legacy" passed down from one generation to the next? Finally, there is the unstated claim that these cultural patterns, developed centuries ago, not only continue down to the present, but also help to explain why many blacks are still mired in poverty (a clear case of spurious causation). Thus, Sowell has piled one unsubstantiated claim upon another, resulting in a weak, if not fallacious argument.

*Implications.* The previous set of questions probe a work "on its own terms"—that is, in terms of its internal logic and validity. A third set of questions probe the implications of a work in terms of a broader range of issues and concerns. Here it is appropriate to introduce whatever background knowledge you have—whether from life experience or from academic sources. To illustrate the kinds of questions that are in order, let us refer to Rosenthal and Jacobson's "Teacher Expectations for the Disadvantaged" (see Chapter 6):

1. Does the study shed light on the issue at hand (why disadvantaged children fail in school)?

[1]Thomas Sowell, *Ethnic America* (New York: Basic Books, 1981), p. 187.

2. How does this study apply to your own life experience? Does "Teacher Expectations for the Disadvantaged" give you any new insight into your own early education? After reading this work, do you think that your social class background worked to your advantage or disadvantage?
3. Does the work conflict with other readings on the subject? If so, can you reconcile these differences?
4. Finally, does the study stir any ideas about related issues? For example, is it possible that math teachers have lower expectations for females than for males? How could this be determined, and what are the implications of such a finding?

## Organizing the Essay

The preceding sets of questions are designed to help you develop a critical perspective on the work, and to generate ideas. The next step is to organize your essay. Using your notes, you might begin by formulating a central idea about the work. Then develop a thesis statement, which is your critical judgment about that central idea. Your thesis statement might affirm, qualify, or perhaps dispute an aspect of the author's argument.

Like all essays, the critical paper has an introduction, a body, and a conclusion. It is usually a good idea to work your thesis into your introduction. In one to three sentences, the thesis should summarize a key idea in the work, along with your response to that idea. In order to sustain your focus, you may have to leave out comments that do not relate to your thesis.

Here is an example of how one student, Sharon Goldstein, incorporated her thesis in her opening paragraph of her critique of Franz Fanon's *Wretched of the Earth:*

> According to Franz Fanon, the only way a person who has been oppressed and dehumanized in a colonial situation can regain his or her humanity is through violence against the oppressor. Whether or not the oppressed individual can regain his or her humanity inevitably depends on one's definition of "humanity." In this essay I will discuss two aspects of what it is to be human, and suggest that in situations where one must resort to violence in order to gain one's freedom, the fulfillment of one of these aspects precludes the attainment of the other.

Thesis Statement

It is possible to introduce a critical paper with a more complete summary of the text, and then go on to develop your commentary of one or two major points. However, this plan forces the reader to wait for the purpose of the essay to become clear. In any event, summary is indispensable. Even when your thesis is included in the introduction, you must accurately represent the author's argument. Be sure to highlight the points essential to your critique.

The body of the critical essay is the development of your critique. As indicated earlier, you may examine the author's assumptions or the implications of an argument. The critique may employ one or more of the rhetorical strategies that we outlined in Chapter 4.

For example, in the critique of Fanon's *Wretched of the Earth* alluded to above, these are some of the rhetorical strategies that the author could have used:

> *Comparison-Contrast.* Sharon could have located a critic of Fanon, compared and contrasted the two positions, and entered the debate either by taking sides or by attempting to reconcile the opposing points of view.
>
> *Cause-Effect.* Sharon could have critically examined Fanon's assumption about the positive psychological effects of violence on the part of the colonized. Is it correct to assume that the rage of the oppressed is purged through violence, and if so, what is the psychological process that is at work?
>
> *Illustration.* Sharon could have illustrated Fanon's point by documenting a specific case of anticolonial violence—for example, by the Algerians against the French. Or she could have found parallels in her own life experience that might have provided a personal basis for assessing Fanon's thesis.

The rhetorical strategy that Sharon actually used to develop her critique was *definition*. She takes issue with Fanon's assumptions regarding a key term—humanity—and suggests that a redefinition of that term leads to a different conclusion. Here is Sharon's essay in its entirety:

### FRANZ FANON AND THE MEANING OF "HUMANITY"

According to Franz Fanon, the only way a person who has been oppressed and dehumanized in a colonial situation can regain his or her humanity is through violence against the oppressor. Whether or not the oppressed individual can regain his or her humanity inevitably depends on one's definition of "humanity." In this essay I will discuss two aspects of what it is to be human, and suggest that in situations where one must resort to violence in order to gain one's freedom, the fulfillment of one of these aspects precludes the attainment of the other. The recognition of this conflict leads me to question the confidence with which Fanon asserts that men, once oppressed, can ever truly capture their humanity.

*Thesis Statement*

Fanon claims that violence "frees the native from his inferiority complex and from his despair and inaction; it makes him fearless and restores his self-respect" (p. 73). When Fanon speaks of "self-respect," he is describing one of the two aspects of humanity alluded to above—that is, the capacity to feel that one has control over one's life, that one is free from arbitrary domination by others. Without this sense, one is left to feel inferior, anxious, and undignified. When individuals have been oppressed through colonization, they inevitably lose their sense of control: their actions are restricted, they are discriminated against, they are treated as inferiors. Under these circumstances the only way for the native to regain control over his life is to overthrow his oppressors.

*Summary of Fanon's position*

There is, however, a second dimension to being human, at least according to this writer: the capacity to be humane—to act in accordance with a feeling of compassion and respect for one's fellow beings. An essential aspect of being humane is to abhor cruelty and brutality, which in turn precludes ever intentionally taking the life of another person. It is this aspect of humanity which is undermined by acts of violence. This is especially true in the case of violence directed against innocent people, for

*Student's critique*

these acts cannot even be rationalized as necessary to destroy the oppressor. By being confronted with one's capacity to maliciously and cold-bloodedly harm another human being, one forever loses a certain innocence—an innocence which is essential to the particular conception of humanity here being discussed—an innocence which the native perhaps knew before the oppression of his people.

Conclusion     In conclusion, I agree with Fanon in his conviction that violence can recreate the dignity of the oppressed. It can do so, however, only at the cost of disillusionment and the destruction of another key aspect of a man or woman's humanity. Fanon underestimates the damage done to the psyche of those who are colonized and oppressed by suggesting that this offense to humanity can ever be rightfully repaired.

Sharon's essay is clearly unified around her critical response to Fanon's thesis regarding violence against the oppressor. On the one hand, she acknowledges the value of Fanon's insight into the psychology of the oppressed, the need of the colonized to fight back in order to reclaim their humanity. On the other hand, she questions Fanon's implicit definition of "humanity." Sharon contends that Fanon's definition is too limited and leads him to underestimate the costs of seeking to restore one's dignity through the use of violence. By redefining this key term, she qualifies Fanon's argument.

Because this is a brief essay, its structure is readily apparent. The introductory paragraph presents an overview of the paper—a brief statement of Fanon's position and the student's critique of this position. The second paragraph elaborates on Fanon's position. The third paragraph elaborates on the student's critique. The concluding paragraph restates the student's main point, culminating with a reassessment of Fanon's position.

## APPLICATION OF A CONCEPT

As we noted in Chapter 1, social scientists have concepts that enable them to see the social world differently from journalists and other observers. Much pedagogy in social science courses consists of introducing students to the key concepts in a particular field of study. To help them develop analytical skills and to deepen their understanding of concepts, students are often assigned papers in which they are expected to *apply* a concept to a particular event or situation.

For example, students in a course on American government might be asked to apply Jefferson's concept of "democracy" to the local government of their community. Students in an economics course might apply the concept of "perfect competition" to the school voucher program. Students in a sociology class might be asked to do an observational study of "alienation" among students at their college. Each of these is a case study involving the original application of a concept, based on observation or life experience.

Indeed, applying concepts in order to shed new and different light is the "stuff" of social science, and professional social scientists have a "mental dictionary" of concepts that they draw upon, applying the ones that seem most relevant to the problem at hand.

The following example comes from an article by two sociologists, Rose and Lewis Coser, on the tragedy at Jonestown, the commune in Guyana where over nine hundred Americans participated in a mass suicide in 1977. The Cosers argued that Jonestown can best be understood as belonging to a class of "greedy institutions." This was a concept that Lewis Coser coined four years earlier in a book by that title:

> Yet the modern world . . . continues to spawn organizations and groups which . . . make total claims on their members and which attempt to encompass within their circle the whole personality. These might be called *greedy institutions*, insofar as they seek exclusive and undivided loyalty and they attempt to reduce the claims of competing roles and status positions on those they wish to encompass within their boundaries. Their demands on the person are omnivorous.[2]

When the Jonestown tragedy occurred, the Cosers realized that this concept applied with chilling exactitude. Thus the subtitle of their article: "A Greedy Institution in the Jungle."

The excerpt below consists of the first eight paragraphs of their article.[3]

### JONESTOWN AS A PERVERSE UTOPIA:
#### A "Greedy Institution" in the Jungle

For 20 days, until December 8, the Jonestown horror story made first-page news in the *New York Times*. In the course of five hours, 911 adults and children were killed or killed themselves. There had been no threat on their lives from the outside, nor was there any strong transcendental cause that leader or followers meant to serve. The leader had claimed he wanted "socialism" and "Marxism," and had mixed his missionary zeal with religion because he allegedly believed the followers "needed it." So for years he gave them "opium for the people," and in the end cyanide.

The questions that are usually being asked are: What kind of people were those commune members? Were they without roots? Were they the rejects of society—the drug addicts, the convicts, the prostitutes, those not embedded in the social fabric of their society? And who was the leader? What manner of man commanded such obedience? How did he grow up in the small town where he was born? Had he given signs of such wickedness earlier in his life?

It turned out that the followers were of all kinds. There were the poor, the rich, and those of the middle. There were convicts and there were lawyers; there were the elderly and young prostitutes; there were physicians and nurses, blacks and whites. There were those with weak moral beliefs, and those with a strong social conscience. The answers about the characteristics of the mem-

---

[2]Lewis Coser, *Greedy Institutions* (New York: The Free Press, 1974), p. 4.

[3]Reprinted by permission of the authors and publisher from Rose Laub Coser and Lewis Coser, "Jonestown as a Perverse Utopia," *Dissent*, 26 (Spring 1979), 158–59.

bers are not satisfactory. At best they tell us who was attracted to Jim Jones, but they cannot tell us why they obeyed him unto death.

Nor do the characteristics of the leader tell us much. It is interesting to hear that as a child he killed animals, and said mass after their death; and that his mother had predicted her son would be a messiah. But surely, the Jekyll-Hyde personality is a frequent figure, and many people have fantasies of omnipotence. Some even become murderers, and occasionally there is one who manages to kill as many as a dozen people. But they do not kill, or are not capable of killing, almost a thousand people in one sweep. This is hard work. While psychological predispositions in the leader and his followers explain some of their mutual attraction, they cannot fully explain this horrible success story.

Let us turn from personal to structural characteristics. Perverse as it was, Jonestown was a species of the genus, *utopian commune*. Ever since the industrial revolution and earlier—already in antiquity—usually at times of widespread discontent with the quality of life, blueprints for a more satisfying social organization were drawn up, from *The Republic* to *Utopia* (which coined the generic name) to *Looking Backward*. These utopias transcended the here-and-now, served as guidelines for social criticism and as foci for human strivings. Yet, as Lewis Coser and Henry Jacoby wrote years ago, "We are appalled to discover that many of the rationalistic fantasies of the world improvers contain a large admixture of what we now recognize as totalitarianism" (*Common Cause*, February 1951).

Not only blueprints but actual experiments in utopian living attracted over the years the socially committed and the morally courageous, the physically and psychologically deprived, and those yearning for a new morality. Yet, in most communes morals and social relations tended to become regulated from above; personal and public allegiances were monopolized by a central authority; and what had started out as an experiment in liberation usually ended in an experiment in the total absorption of personality. Communes have an innate tendency to become, as one of the authors wrote, *greedy institutions*.

Communes did not usually end in the destruction of their members, and some of those inspired by vigorous religious beliefs even managed to survive for several generations. But most ended in splits, fights between factions, acrid disputes, mutual recriminations, and sordid intrigues between rival leaders. Their isolation from other social institutions, their inward orientation, the absorption of the members' total personality often led to a disintegration of the commune, even as it deprived members of the ability to sustain personal relations both within and without.

Jonestown was a community isolated by design. In a sense, if not literally, it was an incestuous community. To survive for even the short period it did, it operated in secrecy, erected strong barriers around itself. Rank-and-file members had to break all ties with the outside. This prevented interference from nonbelievers, but mainly it prevented reality testing. Any personal or social values members brought with them from their previous lives were destroyed. Finally, any personal relations, whether sexual or otherwise affective, were broken up. This assured the absence of interpersonal allegiances. It also assured complete dependency, similar to the dependency of a newborn child, on one person, and one person only.

Note the logical structure of this introductory section. Paragraph 1 summarizes the horrible events at Jonestown. Paragraph 2 alludes to the questions "that are usually being asked" by journalists and others. Paragraphs 3 and 4 show that the answers to these questions, advanced by journalists and other commentators, do not go far enough in explaining this extraordinary event. Paragraph 5 begins with a transitional sentence, "Let us turn from personal to structural characteristics," and begins to develop the thesis statement, explicitly stated in paragraph 6: "Communes have an innate tendency to become . . . greedy institutions." Paragraphs 7 and 8 elaborate on the thesis statement.

The body of the article (not reprinted here) proceeds to show how Jonestown essentially devoured its members, to the point that they lost the capacity to function as independent adults. The Cosers bring their paper to the following conclusion (note how the first paragraph essentially restates the thesis, while the second paragraph explores some of the larger implications of their analysis):

> Jonestown was more "greedy" an institution than has probably ever existed. It successfully "devoured" its members by making total claims on them and by encompassing their whole personality. By claiming, and receiving, undivided loyalty, and by reducing the claims of competing roles and allegiances, it succeeded not merely in totally absorbing members within its boundaries but in reducing them to human pulp as well. Not only did it erect insurmountable boundaries between the inside and the outside, between the "reborn" collective present of the members and their "disreputable" private past; it also succeeded in maiming them by breaking up any mutual attachments, sexual or otherwise. The stable relationship, *voila l'ennemi*.
>
> Even as we recoil in horror at the unfolding of the Jonestown story it behooves us not to look at it in isolation. It did, after all, unfold at this time and in this place. While it would be fatuous to blame what happened on "American society," we must keep in mind that the damned and the lost and the hopeful who flocked to Jones and the People's Temple did so because the society in which they lived had failed to provide satisfactory bonds, meaningful community, and fraternal solidarities. To Jones's followers, the society felt like a desert devoid of love; so they turned to the People's Temple, which they saw as an oasis. Although their quest turned out to be a delusion, we cannot deny that their need was acute.

The Cosers' article is a stunning example of how a concept can be applied to yield new insight. In their hands the concept of "greedy institutions" not only illuminates the grisly events at Jonestown, but in doing so, makes a compelling point about the alienation that is characteristic of American society generally.

It goes without saying that your instructors have less lofty expectations when they ask you to write a paper involving an original application of a concept. Let us examine a successful student paper. In a class on "The Community" students had been assigned two readings on the family that presented conflicting theories concerning the American family. The first, an article by Busacca and Ryan, "Beyond the Family Crisis," argued that the traditional nuclear family is in shambles.[4] The second, a chapter in Claude

[4]Richard Busacca and Mary Ryan, "Beyond the Family Crisis," *Democracy*, 3 (Spring 1983), 79–92.

Fischer's book, *The Urban Experience*, argued that the family has successfully adapted to the stresses of modern society.[5] Students were asked to apply the positions put forward in these two readings to their own life experience. Below is an excerpt from a paper by Bea King:

> Although the family is the most intimate and basic unit of society, some sociologists contend that this ancient institution is on the verge of extinction. According to these writers, urbanism weakens the family and is stripping it of its historic functions, which have been coopted by other social institutions. The workplace, the school, the shopping mall, and the club have all encroached on the family, and people increasingly rely on networks of co-workers and friends rather than family members for emotional support. The end result, as Busacca and Ryan argue, is that the home has become "little more than boarding houses for those with blood ties."
>
> This does not happen to be the case with my family. Although we live in the midst of one of the largest cities in the world, my family still conforms to the ideal-typical nuclear family, consisting of a working father, a housewife/mother, and a child. Although we go our separate ways, we do manage to get together at least once a day to hear what each other has to say. Even if it is for only a few minutes, those few minutes make a big difference.
>
> Although my family is lax in some areas, it is very strong in others, such as holidays and extended family gatherings. In my family it's a must to be home for Christmas and Christmas eve, and there is no possible excuse for not being present, even now that I am an adult. Many of my friends spend holidays with friends and boyfriends, but I spend mine with my family.
>
> Data in Claude Fischer's book indicate that because extended kin live in more dispersed urban areas, the likelihood of family interaction decreases. My extended family is dispersed throughout the city from Long Island to Brooklyn, but we still find ourselves at my grandmother's house every holiday. Most families see each other, if at all, at Christmas and Thanksgiving, and even then only a few relatives turn out. My family comes through not only on these holidays, but also on Easter, Valentine's Day, Mother's Day, the Fourth of July, and my grandmother's birthday. The only holiday we don't get together on is Secretary's Day! Unlike many other families, every member of the family is present, even my cousins who fly in from California and Florida.
>
> Fischer's article also states that there is a breakdown of economic as well as recreational functions within the family. Not only is this statement wrong about my immediate family, but it is wrong in terms of my extended family as well. Whenever anyone in my family is in need of money, someone will be there to help out. Whether it is a few dollars or a few thousand dollars, we are there for each other.
>
> Finally, as stated in both articles, emotional support has become the responsibility of friends and co-workers rather than family members. Emotional support may be one of the strongest factors we have going in our family. If someone is in need of support, other family members will be there. If there is a crisis or tragedy in one household, as recently happened when my great uncle died in Virginia, the whole family will get together to express sympathy. Not over the phone, but in person. Not one person, but the whole family.

[5]Claude S. Fischer, *The Urban Experience* (San Diego: Harcourt, 1984), pp. 141–48.

Recently my grandmother was in the hospital and my family was there in full force every day and all day. Hospital rules permit only two guests in the room at a time, but because the nurses saw the closeness and size of the family, they put my grandmother in a private room and allowed us all in, even before and after visiting hours. The staff of the hospital even mentioned how unusual it was to see such a close family these days.

One last point. When my grandmother came home she needed 24-hour nursing care, but only twelve hours has been available. Instead of putting my grandmother in a home, everyone helped out. Each member of the family took turns spending the night and went straight to work the next day.

What I'm really trying to get across is that at a time when such articles as "The Urban Experience" and "Beyond the Family Crisis" come out with such alarming facts on the disintegration of the family, it's good to know and discover that the family still exists, even an extended family with 36 members. The number of such families may be small, but their spirits make up for it and encourage others. So in response to Fischer, Busacca, and Ryan, I say: "The Family Lives!"

Of course, just because *this* student's family is strong does not mean that Busacca and Ryan are wrong when they argue that the American family is in deep crisis. As Bea herself implies at several points in her paper, her family may be an exception to the rule. Nevertheless, she has done a good job at testing the applicability of a general analysis of *the* family to *her* family.

From a writing standpoint, it is also an effective paper. In the first paragraph Bea paraphrases the analysis put forward in the assigned reading to the effect that urbanism has had a destructive influence on the family system. She ends with a quotation from Busacca and Ryan, who suggest that many homes have become little more than "boarding houses for those with blood ties." This is an effective quotation because it vividly expresses the position that she wishes to challenge.

Bea begins the second paragraph with her thesis statement: "This does not happen in my family." Most of the body of her paper describes the ways in which her family defies Busacca and Ryan's analysis—her father works and her mother is a traditional homemaker, there are powerful family traditions especially on holidays, and the extended family can be relied upon at times of crisis. To assure that this description is relevant to the course, she periodically alludes to specific elements in the reading that do not apply to her family. Finally, in the concluding paragraph, she restates her thesis in somewhat different language, and ends with a somewhat dramatic declaration directed at Busacca and Ryan: "The Family Lives!" In effect, Bea has presented a graphic case study of one family that does not conform to the general pattern, as some social scientists have described it. Implicitly she raises the possibility that social scientists have exaggerated the extent of the family crisis.

The student papers in this chapter involved critical analysis of published works by social scientists. Chapter 12 deals with papers where the student is expected to take on the role of social scientist by conducting original research or by developing an original synthesis of secondary sources.

## SUGGESTIONS FOR WRITING AND THINKING

1.  In their study of "Teacher Expectations for the Disadvantaged" (see Chapter 6), Rosenthal and Jacobson showed how teacher expectations of student performance amounted to "a self-fulfilling prophecy." Apply this concept to a situation or a setting that you have observed firsthand. In writing your essay, you might want to discuss what a self-fulfilling prophecy is, show how it was used by Rosenthal and Jacobson in their study, and then develop a transition to your own application of this concept.

2.  Suppose you disagreed with Polsky's assumption that hustling is comparable to other kinds of work. Develop a critique of his analysis, leading to your own set of conclusions. Be explicit about how you define work, and your criteria for evaluating whether or not an activity constitutes work.

# Chapter 12
# THE RESEARCH PAPER

Research is central to the academic enterprise, since it is through research that knowledge is advanced. As undergraduates, you are not likely to be expected to do original research, at least not on a professional level. However, you are expected to develop research skills. This is explicitly the case in methods courses, which are typically required of social science majors. In these courses you may be asked to go out and collect data using one of the research tools discussed in Chapters 6 to 9: the experiment, observation, the interview, or documents. In all academic courses, however, students are exposed, directly or indirectly, to research conducted by professional social scientists. In these courses you may be asked to write a "research paper" that brings together and analyzes research and writing on a particular topic.

Thus, let us draw a distinction between the *primary research paper*, which is based on original data, and the *secondary research paper*, which is based on the published work of other writers. Each has its own characteristic format, and each presents distinctive problems for the writer.

## THE PRIMARY RESEARCH PAPER

The four sample essays in Chapters 6 to 9 are all examples of primary research, and thus may serve as models for student papers as well. Despite obvious differences, these essays are similar to one another in overall organization. Each one has an *introduction* that provides background and justification for the study and posits the questions or issues that govern the actual research. The *body of the paper* consists of a systematic presentation of research findings. The *conclusion* sums up what has been learned and explores whatever implications flow from the research. In short, there is a logical beginning, middle, and end, consisting of questions, evidence, and answers. This is the "logical structure" of social science writing that we discussed in Chapter 5.

These three divisions can also be subdivided into smaller and more specific parts. The following format is typical of papers based on primary research:

I. INTRODUCTION
 1. Statement of the research problem
 2. Review of the literature
 3. Research objectives
 4. Methods

II. BODY OF THE PAPER
 1. Appropriate subdivisions in terms of content

III. CONCLUSION
 1. Summary
 2. Conclusion

Let us elaborate briefly on each of these categories.

I. *Introduction.* Provides background and justification for the research.
 1. *Statement of the research problem.* What is the overall question or issue that is being addressed?
 2. *Review of the literature.* Places the study within the context of previous research. How does it build on earlier studies? Are there gaps in the literature that this study will fill? Does it test or challenge findings or propositions put forward by earlier studies?
 3. *Research objectives.* Provides a more detailed statement of research objectives. States the hypotheses, if any, or the ideas that are being explored.
 4. *Methods.* Discusses the specific research methods that are employed. How were subjects chosen? What research instruments were used (for example, interviews or questionnaires)?

II. *Body of the Paper.* Consists of a systematic presentation of research findings. These should be arranged under appropriate subheadings. Typically, these subdivisions are drawn in terms of different clusters of findings.

For example, in her article "Emerging Sex-Role Attitudes, Expectations, and Strains" (see Chapter 8), Parelius has four subdivisions in her "Findings" section:

Sex-Role Orientations, 1969 and 1973
Perception of Male Attitudes, 1969 and 1973
Women's Attitudes and Their Perceptions of Men
Emerging Strains

In Ned Polsky's article "The Hustler" (see Chapter 7), subdivisions in the body of the paper conform to various aspects of poolroom hustling:

The Hustler's Methods of Deception
Job-Related Skills and Traits
The Hustler as Con Man

Without these subdivisions, the findings section would be amorphous and confusing. The subheadings provide the reader with points of reference, and thus add clarity and coherence. You will need to decide what subdivisions are most appropriate to your subject.

III. *Conclusion.* This section typically consists of a summary and conclusion, whether or not they are designated as such. The summary repeats, in less detail, the major findings. The conclusion explores implications of these findings, and is therefore more speculative.

The above schema is more or less standard in social science writing based on primary research. This does not mean that it is applied mechanically. Writers modify and adapt it to the requirements of a particular paper, as well as to their prose style. Some writers make explicit use of the key categories—statement of the problem, review of the literature, method, and so on. Others cover the same material, but weave it more subtly into their exposition. As student-writers, you may find it useful to adhere to the schema outlined above, since it will impose discipline and organization on your writing. As you gain expertise and self-confidence, you may decide to be more improvisational.

## THE SECONDARY RESEARCH PAPER

Research does not always involve the collection of original data. In most social science courses the "research paper" involves going to the library and turning up books, articles, and other source materials on a given topic. In your paper you are expected to synthesize this material. This consists of bringing together information and ideas from different sources, usually with the purpose of advancing an interpretation or a statement of your own. Insofar as you are not merely regurgitating information, there is ample room for originality in thought and writing.

Assignments differ, however, in the extent that students are expected to carry the analysis, and to inject their own point of view. In the case of *informative papers,* you are expected merely to summarize—in effect, to present a coherent distillation of a body of material. In the case of *analytical papers,* you will not only summarize this material, but also analyze the relationship among key variables. Finally, in the case of *argumentative papers,* you go an analytical step further and develop your own position or point of view.[1]

As an example, consider three possible papers on the American family:

*Informative paper:* Collects statistical material showing increasing numbers of singles, later marriages, smaller families, rising rates of divorce and out-of-wedlock births, and so on. A title and focus for such a paper might be "Trends in the American Family System."

*Analytical paper:* Explores causes or effects of some of the statistical patterns cited above. Thus, a suitable title might be "Sources of Family Instability," or "Some Consequences of Family Instability."

*Argumentative paper:* Goes further in making judgments about a known set of facts, and advances an argument that must be defended against likely crit-

---

[1]These categories are borrowed from James D. Lester, *Writing Research Papers,* 5th ed. (Glenview, Illinois: Scott, Foresman and Company, 1984), pp. 3–4.

ics. An appropriate title might be: "The Family Crisis in Contemporary American Society."

All three papers deal broadly with the same general subject: changes in the American family. The informative paper essentially documents what these changes are. The analytical paper goes beyond surface description and analyzes some of the sources and/or consequences of these changes. The argumentative paper develops that analysis into a full-fledged argument involving interpretation of the empirical findings. In this last instance, "changes" are construed merely as "symptoms" of deeper problems, and an argument is put forward suggesting that the American family is in "crisis." As papers become more analytical, they necessarily become more abstract and speculative.

## The Process of Writing a Secondary Research Paper

Let us say that you are required to write a research paper for a social science course, and that your instructor has given you wide latitude to write on any topic that fits under the general rubric of the course. Where does one begin? Most students have a linear model of how to proceed: first, you come up with a topic; then you go to the library to look for relevant sources; finally, you write the paper. This, we would submit, is *not* the best way to proceed. Remember what we said in Chapter 2 about the interrelationship between reading, thinking, and writing. Therefore, we suggest a somewhat different approach. Do not begin with a specific topic, but rather with a general subject area from which you will eventually formulate a topic. The next step is to search for relevant sources—books, articles, or other materials; usually this involves several trips to the library. Once you have located some promising sources, you should scan them in order to become familiar with the general terrain. On the basis of this reading, you should be able to formulate a topic that has specific focus.

*Focus* is the key to a successful paper. Without focus, your paper will be difficult to research because you do not have a clear idea of what you are looking for, and it will be difficult to write because you are not clear about what you want to say. On the other hand, a topic with clear focus will give direction to your research and writing.

With this in mind, let us go through the various steps in writing a research paper, remembering that they do not necessarily follow one another in linear sequence. For example, as you read, you should take notes and summarize materials, brainstorm whenever ideas come to you, and freewrite once you have absorbed a body of material. As you formulate your ideas, this in turn will guide subsequent reading and thought.

**1. Choosing a Subject Area.** As already indicated, you should begin not with a specific topic, but with a subject area out of which you will "carve" a specific topic—one that is appropriate for a term paper in a particular course. The first rule is to choose a subject area in which you have genuine interest. This may appear unnecessary to say, but all too often students are capricious in choosing a topic, and lack that spark of curiosity that is necessary to sustain their interest and deepen their understanding.

**2. *Preliminary Reading.*** If the idea for your paper was prompted by something you read, such as a book assigned in your course, this would be a good place to begin your search for relevant sources. Check to see if there are citations (footnotes or bibliography) to sources that you can go to for further information. You might also consult with your instructor or some other knowledgeable person who may be able to give you some titles to get you started. As you turn up a few sources, you can "milk" their citations for still other works that seem relevant.

Now is the time for an initial foray to the library. A common starting point is the card catalog, which lists all the library's holdings by subject as well as by author and title. Look under headings relevant to your subject, and single out titles that look promising. Generally speaking, it is a good idea to begin with recent publications, since they are more likely to present up-to-date information and source material.

Your college library also contains a large array of reference works—specialized encyclopedias, reviews, bibliographies, abstracts, and indices—that can be of immense value in turning up source material on virtually any subject. (See Appendix A of this book, "Selected Reference Works in the Social Sciences.") Some of these reference works include annotations or abstracts. These are especially useful at this stage of the research, since they give you a good idea of the general contents of books and articles while sparing you (for the time being) of having to locate them and read them in their entirety. In this way you can find out what is "out there" and use this source material to think about how to restrict the focus of your own paper.

**3. *Formulating an Appropriate Topic.*** On the basis of this preliminary survey of the subject area of your paper, you should now be able to formulate a specific topic. The importance of restricting the focus of your paper cannot be stressed too much. At the outset of the research process, when you do not have much to say, you might take comfort in defining your topic broadly. Such topics, however, rapidly become unmanageable as you turn up more and more source material. As we commented earlier, only by restricting the focus of your paper will you be able to address the topic in some depth and detail.

In short, it is imperative that you make the transition from *subject* to *topic.* This is done by honing down the subject to more manageable proportions.

For example, let us say that you are assigned a research paper in a course on racial and ethnic minorities. You have always been curious about the Chinese, and decide to write a paper on this group. Unless you plan to devote years to writing a book-length manuscript, it would be unwise to write a paper titled "The Chinese in America." This is simply too broad, too complex a subject to cover in a single paper. "The Chinese in San Francisco" begins to limit the focus, but it is still too broad. "Recent Chinese Immigration to San Francisco" is more focused, and for some purposes this might be an acceptable topic. In doing the research, however, you may turn up more material than you can use in a single paper. Therefore, it might be advisable to focus on a specific aspect of recent Chinese immigration to San Francisco, such as "Health Problems of Recent Chinese Immigrants" or "Conflicts Between Old and New Immigrants in San Francisco's Chinatown."

It is generally advisable to limit the topic in terms of the disciplinary perspective of the course for which you are writing the paper. For example, a history student might focus on "The Origins of the Chinese Laundryman"; an anthropology student on "The Cultural Adjustment of Recent Chinese Immigrants to San Francisco"; a psychology student on "Feelings of Uprootedness Among Recent Chinese Immigrants"; an economics student on "The Role of the Chinese Restaurant in the Economy of San Francisco's Chinatown." Each of these topics is sufficiently narrow to allow a student-researcher to write about it in some depth and detail. Each has a specificity that suggests the kinds of source materials that are relevant, and how they might be integrated into the final paper.

To further illustrate how one goes about formulating an appropriate topic, let us use the student paper that is printed in its entirety in Appendix C. After the paper was written, we interviewed the student, Michael Steinberg, in order to reconstruct his thought process in the conception and evolution of the paper.

Mike was enrolled in a course on American history and literature in the South, and was assigned a term paper in the range of seven to ten pages on a topic of his own choosing. His first thought was to write "something about the Ku Klux Klan." During the semester he had seen *Birth of a Nation*, a film that portrayed the Klan as driven by a righteous desire to redeem white honor and political integrity. He was particularly incensed by one scene that depicted black legislators slobbering over watermelon in the legislative chambers. All of this piqued Mike's interest, and he resolved to write his paper on the KKK.

Thus, Mike had a subject, but had yet to formulate a specific topic. However, his curiosity about the image of the Klan as having rescued the South from the "evils" of Reconstruction suggested one promising direction.

It occurred to him that the assigned reading provided one relevant source: a book by a Southern historian, Thomas Dixon, Jr., called *The Clansmen*, which also glorified the Klan. Mike recalled that his professor had commented that Dixon was typical of a school of historians who uncritically accepted the Klan's self-conception as a "reform group" that sought to wrest power from carpetbaggers and blacks in the name of "white civilization." Though fragmentary, these sources nevertheless represented a promising beginning. Moreover, a focus had begun to emerge. He would challenge the notion, originally advanced by the Klan itself and embraced by some historians, that the Klan was "a reform group."

**4. Back to the Library.** Once you have limited the topic and have a better idea of what you are looking for, you can begin a more systematic search for relevant sources. What does this entail? More trips to the library, and the use of various reference materials that are available, ranging from the card catalog to abstracts in the relevant discipline to bibliographies, indices, and other reference works. Not to be overlooked is the reference librarian who can lead you through the dizzying maze of reference works to the one or two that are most relevant to your paper.

In the case of our student paper on the Klan, Mike began his search for sources where most students begin, that is, with the card catalog. Under the heading "Ku Klux Klan," he found an entry for a 1964 Master's thesis: Lillian M. Lynch, "The Evolution of the Ku Klux Klan in the South." In reading the thesis he encountered a reference to a 1939 book by Stanley Horn called *Invisible Empire* that also glorified the Klan, much as Dixon's *The Clansmen* had done. To Mike's surprise, the book turned up in the stacks. The assigned reading for the course also included an article by one of his professors, Clarence E. Walker, entitled "One Hundred Per Cent Americanism: The Ku Klux Klan's Defense of America."

**5. Evaluating Sources.** If you are resourceful in the use of the library, you will turn up a large number of titles that look promising. Inevitably, you are forced to make judgments about which ones are worth retrieving from the stacks, which of these are worth reading, and which of these are worth incorporating into your paper. Intuition plays a large role in these decisions, but there are also a few principles that come into play.

a. *Be wary of sources that you turn up by combing through the card catalog or browsing through the stacks.* With luck, you may turn up "exactly what you are looking for." But you should also be aware that many of the library's holdings are dated or of marginal quality. For this reason computer searches that indiscriminately churn out lists of references on a given topic are often disappointing. Generally speaking, you will be better served by reference works that apply some principles of selectivity in what is listed or recommended, or that provide annotations or abstracts so that you can make your own judgment regarding a source's value or relevance.

b. *Try to locate reference volumes that come close to your subject.* For example, in researching his paper on the Ku Klux Klan our student would have done well to consult the *Harvard Guide to American History*, published in 1974, which has the following selective list of books and articles about the Klan. Note that one of Mike's sources—Horn's *Invisible Empire*—is among the ten works cited:

**21.12.3.2** Ku Klux Klan

Alexander, Charles C., *Ku Klux Klan in the Southwest* (1965).

Chalmers, David M., *Hooded Americanism: Ku Klux Klan, 1865–1965* (1965).

———— "Ku Klux Klan in the Sunshine State: 1920's," *Fla. Hist. Quar.*, 42 (1964), 209.

Davis, James H., "Colorado under the Klan," *Colo. Mag.*, 42 (1965), 93.

Degler, Carl N., "Century of the Klans," *JSH*, 31 (1965), 435.

Horn, Stanley F., *Invisible Empire: The Story of the Ku Klux Klan, 1866–1871* (1939).

Jackson, Charles O., "William J. Simmons: A Career in Ku Kluxism," *Ga. Hist. Quar.*, 50 (1966), 351.

Jackson, Kenneth T., *Ku Klux Klan in the City, 1915–1930* (1967).

Randel, William P., *Ku Klux Klan* (1965).

Rice, Arnold S., *The Ku Klux Klan in American Politics* (1962).

See also volume two for references to Reconstruction.

For more recent articles, Mike might have consulted other reference volumes, such as *America: History and Life*, a quarterly publication that abstracts research published in scores of journals. For example, the 1986 edition has the following entry of a study of the KKK in Illinois; note that the author's view of the KKK as engaging in "reactionary violence and cultural counterrevolution" is consistent with Mike's own analysis:

23A:6967.                                                                          1870's

Raines, Edgar F., Jr. THE KU KLUX KLAN IN ILLINOIS, 1867–1875. *Illinois Historical Journal 1985 78(1): 17–45.* The Illinois Ku Klux Klan was a movement of reactionary violence and cultural counterrevolution that developed in the 1870's in the southern extreme of the state. It was most successful in isolated communities recently exposed to more cosmopolitan influences, places of evangelical religious traditions, centers of upland Southern migration, and areas characterized by politics strongly Democratic prior to the Civil War but more competitive in the postwar period. At the Klan's peak, there were between two and three hundred members. While heightening existing elite rivalries, the Klan idealized a vigilante response to petty crime and decried the prominence of social injustice and immorality. Map, 5 illus., 2 tables, 110 notes.                                                                          A. W. Novitsky

When you locate a promising source, be sure to scrutinize the citations for other titles that may be relevant to your specific topic. In this way, developing a bibliography on a topic becomes a snowballing process.

c. *Try to identify sources that are "authoritative."* Generally speaking, professional journals are more deserving of attention than popular magazines, since the authors must conform to rules of evidence, and their work is scrutinized by other scholars before it is accepted for publication. Thus, for example, an article on divorce in the *Journal of Marriage and the Family* is more likely to be useful than a similar article in *Family Circle.* News magazines, like *Time* or *Newsweek,* often have feature stories on contemporary issues, and these may contain useful information. However, for a more in-depth analysis, one should rely on scholarly books and journals.

It is also a good idea to identify some of the recognized authorities in the relevant area. Your instructor might supply you with this information, or you might infer this on the basis of your reading. Needless to say, you should never accept a work uncritically merely because its author is a "recognized authority" in the field. In the final analysis, it is up to you as the researcher-writer to assess the validity and significance of a particular source, and to determine how it fits into your own exposition.

*6. Developing a Preliminary Thesis Statement.* Let us say that you have restricted your topic, and garnered various books and articles that relate to it. You have taken notes, written annotated summaries of key works, and periodically brainstormed as promising ideas flashed across your mind. Having assimilated all this material, you have reached a critical phase of deciding what you want your paper "to say." In other words, you need a *thesis statement.* This is a statement—in as little as a single sentence—that encapsulates the central argument of your paper. What is emerging from your research as the answer to the research questions that you posed at the outset of your study? What is it that *you*, as the researcher-writer, have to say on the topic under examination?

For purposes of illustration, let us return to our student paper on the Ku Klux Klan. As Mike read and took notes, he decided that he would challenge the claim that the Klan was ever a "reform group." He had three sources that made this claim: the film *Birth of a Nation* and the two Southern histories that glorified the Klan. On the other side of the issue, he had two sources that were critical of the Klan: the Master's thesis and the Walker article. After reading all this material and ruminating about it, Mike arrived at a preliminary thesis statement, which he wrote down: "While the Ku Klux Klan of the nineteenth century has been called a reform group by its members and by some historians, in reality it was no more than a terrorist organization, dedicated to the restoration of white supremacy." Note that this thesis statement is embodied in the first paragraph of Mike's final paper (see Appendix C).

As this example shows, the thesis statement provides a capsule answer to the primary research question (Is it accurate to portray the Klan as a reform group?). The thesis helps you to be clear about the thrust of your analysis. By developing a *preliminary* thesis statement early in the research, you will be forced to test your assumptions against the evidence. If your preliminary thesis seems correct, you will collect all the evidence you can to support your case. If, on the other hand, the evidence does not support your preliminary thesis, you will need to modify or refine it. In this way the writing process is an integral part of the research process.

*7. Develop an Outline.* Now that you are clear about the thrust of your paper, you should generate a plan—either a "nutshell" of what you intend to write or a formal outline. Like a map, a good outline marks the route of the intellectual journey from beginning to end, pointing up important junctions and landmarks along the way. Some students prefer a "rough outline," one that maps out only major arteries and leaves room for improvisation. Other students opt for a more detailed map, recognizing that there may be unexpected detours along the way. In either event, you need not feel bound by your original outline. Its purpose is to help you get started. In the process of writing the paper, you may find that you need to revise the outline extensively.

*8. The Exposition: The Introduction.* Sometimes the most difficult juncture in writing a paper is the opening sentence or paragraph. Breaking into a paper is not unlike accelerating a car from a dead stop. On the other hand, once you are in motion—once you have some pages behind you—it is easier to maintain your momentum. For this reason you may find it easier to write the introduction after you have drafted the body of the paper and have a better idea of where you are headed.

The opening sentence or paragraph is crucial because it sets the tone and the direction for the entire exposition. In *Writing Research Papers*, James D. Lester suggests a number of techniques that are commonly used in opening paragraphs.[2] Let us illustrate some of these by referring to the four sample essays in Chapters 6 to 9 of this book:

Relate to the Well Known. For example, in "Teacher Expectations for the Disadvantaged," Rosenthal and Jacobson begin their article as follows: "One of the central problems of American society lies in the fact that certain children suffer a handicap in their education which then persists throughout life."

Use a Brief Quotation. Both Gutman ("Send Me Some of the Children's Hair") and Polsky ("The Hustler") begin with epigraphs. These quotations capture the essence of the phenomenon under study and hint at the author's point of view.

Review of the Literature. In "Emerging Sex-Role Attitudes, Expectations, and Strains Among College Women," Parelius begins with a review of the sex-role literature. By pointing up certain gaps in the literature, she provides a rationale for her own study.

Define a Key Term. Polsky's opening sentence, in effect, provides a definition of the hustler: "The poolroom hustler makes his living by betting

[2]Ibid., pp. 99–103.

against his opponents in different types of pool or billiard games, and as part of the playing and betting process he engages in various deceitful practices."

Challenge an Assumption. From the outset of their article on "Teacher Expectations for the Disadvantaged," Rosenthal and Jacobson make it clear that they are challenging the conventional wisdom about why poor children lag in school. As they write: "The reason usually given for the poor performance of the disadvantaged child is simply that the child is a member of a disadvantaged group. There may well be another reason. . . ." In the case of our student paper on the Klan, the opening sentence states the position that will be challenged in his paper: "The Ku Klux Klan of the nineteenth century has been called 'a reform group' both by its own members and by historians."

Still another technique for getting started is to cite statistics that stir the reader's interest. For example, at the outset of the report alluded to in Chapter 10 on drunk driving ("The Party's Over: Controlling Drunk Drivers"), the author notes that drunk drivers were involved in accidents accounting for 25,000 deaths and 750,000 injuries in 1981 alone. This not only conveys important information but alerts readers to the urgency of the problem, which arouses their interest.

*9. Rhetorical Strategies.* In Chapter 4 we examined eight rhetorical strategies that are commonly employed in social science writing. They are:

1. Definition
2. Classification
3. Description
4. Narration
5. Illustration
6. Comparison-contrast
7. Cause-effect
8. Argument

As we have already stated, these are not formulas to be applied mechanically, and you may find yourself employing more than one of them in a single paper. However, thinking through the rhetorical strategies relevant to your paper will enable you to write more effectively.

Our student paper on the Klan combines Definition with Argument. In his second paragraph, Mike wrestles with the meaning of "reform": "If 'reform' is used in its most general and literal sense—that is, 'to form again'—then I would have to say that the KKK was indeed a reform group." However, if "reform" is construed to mean to "change for the better," then a different conclusion is in order. The thrust of the paper uses Argument to advance Mike's view that the KKK was fundamentally a terrorist organization dedicated to the restoration of white supremacy.

*10. Incorporating Sources.* By definition, a secondary research paper is largely based on books and articles written by others. Therefore, it is important that you make explicit reference to these sources, and that you incorporate them into your paper. Basically, there are four techniques for doing this: *quotation, paraphrase, summary,* and *reference.* They differ mainly in the extent to which they rely upon the language of the original source.

Let us illustrate these techniques with our student paper. Mike based his research on four sources, and makes use of quotation, paraphrase, summary, and reference, skillfully weaving them together in order to put forward his analysis of the KKK as a terrorist organization.

Quotation. Direct quotation is the clearest way to incorporate sources into your paper. In the case of our student paper, it was important to provide documentation of the view advanced by some historians that the KKK was originally dedicated to political and moral "reform." In this way readers who might be skeptical that the KKK had its intellectual defenders are allowed to "see for themselves." Thus, through direct quotation Mike establishes the position that he wishes to challenge. Note how he introduces and frames the quotation:

> Stanley Horn, who presents a sympathetic account of the Klan's origins and activities in his Invisible Empire, claims that the "Negro's Loyal League was a primary cause for the white men's Ku Klux Klan." The adjectives used in his description of the League, however, seem more appropriate to the movie "Birth of a Nation" than to a history on the Reconstruction period:
>
> > This was a totally unrestrained and disorderly form of group activity in its Southern manifestation, used by low-grade white men as an instrumentality for organizing the negroes politically and keeping them unified by a steady infusion of inflammatory propaganda by imported flannel-mouthed orators. . . . Bands of League members, armed to the teeth, prowled the country at all times, particularly at night, and the white people were increasingly terrified (Horn, p. 27).

As this example shows, quotation often helps to capture the flavor and nuance, as well as the substance and meaning, of an original source.

Although direct quotation is often effective, it should be used sparingly, and never as a substitute for expressing ideas in your own words. As a general rule, the only reason to quote is when you feel that it is important to preserve the original language. For example, you might want to quote some authority, either to build support for your position, or as in the example above, to highlight conflicting viewpoints. Or you might feel that another writer has stated a point so well that the temptation to quote is irresistible. Unless there is some compelling reason to preserve the original language, however, it is generally better to use your own words and to rely on paraphrase, summary, or reference.

Paraphrase. A paraphrase is like a quotation, except that you translate the original into your own words. Why not, one might ask, simply quote the original source? For a very good reason. By rephrasing, you adapt and tailor the original material to the concerns of your paper, and maintain greater consistency of style as well. In effect, through paraphrasing you have the advantage of someone else's ideas without losing your authorial voice. Consider the following example of paraphrase, also excerpted from our student paper:

> In his apologetic version of the Klan story, Horn also suggests that the Ku Klux Klan had little choice but to take the law into its own hands in order to counter the "lawlessness" of the Negroes and the Radical Republicans. Horn implies that the Klan's acting outside the law was justified because the reforms they were working for were essential to the South's well-being: the KKK "was destined to grow into perhaps the most powerful and extensive organization of its kind that ever existed" (Horn, 30).

Note that the paraphrase includes a short quotation of a key point where it was useful to preserve the original language.

Summary. A summary is more a matter of condensation than of rewording. A large body of material—perhaps an article, or a whole book—is boiled down to a paragraph or two that encapsulates the central argument. For example:

> In The Evolution of the Ku Klux Klan in the South Lillian Lynch exposes abuses that allegedly occurred under the Reconstruction Act. According to Lynch, buying votes and voting twice were common occurrences among carpetbaggers and scalawags. In one case votes were inspected before being placed in the ballot box; all votes for Democrats were withheld. Often leaders would give Blacks pre-marked Republican ballots.

Reference. This is an even more concise allusion to another work, either a specific passage or the work as a whole. For example, in documenting actions taken by the forces opposed to Reconstruction, Mike writes the following:

> In 1871 a Democratic legislature successfully wiped out the Loyal League by calling for the disbandment of all secret organizations (Lynch, 22).

The full reference is found in the bibliography:

> Lynch, Lillian M., The Evolution of the Ku Klux Klan in the South, Master's Thesis, Wesleyan University, Middletown, Connecticut, 1964.

As we noted earlier, it is through these four devices—quotation, paraphrase, summary, and reference—that the writer "incorporates sources" into a research paper. The most important principle to keep in mind is that sources should never dominate your writing. At all times you must be the "master" of your prose. Your central argument should always be apparent, in bold relief against your background sources. You can make liberal use of these sources, but should do so selectively—to illustrate, document, or otherwise elaborate upon an argument or point of view that *you* wish to advance.

**11. Documenting Sources.** If you borrow someone else's ideas, then you have an obligation to acknowledge your intellectual debt. Failing to do so could subject you to the charge of *plagiarism*—that is, claiming someone else's ideas as your own. The way to avoid this is to provide appropriate citations to all sources used in writing your paper. Aside from avoiding the sin of plagiarism, documenting sources adds authority to your paper.

Does one have to footnote "everything"? At the very least, it is necessary to footnote any source that was the basis of a quotation, paraphrase, summary, or reference. Facts or details that are not well known or generally accepted should also be footnoted, since the reader may want to know where this information came from.

What about sources that may have influenced your thinking, but are not specifically incorporated into the text of your paper? Here there is more ambiguity. To be safe, you should list these sources in your bibliography. But you might also want to generate a footnote at the point in your paper where this source clearly shaped your own thinking.

In short, pay your intellectual debts! It will enhance your integrity as a writer and earn the confidence of your readers.

There is no *one* format for documenting sources that is universally accepted, and the prevailing styles vary from one discipline to the next. You should therefore conform to whatever guidelines your instructor lies down. Below we demonstrate two formats that are widely employed (for more detailed information about the nuances of footnoting, consult a style guide).

Most academic journals now require that source references be included in the text. The author's name, the date of publication, and, where relevant, the page number is placed in parentheses at an appropriate juncture in the text (usually at the end of the sentence containing the reference). The full bibliographic reference (the title, publisher, and place of publication) are then included in the bibliography at the end of the paper. For example, Parelius (see Chapter 8) wrote:

> . . . many women have experienced considerable anxiety as they have been caught between conflicting normative definitions of appropriate sex-role behavior (Horner, 1969).

The full reference is then found in the bibliography:

> Horner, Matina, "Fail: bright women." *Psychology Today* 3 (6), 1969, 36–41.

Note that this format incorporates most references into the text of the paper. Footnotes (at the "foot" of the page) or endnotes (at the "end" of the paper) are reserved for comments or other information that the author might wish to add.

Some writers prefer the "traditional" format, which is to have numbered footnotes (or endnotes), thus separating the reference from the text of the paper. Had Parelius used this format, it would have looked as follows:

> . . . many women have experienced considerable anxiety as they have been caught between conflicting normative definitions of appropriate sex-role behavior.[1]

The footnote or endnote would follow:

> 1. Matina Horner, "Fail: bright women," *Psychology Today* 3 (6), 1969, 36–41.

Remember that providing references is more than an academic ritual. It provides readers with important information about the source of information and ideas that are included in your paper. With this information they can better assess your claims and arguments, and just as you did in researching your paper, they may want to use your sources in the conduct of their own research. In this way references help to keep the research process in motion. (For further details regarding bibliographic form, see Appendix B.)

## SUGGESTIONS FOR WRITING AND THINKING

1.  This exercise asks you to lay the groundwork for a primary research paper—one that you may carry to completion at another time. Select an area in which you have some background and interest, and develop a specific topic, following the guidelines spelled out in this chapter. Then, write separate sections under the following headings:

    a. *Statement of the Research Problem*
       What is the overall question or issue that is being addressed?
    b. *Review of the Literature*
       Use at least two references to place your study within the context of previous research. How does it build on these earlier studies? Does it fill a gap? Does it test or challenge findings or propositions put forward in these studies?
    c. *Research Objectives*
       Develop a more detailed statement of your research objectives. What are some of the secondary questions or issues that will be addressed?
    d. *Research Design*
       Discuss the research methods that you plan to employ. How will

subjects be chosen? What are your sources of data? How do these methods relate to your research objectives?

2. Refer back to exercise 1 in Chapter 10, which asked you to develop an annotated bibliography on a social science topic of your own choosing. You can now use this material to write a secondary research paper (2 to 3 pages). First, formulate a topic that addresses a specific question or issue. As a second step, develop a thesis statement that conveys your point of view on the question or issue under examination. Finally, develop a synthesis of the five works around this thesis statement. In doing so, you should explore related threads in the source material, and weave them into a coherent essay that provides an answer to the research question, or attempts to resolve the issue addressed by your paper.

For example, let us say that you decide to do research on the role that women played in the labor force during World War II. To turn up five relevant sources, you make use of reference works such as *Women Studies Abstracts*, the *Social Science Index*, and *America: History and Life: A Guide to Periodical Literature*. You formulate a thesis statement to the effect that labor shortages during the war impelled government, industry, and other major institutions to encourage women to enter the labor force. Finally, you take fragments of information and analysis from your source material, and weave them together to show how economic forces led to a redefinition of "women's place," perhaps ending your paper with a comment about what happened in the aftermath of the war when labor shortages were alleviated.

# Chapter 13
# THE ESSAY EXAM

Pity the student. You have crammed as many as fifteen weeks of book learning and class notes into the memory cells reserved for a particular course. On the appointed day you limp into class, bleary-eyed from a long night of study. A grade is at stake, perhaps much more. A hush descends over the room as the instructor passes out the dreaded blue books. You run your eyes over the exam sheet to see if there is hope. Precious minutes have already slipped away. You tackle the first question. As you write you are relieved to discover that you have a lot to say, but is there enough time? You freeze, and lose time. Or you speed up, and ramble. Each time your instructor records the time on the blackboard, a nervous spasm radiates down your spine. Your body seems under siege. Your hands are clammy. Your arm cramps up. But you persevere and write on. Again, the detestable jotting on the blackboard. Time has run out. You cast your fate on the awaiting pile on the instructor's desk. Another of academia's ritual ordeals has ended—until the instructor reappears one day with a grave expression and a stack of blue books.

For better or worse, exams are a fact of academic life and every student has to learn to field questions and write cogent answers in an exam situation. Some students work well under pressure. Others are unnerved and suffer the consequences. If you are in the latter category, self-pity is no answer. What will help is to improve your skill at writing exams. As you do so, you will have less reason to be anxious, and may even come to enjoy the challenge of testing your wits against the clock.

In major respects an exam essay is no different from other kinds of writing that involve the communication of information and ideas. Thus, as you improve your writing skills, you will find yourself writing better exams. In other respects, however, the exam essay does differ from other kinds of writing. Its chief purpose is to test your mastery of course materials. As with other kinds of writing, remember your audience—in this case, your instructor (or the grader who functions as proxy for your instructor). He or she wants to gauge how well you have grasped key concepts advanced in lecture and reading. This should govern your approach in writing answers to exam questions. For example, you should incorporate specific ideas and information from reading and lecture to demonstrate your proficiency and understanding. In terms of style, an exam is not an occasion for inspirational writing. It *is* an occasion for discipline, precision, and a deliberate, parsimonious prose style.

Aside from these general considerations, there are a number of specific techniques that will improve your performance on exams. In *The Random House Handbook* Frederick Crews enunciates ten principles for writing exam essays.[1] We list them below in italics, adding our own explanations of how they might be applied.

1. *Try to anticipate questions.* Students who do well on exams generally have developed a knack for "psyching out" exam questions in advance. Indeed, this is an important skill, although there is nothing mysterious about it. Many instructors tip off exam questions, and the alert student does not miss these valuable cues. Even when this is not the case, instructors are likely to ask questions that touch on subjects that have been stressed in class, and are so central to the course that their inclusion on an exam is predictable. By anticipating the questions, you come to the exam not only with general knowledge, but also with the language that will allow you to write informed answers under pressure of time. In this sense, the writing process begins even before the exam itself.

2. *Read the question with care.* It might seem gratuitous to remind you to read the question with care, but the most common mistake that students make on exams is that they do not squarely address the question. In their haste they seize upon a "flash word"—a name or term embedded in the question—and write everything they know about it. Needless to say, it does not help to write the right answer to the wrong question. Nor does it help to "know" the answer if you do not get it down on paper. Thus, it is imperative that you read the question carefully, and mull it over before you begin to write.

3. *Gauge your available time.* An exam requires strategy. If some questions are worth more than others, you should allot your time accordingly. Be careful not to dawdle at the beginning of the exam, lest you run out of time toward the end.

[1]Frederick Crews, *The Random House Handbook*, 3rd ed. (New York: Random House, 1980), pp. 383–85.

4. *Plan your essay.* Many students find it helpful to outline their essays on a separate sheet of paper. If this works for you, fine. Other students worry that an outline consumes too much time, and prefer to develop their ideas in the process of writing, rather than mapping them out in advance. If you choose this tack, then be careful not to digress from the question. The key is a good beginning—one that gets to the heart of the question, and sets you off in the right direction.

5. *Don't waste time restating the question.* Some students have an unfortunate habit of copying or restating the question, perhaps as a way of "warming up" before they break into their answer. This wastes valuable time and is annoying to the person reading the exam. How *should* you begin? Pay close attention to the next point.

6. *State your thesis in the opening paragraph.* Just as you ought to be clear about the main thrust of the exam question, you need to be clear about the main thrust of your answer. Begin, if you can, with a general statement, or thesis, that puts your answer in a nutshell. Then, as you develop your answer, you can elaborate on the thesis statement, bringing in substantiating evidence, and exploring other linkages or meanings.

The advantages of stating the thesis in the opening paragraph should be obvious. For one thing, you get to the most important point first, thus establishing a framework for the rest of the answer. For another, it alerts your grader—who is also bleary-eyed from reading umpteen answers to the same question—that you "know your stuff."

7. *Keep to the point.* Again, do not lose sight of the question. Students often get into trouble by "going off on a tangent." If you find yourself drifting from the question, complete your thought, and then begin a new paragraph that puts you back on track. Also, it is generally inadvisable to insert personal asides—anecdotes or opinions—unless you are specifically asked to do so. Remember that the grader must assess your essay in terms of its accuracy and depth of understanding, not whether or not you are an engaging writer or agree or disagree with a particular point of view.

8. *Be emphatic.* As you write your exam essay, it is often a good idea to underscore or highlight key points—those that warrant emphasis and that you want to bring to the attention of your reader-grader. You may do this by employing phrases that add emphasis, such as: "By far the most important reason is . . ." or "Perhaps the major factor was. . . ." Under some circumstances you may find it helpful to present a series of points, preceded by numbers: (1), (2), (3), and so on. This helps you to order your own thoughts, and it demarcates a number of different points that may earn you extra points. As a shorthand device for achieving emphasis, you may simply underline key points. This is perfectly legitimate. After all, underlining script corresponds to italics in a printed volume.

9. *Support your generalizations.* By their very nature, essay exam questions are general in scope. So are the answers. However, it is important that you substantiate general statements with specific details. Remember that your instructors are looking for evidence that you have mastered course materials. You can accommodate them by citing specific points drawn from readings or lectures. Otherwise, you run the risk of stating bald generalizations that, without documentation, seem obvious or ambiguous, rather than grounded in hard fact.

10. *Read through the completed answer.* As professors, we are always perplexed when students leave the exam early. You should use any remaining time to read over the exam and make appropriate revisions. Obviously, there is not enough time or space to do an extensive rewrite. However, you can improve the readability of your essay by doing light editing. This involves deleting superfluous words, substituting a more accurate term, correcting grammatical or spelling errors, and the like. On a second reading, you may realize that you missed a key point. In this event, you can squeeze it in the margin, or still better, place an asterisk referring the reader to an insert at the end of the exam.

It helps to be neat. Leave wide margins and blank space at the end of each question so that you can add material if this becomes necessary. Write legibly. This will ensure that important points are not missed (besides, your grader deserves a little pity too).

As a final admonition, keep in mind that no skill at exam-taking is a substitute for regular class attendance and conscientious study. The "tips" offered in this chapter can only help you make more effective use of what you have learned before the fateful day of the exam. Each time you approach an exam, read over the ten principles spelled out above. Eventually, you will incorporate them into your thinking and writing, and apply them without even being conscious of doing so. And one more thing: Good luck!

## SUGGESTIONS FOR WRITING AND THINKING

The following "exam questions" pertain to the four sample essays in Chapters 6 to 9. When you are done, ask your instructor to assess the strengths and weaknesses of your answers. You may also find it helpful to read the answers of students who wrote exemplary "exams." Probably you will find that you "knew" as much as they did, but were less skillful as a writer. Try to understand where you went wrong so that you can avoid these mistakes on actual exams.

1.  In the introductory section to their article, "Teacher Expectations for the Disadvantaged," Rosenthal and Jacobson wrote:

The reason usually given for the poor performance of the disadvantaged child is simply that the child is a member of a disadvantaged group. There may well be another reason.

What, according to Rosenthal and Jacobson, is the reason for the poor performance of disadvantaged children? How did they arrive at this conclusion? What are the implications of their study for educators and other policymakers?

2. In "Emerging Sex-Role Attitudes, Expectations, and Strains Among College Women," Ann Parelius found that college women in her sample had become increasingly "feminist" in their sex-role orientations. But she also contended that women were experiencing a great deal of "strain." What were the sources of this strain? Do you think her findings would apply to women at your college today? Why or why not?

3. On the basis of your reading of Ned Polsky's "The Poolroom Hustler," discuss how Polsky's "insider account" differs from the way poolroom hustlers are perceived by outsiders.

4. At the outset of *The Black Family in Slavery and Freedom*, Herbert Gutman comments that his study was prompted by the controversy surrounding the Moynihan report, a government study that contended that slavery destroyed the black family. Discuss how his findings are at odds with this assumption. What are some of the implications of Gutman's study for understanding the troubles that beset black families today?

## *Appendix A*
# SELECTIVE REFERENCE WORKS IN THE SOCIAL SCIENCES

It is perhaps symptomatic of the "knowledge industry" that every college library is stocked with a dizzying array of reference works: encyclopedias, dictionaries, handbooks, yearbooks, annual reviews, abstracts, indexes, research guides, book review digests, bibliographies, even bibliographies of bibliographies. The purpose of these works is to help readers locate relevant source material, but the sheer number of these volumes can itself defeat the purpose for which they are intended. Many writing texts and research guides also include so many entries that they overwhelm their student-readers.

With this in mind, we have been highly selective in compiling a list of recent sources that are likely to be of most value to students. The list covers the six fields that received emphasis in this book: anthropology, economics, history, political science, psychology, and sociology. For a more extensive interdisciplinary guide, see *Sources of Information in the Social Sciences: A Guide to the Literature*, Third Edition (Chicago: American Library Association, 1986). This volume covers eight disciplines: history, geography, economics and business administration, sociology, anthropology, psychology, education, and political science. It presents an extensive survey of each discipline and its major subdivisions, as well as a survey of both comprehensive and specialized reference books.

### ENCYCLOPEDIAS:
Consist of articles, usually arranged alphabetically by topic, that attempt to provide comprehensive summaries of knowledge.

THE BLACKWELL ENCYCLOPAEDIA OF POLITICAL INSTITUTIONS. Ed. Vernon Bog-
danor. New York: Blackwell Reference, 1987.

THE BLACKWELL ENCYCLOPAEDIA OF POLITICAL THOUGHT. Ed. David Miller. New York: B. Blackwell, 1987.

ENCYCLOPEDIA OF AMERICAN HISTORY, 6th ed. Ed. Richard B. Morris. New York: Harper & Row, 1982.

ENCYCLOPEDIA OF ANTHROPOLOGY. Eds. David E. Hunter and Philip Whitten. New York: Harper & Row, 1976.

ENCYCLOPEDIA OF ECONOMICS. Ed. Douglas Greenwald. New York: McGraw-Hill, 1982.

ENCYCLOPEDIA OF PSYCHOLOGY, 4 vols. Ed. Raymond J. Corsini. New York: Wiley, 1984.

HARVARD ENCYCLOPEDIA OF AMERICAN ETHNIC GROUPS. Ed. Stephan Thernstrom. Cambridge: Belknap/Harvard University Press, 1980.

INTERNATIONAL ENCYCLOPEDIA OF SOCIOLOGY. Ed. Michael Mann. New York: Continuum, 1984.

INTERNATIONAL ENCYCLOPEDIA OF THE SOCIAL SCIENCES, 17 vols. Ed. David L. Sills. New York: Macmillan, 1968. Biographical Supplement, 1979.

## DICTIONARIES:
Provide concise definitions of specialized terms and key concepts, often supplemented with other relevant information.

THE AMERICAN DICTIONARY OF CAMPAIGNS AND ELECTIONS. Michael L. Young. Lanham, MD: Hamilton Press: Abt Books, 1987.

AMERICAN POLITICAL DICTIONARY, 4th ed. Jack C. Plano and Milton Greenberg. New York: Holt, Rinehart and Winston, 1976.

CONCISE DICTIONARY OF AMERICAN HISTORY. New York: Scribner, 1983.

DICTIONARY OF AMERICAN HISTORY, rev. ed., 7 vols. Ed. James Truslow Adams. New York: Scribner, 1976.

A DICTIONARY OF POLITICS. Walter Lacquer. New York: Macmillan, 1974.

A DICTIONARY OF POLITICAL ANALYSIS. Jack C. Plano, Robert E. Riggs, Helenan Robin. Santa Barbara, CA: ABC-CLIO, 1982.

A DICTIONARY OF POLITICAL THOUGHT. Roger Scruton. New York: Harper & Row, 1982.

DICTIONARY OF PSYCHOLOGY, rev. ed. James P. Chaplin. New York: Dell Publishing Co., 1975.

MACMILLAN DICTIONARY OF ANTHROPOLOGY. Ed. Charlotte Seymour-Smith. London: Macmillan Reference Books, 1986.

THE MIT DICTIONARY OF MODERN ECONOMICS. Ed. David W. Pearce. Cambridge: MIT Press, 1986.

A NEW DICTIONARY OF THE SOCIAL SCIENCES. Ed. Geoffrey Duncan Mitchell. New York: Aldine Publishing Co., 1979.

THE PENGUIN DICTIONARY OF SOCIOLOGY. Nicholas Abercrombie, Stephen Hill, and Bryan S. Turner. London: A. Lane, 1984.

## INDEXES AND ABSTRACTS:

List recent books and/or journal articles according to subject. Abstracts provide capsule summaries, whereas indexes merely list works or provide brief annotations.

ABSTRACTS IN ANTHROPOLOGY

AMERICA: HISTORY AND LIFE: A GUIDE TO PERIODICAL LITERATURE

CURRENT INDEX TO JOURNALS IN EDUCATION

EDUCATION INDEX

EDUCATION ABSTRACTS

ERIC (Educational Resources Information Center). CURRENT INDEX TO JOURNALS IN EDUCATION (CIJE)

HISTORICAL ABSTRACTS

INDEX OF ECONOMIC ARTICLES

PSYCHOLOGICAL ABSTRACTS

PUBLIC AFFAIRS INFORMATION SERVICE BULLETIN (PAIS)

SAGE ABSTRACTS: FAMILY STUDIES

SAGE ABSTRACTS: RACE RELATIONS

SAGE ABSTRACTS: URBAN STUDIES

READERS' GUIDE TO PERIODICAL LITERATURE

SOCIAL SCIENCES INDEX

SOCIOLOGICAL ABSTRACTS

WOMEN STUDIES ABSTRACTS

## BOOK REVIEWS:

Contain scholarly reviews of recent books, generally classified by subject area within a discipline. For indexes of reviews of social science books, see the *Social Science Index, Book Review Index,* and *Book Review Digest.*

AMERICAN ANTHROPOLOGIST

AMERICAN POLITICAL SCIENCE REVIEW

CONTEMPORARY PSYCHOLOGY: A JOURNAL OF REVIEWS

CONTEMPORARY SOCIOLOGY: A JOURNAL OF REVIEWS

JOURNAL OF AMERICAN HISTORY

JOURNAL OF ECONOMIC LITERATURE

REVIEWS IN AMERICAN HISTORY

## MAJOR JOURNALS:

Publications of recent research or thought within particular disciplines or subdivisions within a discipline.

A. **General Audience**: Intended for lay readers as well as scholars.

ANTHROPOLOGY TODAY (Anthropology)

AMERICAN HERITAGE (History)

ARCHAEOLOGY (Archaeology and Anthropology)

CHALLENGE (Economics)

CHANGE (Education)

DOLLARS AND SENSE (Economics and Public Policy)

ELECTION POLITICS (Political Science)

FRONTIERS (Women's Studies)

PSYCHOLOGY TODAY (Psychology)

SOCIETY (Sociology)

SOCIAL POLICY (Politics and Public Policy)

B. **Professional Journals**: Intended mainly for professional social scientists.

### 1. Anthropology

AMERICAN ANTHROPOLOGIST

AMERICAN ETHNOLOGIST

CURRENT ANTHROPOLOGY

### 2. Economics

AMERICAN ECONOMIC REVIEW

JOURNAL OF POLITICAL ECONOMY

QUARTERLY JOURNAL OF ECONOMICS

### 3. History

AMERICAN HISTORICAL REVIEW

JOURNAL OF AMERICAN HISTORY

JOURNAL OF SOCIAL HISTORY

### 4. Political Science

AMERICAN POLITICAL SCIENCE REVIEW

POLITICS AND SOCIETY

POLITY

## 5. Psychology

AMERICAN JOURNAL OF PSYCHOLOGY

JOURNAL OF ABNORMAL PSYCHOLOGY

JOURNAL OF EXPERIMENTAL PSYCHOLOGY

JOURNAL OF PERSONALITY AND SOCIAL PSYCHOLOGY

JOURNAL OF SOCIAL PSYCHOLOGY

## 6. Sociology

AMERICAN JOURNAL OF SOCIOLOGY

AMERICAN SOCIOLOGICAL REVIEW

PUBLIC OPINION QUARTERLY

SOCIAL FORCES

SOCIAL PROBLEMS

## RESEARCH GUIDES AND HANDBOOKS:

Provide a general introduction to a field and its bibliographic resources.

A GUIDE TO LIBRARY SOURCES IN POLITICAL SCIENCE. Clement E. Vose. Washington: American Political Science Association, 1975.

HANDBOOK FOR RESEARCH IN AMERICAN HISTORY. Francis Paul Prucha. Lincoln: University of Nebraska Press, 1987.

HARVARD GUIDE TO AMERICAN HISTORY. Ed. Frank Freidel. Cambridge: Belknap/ Harvard University Press, 1974.

INFORMATION SOURCES IN ECONOMICS, 2nd ed. Ed. John Fletcher. London: Butterworths, 1984.

INFORMATION SOURCES OF POLITICAL SCIENCE, 3rd ed. Frederick L. Holler. Santa Barbara, CA: ABC-CLIO, 1981.

INFORMATION SOURCES IN POLITICS AND POLITICAL SCIENCE. Eds. Dermot Englefield and Garvin Drewry. London: Butterworths, 1984.

INTRODUCTION TO LIBRARY RESEARCH IN WOMEN'S STUDIES. Susan E. Searing. Boulder: Westview Press, 1985.

SOURCES OF INFORMATION IN THE SOCIAL SCIENCES: A GUIDE TO THE LITERATURE, 3rd ed. Chicago: American Library Association, 1986.

THE STUDENT SOCIOLOGIST'S HANDBOOK, 4th ed. Pauline B. Bart and Linda Frankel. New York: Random House, 1986.

URBAN POLICY: A GUIDE TO INFORMATION SOURCES. Dennis J. Palumbo and George A. Taylor. Detroit: Gale Research Co., 1979.

URBAN POLITICS: A GUIDE TO INFORMATION SOURCES. Ed. Thomas P. Murphy. Detroit: Gale Research Co., 1978.

# *Appendix B*
# BIBLIOGRAPHIC FORM

The pursuit of knowledge is a cumulative process in which scholars build upon the work of other scholars. As students you will be expected to make effective use of the relevant literature, and to incorporate the ideas of previous writers into your own writing. Whenever you do so, you are obliged to have an appropriate citation to the original source, and to include it in your bibliography. This is true whether you quote, paraphrase, or summarize another work. As we suggested in Chapter 12, by documenting the sources that informed your writing, you not only avoid plagiarism but you also give your readers access to these sources and add authority to your voice.

For better or worse, there is no single documentation style that is universally accepted among social scientists. Two styles are widely used: (1) the APA style is used in all publications issued by the American Psychological Association, and (2) the University of Chicago's *Manual of Style* is commonly used in the other social sciences. Let us illustrate these two styles with the four sample essays presented in Chapters 6 to 9.[1]

## APA STYLE
### References

GUTMAN, H. (1976) The black family in slavery and freedom. New York: Pantheon, 3–11.

PARELIUS, A.P. (1975). Emerging sex-role attitudes, expectations, and strains among college women. *The Journal of Marriage and the Family, 37,* 146–153.

[1]For a more detailed description of these editorial styles, see the *Publication Manual of the American Psychological Association*, 3rd ed. (Washington, D.C.: American Psychological Association, 1983), pp. 118–133; and *A Manual of Style*, 13th ed. (Chicago: University of Chicago Press, 1982), pp. 485–510.

POLSKY, N. (1985). The Hustler. In *Hustlers, beats, and others* (pp. 31–108). Chicago: University of Chicago Press.

ROSENTHAL, R. & JACOBSON, L.F. (1968). Teacher expectations for the disadvantaged. *Scientific American, 218,* 19–23.

## CHICAGO MANUAL OF STYLE
### Bibliography

GUTMAN, HERBERT. *The Black Family in Slavery and Freedom.* New York: Pantheon Books, 1976: 3–11.

PARELIUS, ANN P. "Emerging Sex-Role Attitudes, Expectations, and Strains Among College Women." *The Journal of Marriage and the Family* 37 (February 1975): 146–153.

POLSKY, NED. "The Hustler." In *Hustlers, Beats, and Others.* Chicago: University of Chicago Press, 1985: 31–108.

ROSENTHAL, ROBERT and LENORE F. JACOBSON. "Teacher Expectations for the Disadvantaged." *Scientific American* 218 (April 1968): 19–23.

# *Appendix C*
# STUDENT
# RESEARCH PAPER

### THE KU KLUX KLAN OF THE NINETEENTH CENTURY:
### REFORM GROUP OR TERRORIST ORGANIZATION?

Essential background information leading to thesis
    The Ku Klux Klan of the nineteenth century has been called "a reform group" both by its own members and by historians. According to this view, the KKK sought to restore white supremacy in the South by destroying the radical reconstruction "regime" which it saw as corrupt and abusive. The methods used to bring these social, political, and moral "improvements" have been romanticized in movies, novels, and historical accounts.

Thesis statement
    However, in this paper I will argue that the Klan was no more than a terrorist organization dedicated to the restoration of white supremacy.

Definition of a key term
    As implied in the preceding paragraph, using the term "reform" to describe the activities of the Ku Klux Klan can be challenged. If "reform" is used in its most general and literal sense—that is, to mean "to form again"—then I would have to say that the KKK was indeed a reform group. If, on the other hand, "reform" is used to mean "change for the better," then this term hardly fits the KKK's efforts to restore white supremacy in the postbellum South.

Elaboration of background material
    Let us first examine why the Ku Klux Klan wanted to "reform" the South. Most sources agree that the Reconstruction Act of 1867, enacted by the northern radical Republicans to "teach the South a lesson," prompted a small group of young ex-Confederate soldiers to transform their social club into a "defender of white civilization." This group had originally been formed solely as a source of "harmless amusement" in Pulaski, Tennessee in June, 1866. The Reconstruction Act brought Federal troops to the South, enfranchised Black adult males, disfranchised ex-Confederates, and stipulated that each Southern state would not be readmitted to the Union until it accepted the Fourteenth Amendment. The ruling white Southerners saw their power being taken from them with the passage of the Act and reacted accordingly.

Introduction of relevant source material
    In The Evolution of the Ku Klux Klan in the South Lillian Lynch exposes abuses that allegedly occurred under the Reconstruction Act. According to Lynch, buying votes and voting twice were common occurrences among carpetbaggers and scalawags. In one case votes were inspected before being

placed in the ballot box; all votes for Democrats were withheld. Often leaders would give Blacks pre-marked Republican ballots (Lynch 4–5).

Whites often interpreted these abuses as attempts by Negroes to seek revenge and oppress them the way whites had oppressed Negroes under slavery. Memories of slave revolts, such as that of Nat Turner, were still ingrained in the ex-slaveholders' minds and often provoked paranoia.

Stanley Horn, who presents a sympathetic account of the Klan's origins and activities in his Invisible Empire, claims that the "Negro's Loyal League was a primary cause for the white men's Ku Klux Klan" (Horn, 27). The adjectives used in his description of the League, however, seem more appropriate to the movie Birth of a Nation than to a history on the Reconstruction period:

> This was a totally unrestrained and disorderly form of group activity in its Southern manifestation, used by low-grade white men as an instrumentality for organizing the negroes politically and keeping them unified by a steady infusion of inflammatory propaganda by imported flannel-mouthed orators. . . . Bands of League members, armed to the teeth, prowled the country at all times, particularly at night, and the white people were increasingly terrified (Horn, 27).

This account, like Birth of a Nation, greatly exaggerates the role that Blacks played during Reconstruction. Birth of a Nation shows drunk, disorderly, and ignorant blacks dominating the state legislatures, when in reality, they held very few offices. Myths like these, however, helped to legitimate the Klan's actions.

*Key inference*

Another myth accused blacks of raping white women. This unfounded fear—such an occurrence was rare, according to Clarence Walker—is fully exploited in Dixon's novel The Clansmen—the book from which Birth of a Nation was made (Walker, 5). Throughout the book Dixon portrays the black male as a "sensuous beast whose every physical feature was the mark of the jungle and the untamed animal." In one scene Gus, an ex-slave, along with other "black brutes," break into a house where Marion and her mother are alone. Marion pleads that they do not have any money:

> Gus stepped closer, with an ugly leer, his flat nose dilated, his sinister bead-eyes wide apart gleaming ape-like, as he laughed:
> "We ain't atter money!"
> The girl uttered a cry, long, tremulous, heart-rendering, piteous.
> A single tiger-spring, and the black claws of the beast sank into the soft white throat and she was still. (Dixon 304)

*Key inference*

Thus, the KKK evolved as a "reform group" partly in response to the abuses which occurred under radical reconstruction, but mostly because whites feared losing their superior status to their former slaves. Myths were created and exploited to justify white reaction. Logically, the next questions are: what type of "reforms" did the Klan seek and how did they carry out these "reforms"?

*Additional documentary material*

The revised and amended Precept of the Ku Klux Klan, which described the character and the objectives of the organization, declares that it is an institution of "Chivalry, Humanity, Mercy, and Patriotism." It protects and defends the innocent, defenseless, oppressed, and suffering ("especially widows and orphans of Confederate soldiers"). The Precept also states that the Klan upholds the Constitution of the United States and aids "in the execution of all constitutional laws."

Works of fiction like The Clansmen make it seem as though Klansmen were exactly as the Precept portrayed them. In the novel the Klansmen do not take action until Marion is attacked. They are made out to be courageous as they exact vengeance by killing Gus in a religious-like ceremony, dressed in mysterious white robes. Such an act was seen as vital to protect the "womenhood" of the innocent southern belles. The other deeds of the Klansmen—the disarmament of the Ulster county Negroes, the whipping of the mayor and the forcing of him to leave town, the intimidation of the sheriff, the gaining of the friendship of the western soldiers, and the terror struck into "the heart of every negro, carpet-bagger, and scalawag" (Horn, 30)—were portrayed as chivalrous, patriotic and necessary actions to regain control of the legislature. At the end of the novel Ben Cameron, the hero, proclaims that the Klan saved white civilization and redeemed southern white honor.

In his apologetic account of the Klan, Horn also suggests that the Klan had little choice but to take the law into its own hands in order to counter the "lawlessness" of the Negroes and the Radical Republicans. Horn implies that the Klan's acting outside the law was justified because the reforms they were working for were essential to the South's well-being: the KKK "was destined to grow into perhaps the most powerful and extensive organization of its kind that ever existed" (Horn, 30). As in The Clansmen, Horn suggests that the Klan carried out its reforms in a dignified manner. He romanticizes the secrecy and mystery behind which the Klan worked, and uses examples of how they cleverly intimidated Blacks from voting by "playing" with their superstitions about hell. Elsewhere Horn describes a Mississippi carpetbagger who was whipped by the Klan, and afterwards "commented on their discipline and generally good behavior when they honored him with their attention" (Horn, 45). Horn downplayed the violence of the KKK and emphasized its "successes." He explains their suppression in most states as the result of the Klan's having fulfilled its purposes—that is, bringing pride back into the South by restoring the Democrats to power, evicting the carpetbaggers and scalawags, and extinguishing the Loyal Leagues.

Transitional sentence leading to writer's argument

The Ku Klux Klan's methods of "reform," despite the lofty rhetoric in its Precept, or its romanticization in novels such as The Clansmen and historical accounts such as Invisible Empire, were anything but noble. As Professor Walker points out in his article, "One Hundred Per Cent Americanism: The Ku Klux Klan's Defense of America," the Klan was actually "a terrorist organization dedicated to the overthrow of Congressional or radical reconstruction" (Walker, 5). Walker shows that the

Key documentary source quoted

Klan's principle targets were Negro Republicans who southern whites feared would become their social equals after the passage of the Reconstruction Act of 1867. This fear was connected to the fact that whites—who were supposed to be sexually restrained, moral, intelligent and industrious compared to the inferior, lazy, stupid, and sex-crazed blacks—could not admit that miscegenation had occurred for centuries during slavery. That the children who were products of this "illicit" sex and "sinful" activity were able to "come back and haunt them" as equals horrified the white South.

The KKK, as most terrorist groups, reacted by using ruthless methods to achieve power. It is ironic, in view of the fears just mentioned, that the myth of black men raping white women would be used to help propagate

Klan activity. The actions of the Klan can be seen as even more hypocritical, however, when some of their tacks of intimidation are revealed. Sexual violence, against both male and female Blacks, was a common form of Klan "punishment." Blacks were also "beaten, tarred and feathered, driven from their homes, and murdered" (Walker, 5).

Lillian Lynch describes methods used by the Klan where men who were sympathetic to radical reconstruction would be dragged from their beds at night and whipped. There are also cases of Blacks being dragged from jails to be murdered. This was far from the sanctimonious ideals projected in the Precept.

velopment
of writer's
argument

The Klan's real objectives were not to defend law and liberty; nor did they have anything to do with upholding constitutional values. It was hardly self-evident to the Klan that all men were created equal. Beneath all the Klan's rhetoric was, as the investigation committee from Congress recognized, a plan to "persecute Republicans, both Black and White, and especially Negro voters" (Lynch, 19). By intimidating Blacks to accept second class citizenship, and by scaring away the carpetbaggers and scalawags, the Klan was largely successful in regaining control of state legislatures. Not only did they use violence to keep Republicans from voting but they also made sure that either a Klan member or at the very least a Klan-sympathizer was elected. In 1871 a Democratic legislature wiped out the Loyal League by calling for the disbandment of all secret organizations (Lynch, 22).

Cites
authority
o reinforce
thesis

Clarence Walker argues that the Klan involved more than the overthrow of radical reconstruction: "It was also the assertion of a particular moral and cultural vision of America" (Walker, 8). The Ku Klux Klan would punish all who deviated from the moral and social norm personified by White Anglo-Saxon Protestants. On the other hand, Blacks personified "evil and moral degeneracy," so they bore the brunt of the Klan's moral tyranny. However, nonconforming whites were also susceptible to the organization's hatred and violence.

Conclusion

Reiteration
of thesis
using
inferences
developed
throughout
paper

In conclusion, the Ku Klux Klan of the reconstruction years was by no means an institution of "Chivalry, Humanity, Mercy, and Patriotism." Rather, it was a counter-revolutionary movement of whites who sought the restoration of white power. The Klan used terror and violence in the most extreme forms throughout the South to maintain their racist values, and Negro Republicans were their primary targets. Unfortunately, their tactics of "reforming" the South were largely successful as the Democrats regained control of state legislatures and reinstituted white supremacy.

## REFERENCES

DIXON, THOMAS JR., The Clansmen (Lexington: University Press of Kentucky, 1970). Originally published in 1905.

HORN, STANLEY F., Invisible Empire (Boston: Houghton Mifflin & Co., 1939).

LYNCH, LILLIAN M., The Evolution of the Ku Klux Klan in the South, Master's Thesis, Wesleyan University, Middletown, Connecticut, 1964.

WALKER, CLARENCE E., "One Hundred Per Cent Americanism: The Ku Klux Klan's Defense of America," unpublished manuscript.

# INDEX

## SUBJECT INDEX

## NAME INDEX